ADVANCE PRAISE FOR
# Becoming an Integrated Educational Leader

"This important work on leadership and education is less about what teachers ought to do and more about what teachers can do to grow personally and professionally and to engage their students more effectively and holistically. The text is replete with helpful strategies to create a positive learning environment while also focusing on the well-being of the educator. The weave of important theories, practical suggestions, research data, relevant facts, trends, policies and issues makes the book both scholarly and applicable to everyday life." — Tim Davidson, Associate Professor and Graduate Liaison, University of Oklahoma

"As an educator for over 40 years, I have seen the latest come, go, and simply change names. But *Becoming an Integrated Educational Leader* addresses an area that needs our attention. Teachers, lead not only in their classrooms, but also in their schools and communities, and can have a wonderfully positive impact on all. This book addresses something new and can help educators become those leaders." — Debby Stine, retired educator

# Becoming an Integrated Educational Leader

Critical Pedagogical Perspectives

Greg S. Goodman, *General Editor*

Vol. 26

The Educational Psychology series is part of the Peter Lang Education list.
Every volume is peer reviewed and meets
the highest quality standards for content and production.

PETER LANG
New York • Washington, D.C./Baltimore • Bern
Frankfurt • Berlin • Brussels • Vienna • Oxford

MICHELLE ROSSER & TOM MASSEY

# Becoming an Integrated Educational Leader

PETER LANG
New York • Washington, D.C./Baltimore • Bern
Frankfurt • Berlin • Brussels • Vienna • Oxford

Library of Congress Cataloging-in-Publication Data
Rosser, Michelle.
Becoming an integrated educational leader / Michelle Rosser, Tom Massey.
pages cm. — (Educational psychology: critical pedagogical perspectives; vol. 26)
Includes bibliographical references.
1. Educational leadership. 2. Educational accountability.
3. Educational change. I. Massey, Tom. II. Title.
LB2806.R673   371.2—dc23   2013038200
ISBN 978-1-4331-2162-3 (hardcover)
ISBN 978-1-4331-2161-6 (paperback)
ISBN 978-1-4539-1232-4 (e-book)
ISSN 1943-8109

Bibliographic information published by **Die Deutsche Nationalbibliothek**.
**Die Deutsche Nationalbibliothek** lists this publication in the "Deutsche
Nationalbibliografie"; detailed bibliographic data is available
on the Internet at http://dnb.d-nb.de/.

© 2014 Peter Lang Publishing, Inc., New York
29 Broadway, 18th floor, New York, NY 10006
www.peterlang.com

All rights reserved.
Reprint or reproduction, even partially, in all forms such as microfilm,
xerography, microfiche, microcard, and offset strictly prohibited.

# TABLE OF CONTENTS

| | |
|---|---:|
| **Preface** | vii |
| **Introduction** | 1 |
| **Section I. The Integrated Leadership Model** | **5** |
| Chapter 1: Learning from Where We Have Been | 15 |
| Chapter 2: Integration and Leadership Development | 25 |
| Chapter 3: Cultural Competence | 37 |
| Section I Review | 49 |
| **Section II. Integration Through Self-Awareness** | **51** |
| Chapter 4: Beliefs, Personality, and Knowing Yourself | 55 |
| Chapter 5: Evaluating and Managing Stress | 65 |
| Chapter 6: Awareness and Your Mental Health | 75 |
| Chapter 7: Self-Motivation | 81 |
| Chapter 8: Importance of Self-Care | 85 |
| Section II Review | 95 |
| **Section III. Integration Through Social Awareness and Management** | **99** |
| Chapter 9: Your Learners | 103 |
| Chapter 10: Awareness and Learner Safety | 115 |
| Chapter 11: Managing Social Relationships | 129 |
| Chapter 12: Managing Cultural Differences | 145 |
| Section III Review | 159 |
| **Section IV. Developing the Leader in You** | **161** |
| Chapter 13: Inevitability of Social Change | 167 |
| Chapter 14: A Leader with Vision | 179 |
| Chapter 15: Integrate and Lead | 189 |
| Section IV Review | 201 |
| **Appendix** | 205 |
| **References** | 209 |
| **About the Authors** | 227 |

# PREFACE

> *Education is the mother of leadership.*
> —Wendell L. Willkie

Becoming a successful educational leader requires the development of multiple skills and personal characteristics. Decision making, organizational facility, creative abilities, intrapersonal skills, interpersonal communication, emotional balance, physical conditioning, and critical thinking all need to be honed in an intricate manner for you to be what we refer to as an integrated educational leader. From this "wholistic" perspective, great teachers are worth more than simply the sum of their individual parts. The educators of tomorrow must recognize, understand, and adapt to the complexity of issues they face in a world that is rapidly changing with new demographics, technologies, and generational perspectives. All of these issues will require new thought on the part of our educational system. To quote Einstein, "We can't solve problems by using the same kind of thinking we used when we created them."

Each year in-service teachers attend training with presentations on the "latest and greatest" ideas. Unfortunately, these so-called new ideas are pushed for a semester and then forgotten as pressures force teachers and administrators to try to balance their academic load with the intricacies of student personalities, differing cultural variables, and parental pressures. Once school scores are received, relief (or panic and frustration) hovers in the hallways, and the cycle begins again to search for a newer and greater program next year.

This cycle gives rise to a plethora of theories about best practices, appropriate pedagogy, cultural competency, and who knows what else, which can be quite confusing for both educators and learners. Even the best teaching practices are not applicable to all students, nor do all of them understand or value the importance of great learning experiences. Furthermore, beliefs and cultural perceptions about teaching are not defined in the same way by all teachers, administrators, or parents. Historically the contingencies surrounding education have swelled. Programs initiated by legislators and/or educators to enhance learning and promote social justice (e.g., No Child Left Behind [NCLB]) become elephants in the room as initial ideas and plans become distorted and sometimes demotivating to learners and educators. When new ideas don't pan out people sometimes lose faith, which leads to fear. Teachers have anxieties about teaching to the test in fear of failure. Students fear not doing well and disappointing their parents, who in turn fear their child won't be able to compete in a global economy. The cycle of fear can lead to a circle of blame. Parents blame teachers and educational institutions for "not getting the job done," while parents are blamed for their lack of participation in the school environment.

We contend that it is time for the fear and blame to stop. Over the past 30 years, we as a nation have become increasingly aware of the need for encouraging educational success by all students. Historically it has taken centuries to get to a place where we are actually addressing what it will take to get there. The one stone that has been virtually unturned is you—the fully integrated educational leader. In the past educators have been trained to know and apply best teaching practices, universal lessons, and diverse activities in the classroom. Our aim is to prepare you to be a leader who believes in and practices self-care, understands and nurtures human needs and motivations, and is a catalyst for positive change. That is how you will make the greatest difference in the lives of children, as well as your own.

Through your training, you will be introduced to some theoretically sound teaching practices that encourage culturally competent pedagogy and classroom management. Although no amount of theory or experience will be able to fully prepare you for the challenges ahead, every piece of information you gain will make you a better teacher. Do you need the knowledge that preparation programs offer? Yes. Will that knowledge sustain you over time? Probably not. Half of all teachers leave the profession within their first five years. You may be enthusiastic right now and think that won't happen to you, but they had the same excitement about teaching in the beginning. So what happened? Some would call it burnout or, as they say in the South, "they got a belly full!" We contend it can happen to anyone, even you. That is why it is important to become an integrated educational leader who focuses on meeting your own needs as well as your students'. Are you willing to put your own well-being first? We will explain later why that is vitally important.

There is little question that education is in a state of unrest, and teachers as well as students are feeling the pressure. Like it or not, the rapidly changing demographics in our society have shattered traditional sources of belonging for the students and the teachers. The breakdown of the nuclear and extended families, an increase in single parenthood, the increase in the number of hours that working parents are away from the home, and the growing transience and mobilization of society have left the children of the United States with a sense of disconnection, and the teachers with feelings of frustration. At the same time we boast about the great technological achievements of this century, there is a growing sense of alienation and apathy among our youth and a lack of communication skills in our adults. Drug and alcohol abuse, violence and gang membership, high-risk sexual activity, depression, and suicide are all signs that something is awry. We understand that your challenge may be daunting and filled with uncertainty. There are no guarantees that this profession will be blissful for you. (If you want a guarantee, buy a toaster!) However, one thing is certain: Teachers are instrumental in developing tomorrow's leaders, but first you must develop yourself into a leader who will make a difference.

This book is designed to help redefine your understanding about yourself as a future educator and the nonnegotiable necessity to meet your own needs as a living, breathing, and caring human being, before you can be the teacher that the present educational system needs. We will address the collective consciousness of the educational community and expand your understanding of how to apply "purposeful intention" into becoming a fully integrated leader. We hope you will find encouragement in these pages as you tap into an inner strength to find personal fulfillment in your career as a teacher. As we prepared this manuscript we were filled with enthusiasm to introduce new ideas and real-to-life applications to the educational preparation context. Teacher performance is more than just checking off a list; it includes understanding who you are and how to become an education leader who finds hope and success within your classroom walls—every day of your career.

# INTRODUCTION

*I have come to believe that a great teacher is a great artist...*
*Teaching might even be the greatest of the arts since the medium*
*is the human mind and spirit.*
—John Steinbeck

Becoming a successful educator will be one of your most fulfilling life experiences. Although times have changed in the educational context, the importance of what educators do has not. As a future teacher, you have an inner devotion, power, and dedication to help those around you and to make a difference. However, to gain strength as an educator it is necessary to evaluate and understand why your development toward this goal is so important. You must dedicate yourself not only as a developing teacher but also as an integrated leader, ready to give of yourself to those you will teach and mentor.

Understanding yourself, your learners, and the educational environment will be foundational to your success as an integrated educational leader. This will take dedication and purposeful intention as you begin to prepare yourself for a career in teaching. You, as a future teacher, have the ability and the motivational charge to change lives. You will spend more time with your students than many of their parents, and your passion for learning can change their lives forever.

This book took life based on the many teachers entering the classroom who express feelings of unpreparedness as well as the current attrition rates of teachers who started out just like you: excited to step into the classroom. The Integrated Educational Leadership Model presented in this book will assist you in gaining the confidence and the skills you will need once you earn your certification rights to teach so that all of theories, strategies, and time in your preparation program will not be wasted, but you must intentionally take ownership of your training opportunities. Your readiness is not only based on books and your professors. It is your decision whether you want to develop your skill set. Whether you teach early, elementary, or secondary education, this book is designed to help you see this bigger picture and build fortitude to assist you in meeting your future goals and aspirations, as well as meet the needs of all your students. You can be successful and fulfilled.

The first section of this book, **The Integrated Leadership Model**, first addresses how the past invested in the model of becoming an integrated leader in education and an introduction of the model, and it outlines how this model can assist you in becoming fully prepared to be a leader in education. It disseminates, through the theoretical frameworks it entails, how to apply self-awareness and development your participation in this process. To become a more powerful individual who finds hope for education within yourself, you must use your personal leadership abilities and become catalysts for positive change. The most important part of this is looking at the "bigger picture" of who you are, as a person, as an intimate part of this global society, and as a future teacher. By better understanding your abilities, biases, emotional responses, and basis for forming beliefs, you can then begin to better understand the environment and those who surround you.

This section continues by addressing in more detail the foundations of the Integrated Educational Leadership Model: cultural competence development. You cannot build anything in your life without a foundation, and the premise of cultural competence development is this foundation. With the right skills and focus, you have the power to make a difference in your classrooms, with your students, with their parents, in your communities, and with each other, as the "chosen ones": the teachers of tomorrow who will be confident in their leadership abilities as they walk into their learning environments, stand proudly as they share their knowledge, and have peace knowing that they offer value and hope to young people.

This section also addresses information that helps you better understand why this model is important to your success. For example, according to the National Center for Education Information (2005), the number one reason teachers teach is because they want to help young people learn and develop. However, 40% of public school teachers expect not to be teaching in K–12 schools within five years. To be clear, these teachers, once in their career, although passionate about it in the beginning, quickly resigned their enthusiasm based on the reality of their new challenge. This does not sound like a statistic that describes a person who is fulfilling a lifelong dream of helping. It is time to change these statistics and to learn how to live healthy, happy, and fulfilled as an educator by searching and assessing yourself, by staying healthy, and by loving what you do and why you have chosen to do it.

The second section, **Integration Through Self-Awareness**, disseminates, through numerous theoretical frameworks, the importance of self-awareness to your development and how to apply this self-awareness to your own life and growth. To become a more powerful individual who finds hope for education within yourself, you must use your personal leadership abilities and become catalysts for positive change.

Section 3, **Integration Through Social Awareness**, will address how to develop yourself though social awareness of others and their needs. Successful leadership often requires you to wear many hats. Better understanding of social awareness will increase the likelihood that you will maintain happiness and health, which in turn will encourage and provide positive momentum for your success as a teacher.

Social awareness also includes a better understanding about education today, as this too is a part of the much larger picture of how our educational system has changed through time. The past decisions of our nation have effects on today's educational stature; however, the past does not dictate your futures as educators. This nation was founded on the right that everyone deserves to be free and that includes free education: the right to learn how to read, how to write, how to think. This is a privilege but yet also a constitutional right in our country, and some privileges and rights do bring trials and consequences that can make things more complicated, but not impossible. Society is diverse. Your classrooms are diverse. Minority and immigrant influxes, socioeconomics, and diverse values have made the classroom challenging, but we encourage you to look at it as an opportunity. It is time to reconsider what your role is as an educator, which includes leading your learners, being successful, and finding joy in your chosen career.

The final section, **Developing the Leader in You**, will empower you not to be submissive to the status quo, but to address positive change head-on and to apply integrated leadership skills to your chosen career. It will introduce proven leadership skills, based on the model, such as vision and goal-setting that can be personally and professionally applied to your life. Although these ideas are many times not addressed in typical teacher preparation or continuing education protocols as important for you to apply, it is often addressed in regard to how to encourage your learners. This builds a bridge for you to better understand that the many skills that you will learn to motivate your future students must first be applied to your own life. It will, in essence, complete the circle of understanding about how the components of the Integrated Educational Leadership Model are highly important to your development and future success as an integrated educational leader. You cannot become a leader overnight, but an important part of becoming a leader is gaining a better understanding about what affects your chosen field; it is not only your learners.

Throughout this book we will use the terms *educator* and *leader* interchangeably, because that is what you must become to be successful. Your ability to lead will be the pendulum that shifts education into the future—successfully and positively. Noah Porter, an American academic, philosopher, author, and president of Yale College (1871–1886), once said:

> Rely on your own strength of body and soul. Take for your star self-reliance, faith, honesty and industry. Don't take too much advice—keep at the helm and steer your own ship, and remember that the great art of commanding is to take a fair share of the work. Fire above the mark you intend to hit. Energy, invincible determination with the right motive, are the levers that move the world.

We encourage each of you to be steadfast and never let go of the reasons you have chosen to teach. Your motivations are your levers; now all you need are the right skills to "captain the ship" successfully. It is time that all educators discover their individual power of influence and become intentional leaders in a career that is honorable and of utmost important to this country's success. It is time to become more proactive in our understanding that the educational environment is not only about the learners and parents; it is also about those who choose to teach: their wholeness, happiness, and motivation.

We also encourage you to take a step back, look at where you are in this dynamic, and reflect on what you need now, and in the future, as a person first, teacher second. Yes, second. Do not negate the necessity of your own integration, wholeness, and preparedness as keys to leading others to success. Find your personal strength as you prepare to implement your personally and altruistically based motivations for making a difference: to change and develop the lives of your students. As you approach this text, we encourage you to be open to the realities that have been set before you and the emotional well-being you must develop to walk successfully through the journey you have chosen. Our intentions are that you will discover that you are more than you may think you are as you discover your inner strength and your power to make a difference in the lives of learners. We feel confident you will begin to see a difference in how you approach your daily life, teacher preparation, and future classrooms. You can become the educational leader of tomorrow.

# SECTION I

## The Integrated Leadership Model

*A leader is someone who demonstrates what's possible.*
—*Mark Yarnell*

For years education has been greatly based on what this country viewed as a need, but needs change, and sometimes quickly, leaving education in a quandary for how to best educate a multitude of learners. Although historical actions did not always support the idea of a country based on equality for all, this premise has always been the stitching to our country's ideals. Defining what equality for all means has been complicated for many, as the economical consequences were usually driving the definition. But one thing through all of our advancements and trials that we have learned is that in the case of the learner, it is about much more than the dollar.

Teachers work around the clock, for little pay and for little gratitude, to educate our youth. What they do, although the hope is that someday it will be more monetarily rewarded, is based on altruistic motivations, such as caring for learners, wanting better for tomorrow, and devotion to what learning bestows. It is important to understand the history of events that have occurred in this nation that drive the decisions we make if progress is to be made within education. This history also denotes the complexities of situations that have devalued what a teacher does and why. It is our history that now calls teachers to become integrated leaders: taking a stand for what they are and what they must do.

This text cannot cover every event in our history, but does effectively insight us to many events and how events and decisions, in themselves, can affect positive progression in educating learners who have diverse needs, abilities, and goals. It is only by gaining the skills to become the integrated educational leader that you will truly access all that you have to offer the future of education and learners.

### Something to Think About

Lyndon B. Johnson was considered by some as very complicated and emotionally touted. Being a leader who fights for justice is not easy for anyone, and this must be clear before you begin. Even this White president who wanted to address civil right issues was judged by many, especially other White men. He was scorned as an immoral politician, offensive and ambitious with a longing for power, was he actually a hurting man with deep ability to feel the pains of others. He was a teacher and as we will discuss in later chapters, teachers are a unique people with altruistic motivations for their goals about teaching others.

On January 20, 1965, the night of Johnson's inaugural gala, he promised to wipe out poverty and segregation and educate our youth. He did make great progress but it did come with a price and we encourage you to all learn more about this once educator. In the following speech exerts, when read with an open heart about the passionate empathy Johnson employed for minorities and social justice, it sheds light on why possibly, he was a frustrated and emotionally touted man.

> I speak tonight for the dignity of man and the destiny of Democracy. I urge every member of both parties, Americans of all religions and of all colors, from every section of this country, to join me in that cause.
>
> At times, history and fate meet at a single time in a single place to shape a turning point in man's unending search for freedom. So it was at Lexington and Concord. So it was a century ago at Appomattox. So it was last week in Selma, Alabama. There, long suffering men and women peacefully protested the denial of their rights as Americans. Many of them were brutally assaulted. One good man—a man of God—was killed.
>
> There is no cause for pride in what has happened in Selma. There is no cause for self-satisfaction in the long denial of equal rights of millions of Americans. But there is cause for hope and for faith in our Democracy in what is happening here tonight. For the cries of pain and the hymns and protests of oppressed people have summoned into convocation all the majesty of this great government—the government of the greatest nation on earth. Our mission is at once the oldest and the most basic of this country—to right wrong, to do justice, to serve man. In our time we have come to live with the moments of great crises. Our lives have been marked with debate about great issues, issues of war and peace, issues of prosperity and depression.
>
> But rarely in any time does an issue lay bare the secret heart of America itself. Rarely are we met with a challenge, not to our growth or abundance, or our welfare or our security, but rather to the values and the purposes and the meaning of our beloved nation. The issue of equal rights for American Negroes is such an issue. And should we defeat every enemy, and should we double our wealth and conquer the stars, and still be unequal to this issue, then we will have failed as a people and as a nation. For, with a country as with a person, "what is a man profited if he shall gain the whole world, and lose his own soul?"
>
> There is no Negro problem. There is no Southern problem. There is no Northern problem. There is only an American problem.
>
> And we are met here tonight as Americans—not as Democrats or Republicans; we're met here as Americans to solve that problem. This was the first nation in the history of the world to be founded with a purpose.
>
> The great phrases of that purpose still sound in every American heart,

North and South: "All men are created equal." "Government by consent of the governed." "Give me liberty or give me death." And those are not just clever words, and those are not just empty theories. In their name Americans have fought and died for two centuries and tonight around the world they stand there as guardians of our liberty risking their lives. Those words are promised to every citizen that he shall share in the dignity of man. This dignity cannot be found in a man's possessions. It cannot be found in his power or in his position. It really rests on his right to be treated as a man equal in opportunity to all others. It says that he shall share in freedom. He shall choose his leaders, educate his children, provide for his family according to his ability and his merits as a human being.

To apply any other test, to deny a man his hopes because of his color or race or his religion or the place of his birth is not only to do injustice, it is to deny Americans and to dishonor the dead who gave their lives for American freedom. Our fathers believed that if this noble view of the rights of man was to flourish it must be rooted in democracy. This most basic right of all was the right to choose your own leaders. The history of this country in large measure is the history of expansion of the right to all of our people.

Many of the issues of civil rights are very complex and most difficult. But about this there can and should be no argument: every American citizen must have an equal right to vote. There is no reason which can excuse the denial of that right. There is no duty which weighs more heavily on us than the duty we have to insure that right. Yet the harsh fact is that in many places in this country men and women are kept from voting simply because they are Negroes.

Every device of which human ingenuity is capable, has been used to deny this right. The Negro citizen may go to register only to be told that the day is wrong, or the hour is late, or the official in charge is absent. And if he persists and, if he manages to present himself to the registrar, he may be disqualified because he did not spell out his middle name, or because he abbreviated a word on the application. And if he manages to fill out an application, he is given a test. The registrar is the sole judge of whether he passes this test. He may be asked to recite the entire Constitution, or explain the most complex provisions of state law.

And even a college degree cannot be used to prove that he can read and write. For the fact is that the only way to pass these barriers is to show a white skin. Experience has clearly shown that the existing process of law cannot overcome systematic and ingenious discrimination. No law that we now have on the books, and I have helped to put three of them there, can insure the right to vote when local officials are determined to deny it. In such a case, our duty must be clear to all of us. The Constitution says that no person shall be kept from voting because of his race or his color.

We have all sworn an oath before God to support and to defend that Constitution. We must now act in obedience to that oath. Wednesday, I will send to Congress a law designed to eliminate illegal barriers to the right to vote. The broad principles of that bill will be in the hands of the Democratic and Republican leaders tomorrow. After they have reviewed it, it will come here formally as a bill. I am grateful for this opportunity to come here tonight at the invitation of the leadership to reason with my friends, to give them my views and to visit with my former colleagues…

But experience has plainly shown that this is the only path to carry out the command of the Constitution. To those who seek to avoid action by their national government in their home communities, who want to and who seek to maintain purely local control over elections, the answer is simple: open your polling places to all your people. Allow men and women to register and vote whatever the color of their skin. Extend the rights of citizenship to every citizen of this land. There is no Constitutional issue here. The command of the Constitution is plain. There is no moral issue. It is wrong—deadly wrong—to deny any of your fellow Americans the right to vote in this country.

There is no issue of state's rights or national rights. There is only the struggle for human rights…

We cannot, we must not, refuse to protect the right of every American to vote in every election that he may desire to participate in…

Their cause must be our cause too. Because it's not just Negroes, but really it's all of us, who must overcome the crippling legacy of bigotry and injustice.

And we shall overcome.

As a man whose roots go deeply into Southern soil, I know how agonizing racial feelings are. I know how difficult it is to reshape the attitudes and the structure of our society. But a century has passed—more than 100 years—since the Negro was freed. And he is not fully free tonight. It was more than 100 years ago that Abraham Lincoln—a great President of another party—signed the Emancipation Proclamation. But emancipation is a proclamation and not a fact.

A century has passed—more than 100 years—since equality was promised, and yet the Negro is not equal. A century has passed since the day of promise, and the promise is unkept. The time of justice has now come, and I tell you that I believe sincerely that no force can hold it back. It is right in the eyes of man and God that it should come, and when it does, I think that day will brighten the lives of every American. For Negroes are not the only victims. How many white children have gone uneducated? How many white families have lived in stark poverty? How many white lives have been scarred by fear, because we wasted energy and our substance to maintain the barriers of hatred and terror?

And so I say to all of you here and to all in the nation tonight that those who appeal to you to hold on to the past do so at the cost of denying you your future. This great rich, restless country can offer opportunity and education and hope to all—all, black and white, North and South, sharecropper and city dweller. These are the enemies: poverty, ignorance, disease. They are our enemies, not our fellow man, not our neighbor.

And these enemies too—poverty, disease and ignorance—we shall overcome.

Now let none of us in any section look with prideful righteousness on the troubles in another section or the problems of our neighbors. There is really no part of America where the promise of equality has been fully kept. In Buffalo as well as in Birmingham, in Philadelphia as well as Selma, Americans are struggling for the fruits of freedom.

This is one nation. What happens in Selma and Cincinnati is a matter of legitimate concern to every American. But let each of us look within our own hearts and our own communities and let each of us put our shoulder to the wheel to root out injustice wherever it exists. As we meet here in this peaceful historic chamber tonight, men from the South, some of whom were at Iwo Jima, men from the North who have carried Old Glory to the far corners of the world and who brought it back without a stain on it, men from the east and from the west are all fighting together without regard to religion or color or region in Vietnam.

Men from every region fought for us across the world 20 years ago. And now in these common dangers, in these common sacrifices, the South made its contribution of honor and gallantry no less than any other region in the great republic.

And in some instances, a great many of them, more. And I have not the slightest doubt that good men from everywhere in this country, from the Great Lakes to the Gulf of Mexico, from the Golden Gate to the harbors along the Atlantic, will rally now together in this cause to vindicate the freedom of all Americans. For all of us owe this duty and I believe that all of us will respond to it.

Your president makes that request of every American.

The real hero of this struggle is the American Negro. His actions and protests, his courage to risk safety, and even to risk his life, have awakened the conscience of this nation. His demonstrations have been designed to call attention to injustice, designed to provoke change; designed to stir reform. He has been called upon to make good the promise of America.

And who among us can say that we would have made the same progress were it not for his persistent bravery and his faith in American democracy? For at the real heart of the battle for equality is a deep-seated belief in the democratic process. Equality depends, not on the force of arms or tear gas, but depends upon the force of moral right—not on recourse to violence, but on respect for law and order…

The bill I am presenting to you will be known as a civil rights bill. But in a larger sense, most of the program I am recommending is a civil rights program. Its object is to open the city of hope to all people of all races, because all Americans just must have the right to vote, and we are going to give them that right.

All Americans must have the privileges of citizenship, regardless of race, and they are going to have those privileges of citizenship regardless of race.

But I would like to caution you and remind you that to exercise these privileges takes much more than just legal rights. It requires a trained mind and a healthy body. It requires a decent home and the chance to find a job and the opportunity to escape from the clutches of poverty.

Of course people cannot contribute to the nation if they are never taught to read or write; if their bodies are stunted from hunger; if their sickness goes untended; if their life is spent in hopeless poverty, just drawing a welfare check.

So we want to open the gates to opportunity. But we're also going to give all our people, black and white, the help that they need to walk through those gates. My first job after college was as a teacher in Cotulla, Texas, in a small Mexican-American school. Few of them could speak English and I couldn't speak much Spanish. My students were poor and they often came to class without breakfast and hungry. And they knew even in their youth the pain of prejudice. They never seemed to know why people disliked them, but they knew it was so because I saw it in their eyes.

I often walked home late in the afternoon after the classes were finished wishing there was more that I could do. But all I knew was to teach them the little that I knew, hoping that I might help them against the hardships that lay ahead. And somehow you never forget what poverty and hatred can do when you see its scars on the hopeful face of a young child.

I never thought then, in 1928, that I would be standing here in 1965. It never even occurred to me in my fondest dreams that I might have the chance to help the sons and daughters of those students, and to help people like them all over this country. But now I do have that chance.

And I'll let you in on a secret—I mean to use it. And I hope that you will use it with me...

**President Lyndon B. Johnson - March 15, 1965**

You too will experience frustration as you move forward. You may not realize it now, but your level of empathy for the learners in your future can make success complicated. Learn from our past. It looks often parallel to our present. You will not be the first or the last to find frustration when supporting social justice to your learning environment. It is a long-time issue. You must stand strong. You must become an Integrated Educational Leader.

*Chapter 1*

# Learning from Where We Have Been

*An increase in light gives an increase in darkness.*
—Sam Francis

Although community awareness and concern about the education of our youth have become dominant throughout the country, oppositional ideas and stakeholder opinions characterize and complicate the current educational system. Understanding where we are today, both the positive and negative, will prepare future educators to be fully integrated leaders in and outside of the classroom.

Educational researchers tend to focus on low test scores as a primary factor in evaluating the efficacy of teaching and learning in the classroom. In a 2005 test of student science understanding administered by the National Assessment of Educational Progress, 32% of U.S. fourth-grade students performed below the "basic" achievement cutoff level (the lowest of three levels defined for the test). Among eighth graders, the share increased to 41%, and by the 12th grade the underachiever population grew to 46%. In mathematics, the same test revealed that less than one-fourth of high school seniors perform at or above their grade level. Interestingly, in the United States, 69% of fifth- through eighth-grade students are being taught arithmetic by teachers who do not possess a degree or certificate in this area; in physical science, 93%. Those ratios in high school do not fare much better: 31% in mathematics, 61% in chemistry, and 67% in physics. The low test scores, in addition to other factors that negatively affect the learning experience, are attributed to numerous educational groups including teachers (Kumashiro, 2012).

## Teacher Preparation

Teachers may be accused by some of being unready to meet classroom challenges. However, current research suggests that teachers are more prepared for the classroom today than ever before in history: teacher training is more extensive, more expensive, and more research based than in the past. Most teacher preparation programs now require a minimum of five years and cost more than many other careers that receive higher pay in today's society. Additionally, in the area of graduate level education, in 2007–2008, 49% of elementary school teachers and 54% of secondary school teachers held a post-baccalaureate degree. Given those statistics, is our current teacher preparation system effective? Only marginally so, according to the study, *A Sense of Calling: Who Teaches and Why* (2000), reporting that only 44% of administrators stated new teachers are ready to effectively lead an "orderly" classroom and only 52% o report that the quality of beginning teachers has improved over past years.

No doubt we need well-prepared teachers who exhibit efficient knowledge of teaching and learning, in addition to expert content knowledge and experience, which lead to positive student achievement (Darling-Hammond, 2006b). Ironically, those same teachers do not control curricula, performance standards, or assessment procedures within their educational institutions; they are also increasingly being required to teach outside of their content areas, which results in lower performing students (Fetler, 1999).

## The Economy and Attrition

The economy of the country drives teacher pay, federal and state funding, grant availability, and special program support. Unfortunately teachers who reportedly don't plan to continue teaching until retirement (37%) blame low pay for their decision to leave the profession (NEA, 2012), yet at the same time, research confirms that experienced educators are critically vital to students' achievement, especially in the areas of science and math where teacher shortages and attrition rates have grown by 50% over the past decade (NCTAF, 2004). Between 1990 and 2000, 2.1 million teachers left their jobs to pursue other careers (Useem, Offenberg, & Farley, 2007). Besides causing a financial burden to the educational system, high turnover is a huge contributing factor to the stagnancy of learning in schools (Alliance for Excellent Education, 2005; NCTAF, 2004; U.S. Department of Education, 2005)

The National Commission on Teaching and America's Future (NCTAF) published a policy brief titled *The High Cost of Teacher Turnover* (Carroll, 2004), which states:

Until we recognize that we have a retention problem we will continue to engage in a costly annual recruitment and hiring cycle, pouring more and more teachers into our nation's classrooms only to lose them at a faster and faster rate. This will continue to drain our public tax dollars, it will undermine teaching quality, and it will most certainly hinder our ability to close student achievement gaps. (p. 1)

Throughout the nation the average earnings of workers with at least four years of college are now over 50% higher than the average earnings of an educator (National Association of Colleges and Employers, 2012). However, teachers report they do not choose the teaching profession specifically for the money, so increases in salaries may be no guarantee for higher performance or higher retention rates. Consequently any focus on attrition in the future must be on better meeting the needs of teachers, in addition to removing demotivating factors that occur within the system once teachers enter the classroom.

### Motivational Considerations

Workplace theorists assert various motivational aspects of why people do or do not stay in a career. Equity theory (Adams, 1965) emphasizes that people must equitably receive back what they put in, whether monetarily, time, success, etc. Self-determination theory (Ryan & Deci, 2000) asserts that feelings of autonomy, competence, and belonging play a key role in the motivation of an employee. Maslow's hierarchy of needs theory suggests that individual needs must be met before there is an increase in motivation (e.g., job security and safety). We will elaborate in later chapters about how those specific theories play key roles in becoming an integrated leader. The economy, salaries, success of students, test performance demands, time demands, and physical and psychological health of teachers all play a role in motivation, in addition to increased accountability for high-stakes testing and support from school administrators (Kieschke & Schaarschmidt, 2008).

### Time Versus Pay

Teachers spend an average of 50 hours per week on instructional duties. These include an average of 12 hours each week on non-compensated school-related activities such as grading papers, bus duty, and club advising. Additionally, "breaks" are often used to prepare for upcoming teaching semesters, including continuing education credits and earning college hours, often at their own expense. Although there is much debate over how much teachers make and how many hours they work, few teachers enter the field to become wealthy. However, when pay is linked with other factors such as the amount of teaching freedom, job stability, administrative support, and media attention, teachers can be drastically affected by it.

### Teaching to the Test: A Loss of Autonomy

The 2002 federal No Child Left Behind Act (NCLB) was originally intended to encourage schools and teachers to "be accountable" for the jobs they do as educators. It resulted in rigorous standardized student testing, which has caused a certain amount of public criticism that educators simply teach information and memorization so that their students can pass exams. In some cases that may be true because the law does not allow educators to deviate from the state standards and benchmarks. It also reportedly led to a declined sense of autonomy and safety by teachers (Anderson, 2003; Faber, 1991; Troman & Woods, 2000, 2001). In Atlanta, the Georgia Bureau of Investigation (GBI) reported that some local schools exhibited a culture of "fear, intimidation and retaliation spread throughout the district" (GBI, 2011), and later released another report documenting widespread cheating where they found evidence of teachers being coerced into correcting students' wrong answers and reflected that the "pressure to meet adequate yearly progress under the No Child Left Behind Act" was key to the scandal. The intent of the act was good, but the implementation must be carried out in a way that does not threaten job stability or federal funding or put into question teachers' competence and self-confidence.

### Educator Value

Respect for the professional educator by youth, parents, and the community is paramount to the success of our educational future. Teachers must not only teach but also excel at translating their knowledge into classroom teaching strategies that assist students of all intelligence, psychological, and experience levels, which requires, at the least, creativity, adaptability, organization, time management skills, conflict management skills, relational skills, problem-solving skills, helper/counseling skills, and purposeful planning.

### Economics

Economics have always played a role in education. Despite the need for a clear vision for how success is measured and defined, in U.S. schools, current standards of education are often the center of debate. Society often defines such standards by the predicted economic effects that said education will contribute to the future of its country. Since our country is considered a leader in a global society, the concerns are not only based on the abilities of each child, but what the consensus of positive productivity will be. This is difficult to measure; how much should one know to be a positive contributor to the national economic goals? Do manual laborers significantly contribute to our nation? Do strong family units generate future positive growth and citizenship? Has our past, even with its continual pendulum of highly debated educational successes, been decorated with great leaders, inventors, creative minds, and entrepreneurs? The answer to those questions is a resounding yes. However, learning introduces opportunities to engage positively in society in multifaceted ways. We as a nation do not yet know how students who began school in the 1990s and thereafter will fare as tomorrow's leaders. That was a time when our educational agenda started to implement acknowledgment of individual learner needs, diversity management, and social justice ideologies bathed in constructivism.

Fortunately total educational funding has increased in recent years at all levels of government, even in the face of enrollment increases and inflation. By the end of the 2004–2005 school year, national K–12 educational spending support increased an estimated 105% since 1991–1992; 58% since 1996–1997; and 40% since 1998–1999. On a per-pupil basis and adjusted for inflation, public school funding increased 24% from 1991–1992 through 2001–2002; 19% from 1996–1997 through 2001–2002; and 10% from 1998–1999 through 2001–2002 (Kline, 2012). Federal funding for Title I, which provides grants to help disadvantaged children, increased from under $3 billion in 1980 to more than $7 billion in 2000 and almost $14 billion in 2005 (USDE, 2012). Spending on education from all sources—local, state, federal, and others—ascended from $249 billion in 1990–1991 to $442.7 billion in 2000–2001 and $501.3 billion in 2003–2004 (U.S. Budget, Historical Tables, 2006). The federal investment in the Elementary and Secondary Education Act rose from under $2 billion in 1966 to $15 billion in 2000 to $25 billion in 2005 (U.S. Budget, Historical Tables, 2006). Special education federal grants were under $250 million in 1977 but rose to $5 billion in 2000 and almost $12 billion in 2005 (U.S. Budget, Historical Tables, 2006).

In 2008, expenditures per student for the United States were $10,995 at the combined elementary and secondary level, which was 35% higher than the average of $8,169 for the Organization for Economic Co-operation and Development (OECD) member countries reporting data. (See http://www.oecd.org for a list of these countries.)

On the downside, the needs of socioeconomically diverse learners continues to be a challenge as each group has its own special needs. Prior to the Great Recession (2007–2009), more white children lived in poverty than Hispanic children (Lopez & Velasco, 2011). However, between 2007 and 2010, Hispanic children living in poverty increased by 36.3%. By contrast, even though the number of white and black children living in poverty also grew, their numbers grew more slowly—up 17.6% and 11.7%, respectively. Additionally, 34% of immigrants in this nation currently lack health insurance, compared to 13% of natives. Immigrants and their U.S.-born children account for 71% of the increase in the uninsured since 1989 (Center for Immigration Study, 2007). As seen throughout history the U.S. economy is an important factor that affects education, especially as the gap between socioeconomic groups increases (Weissmann, 2012).

Immigration has and will continue to play a key role in the economy of our country while presenting challenges to the educational system. The number of factories/plants that depend on Mexican immigrant workers has continued to grow from about 2,700 to about 3,700 in 2001 and of the 6.1 million Latino children who are living in poverty, more than two-thirds (4.1 million) were the children of immigrant parents (Lopez & Velasco, 2011), of which the vast majority (86.2%) were born in the United States (Lopez & Velasco, 2011). These factors have affected how classes are taught because of both the cultural and socioeconomic diversities, which often breed stereotypical thinking and class rivalry within communities.

The foreign-born population growth rate in every decade since 1970 has been higher than at any other time in history, surpassing the 31% increase between 1900 and 1910 (Center for Immigration Study, 2007). This presents a pivotal question to educational leaders today: How do we, as a nation, educate everyone successfully? With the ease of transportation and the predominance of the Internet age, the process and definition of the culture of a community will change. That change will present both challenges and opportunities for future educators who will be working with a growing diversity of learners.

### Cultural Changes and Adaptation

Prior to 1980, there was little concern about cultural diversity in the educational system. Geographical settling dictated societal unity and the adherence to a common set of goals and values. If someone different arrived, he or she was expected to conform to the homogeneous environment. Those expectations have changed dramatically today. Due to area population shifts and changing community needs, those homogeneous schools have become the exception and not the norm.

We have transformed as a society yet admittedly still have a ways to go with cultural adaption. There are still arguable differences over what constitutes "politically correct" in addition to the growing language barriers and differences in parenting norms, to name a few. Sociological research has inspired many new ideas and teaching practices to assist with cultural changes, but we are learning there is no "cookie cutter" answer. Diversity is a complex issue.

The ease of relocation for all learners creates questions in how to create a positive school culture without forcing assimilation and infringing on individual needs. In poverty-driven schools, a high socioeconomic child may have difficulty learning, simply based on the differing practices existent in the new culture. In a farming community, a child who strives to attend postsecondary education could also struggle as he or she muddles through the inconsistent value-based core of the community, which inoculates its educational goals. As will be addressed later, additional factors such as cultural shock are also a possibility to consider as students and families switch school environments more easily. This climate of change in the culture of schools will continue to be challenging as we evolve into a more diverse and mobile society. It is no longer just the racial minorities who can experience oppression within education. Children in poverty, children with one parent, children with same-sex parents, and children in abusive homes are all now a part of our "minority" sectors that increase the challenge to encourage positive learning, since one must first meet the learners where they are, and so many learners are starting at differing points with differing needs. Even positive labeling of students has led to further segregations of children (e.g., the gifted and "wealthy"). Many variables must be considered in the overall schema of the classroom to be successful.

## The Good News

Regardless of the negative reports, there is much reason for teachers to be encouraged and hopeful about the future. Often it is how we look at a situation: great problems create great opportunities. Changing how a system works takes time, energy, money, and belief that the right changes are being made. We must also focus on the right pieces of the puzzle.

Despite negative reports and discrepant scores in the past between cultural groups, all students are improving. This seems reasonable considering they all received the same instruction, same amount of time in class, and the same resources, which was not always the case historically. The inconsistency of scores lies primarily in the starting points for each of the groups. Students of Hispanic and African American descent may have entered classes behind their white counterparts, and all students are now finishing the race and they are making measurable progress. In the past two decades, we have learned to let go of intellectual biases and provide learning resources and opportunities for all students instead of only a select few.

The efforts are paying off. The Hispanic/white achievement gap for fourth and eighth graders in reading closed by 2% from 1992 to 2009; Hispanic scores in reading achievement rose between grade 4 and grade 12; and African American students raised their proficiency 81 points in 1992 (NCES, 2001). In 2009, Hispanics raised their reading proficiency scores by 69 points, African Americans by 64 points, Alaska Native students by 79 points, and whites by 63 points (NCES, 2012). From 1999 to 2008, the total number of black and Hispanic students taking an Advanced Placement (AP) exam more than tripled, from 94,000 to 318,000 students. In 2008, Asians had the highest mean AP exam score (3.08) across all exams (NCES, 2012).

According to the U.S. Census Bureau, in 1980, more than 58 million children enrolled in school preK–12; in 1990, 60.5 million; in 2000, 68.5 million; and in fall 2012, more than 75 million students attended public and private elementary and secondary schools (NCES, 2012). This is a drastic change from our past. Additionally, dropout rates for students have decreased significantly as well: dropout rates have trended downward, from 12% in 1990 to 7.4% in 2010; additionally, although the fluctuations occurred at differing time periods in our past, all ethnicity dropout rates have decreased (Chapman, Laird, Ifill, & Kewal-Ramani, 2011; NCES, 2012).

Equal educational access was a conceptual idea at the birth of this nation but not a reality for close to 500 years. We credit the teachers and the educational system for turning this around in the past two decades and encourage you as leaders in the classroom to continue to take ownership of the educational process and dedicate your efforts to the success of all your students. Don't allow self-fulfilling media platforms that negatively taint poor performance reports and teacher preparedness to affect your motivations. Plant your roots strongly in the positive. You as an educator deserve respect and your value quotient in society will continue to rise.

> **Remember: Educators are making headway and positive steps forward to educating our children—ALL children. Hold on to this TRUTH as you prepare for your career.**

We are continuing to understand more of what it takes to be successful when inspiring children to learn and positively develop. What you do as teacher does matter. Be encouraged that all students in the American educational system **are** learning. Fortunately our nation as a whole is beginning to better understand the complexities of what teachers are being asked to do. The democracy of our country makes us great and the ever-changing contexts of the learners, coupled with passionate beliefs about education, teaching, and learning by stakeholders, will continue to make the process challenging but infinitely rewarding.

### Summary

We are currently undergoing a massive rethinking of how we prepare teachers for the ever-changing levels of learners within their future classrooms. The issue is highly complex and must be dealt with through multifaceted strategies. First, educators must let go of old paradigms of a homogenous society where "one size fits all" for the students they teach. With changing demographics and population shifts, we need to be prepared to embrace a diversity of backgrounds and values. Additionally, change is difficult and teachers must learn to maintain self-motivation in the face of a demanding career. There will be frustrations with the process and outcomes that will be experienced by teachers, parents, and communities. We as educators must continue to take our thinking to new levels and become more innovative about meeting the learners' needs while maintaining a work/life balance that makes teaching a rewarding experience for everyone.

It is good to look back and learn from our history, but what lies behind us is not as important as what lies ahead. We are moving forward. We are redefining success. We are making a positive difference.

# Chapter 2

# Integration and Leadership Development

> *You never change things by fighting the existing reality.*
> *To change something, build a new model that makes the existing model obsolete.*
> — *Richard Buckminster Fuller*

We can no longer look to only one method or a single theory to answer all of the questions in education. Focusing teacher preparation on building integrated leaders, not just content experts, is pivotal in this process. We suggest a combination of multiple theoretical development models be used as a tool to guide you through an integration of motivational, cognitive, and psychological development. Becoming an integrated educational leader will improve your confidence, emotional health, and teaching skills prior to entering the classroom. This development will enhance your ability to facilitate successful learning experiences for your students, as well as provide you with skills to create a healthy work/life balance to maintain high motivation and energy in a demanding field.

Unlike previous models, the Integrated Educational Leadership Model (IELM) incorporates the needs of both the teacher and stakeholders (defined to include students, parents, and community members) with an emphasis on building effective leadership skills designed to enhance learners' success. Significant to the IELM are the following theories:

1. **Hierarchy of Needs Theory (HNT)**—incorporating key components to one's personal needs, both of the leader and the learner: safety, security, belonging, personal esteem, and self-actualization (Maslow, 1943).

2. **Emotional Intelligence (EI)**—incorporating key components to one's behavior and thoughts: self-awareness, self-management, social awareness, and relationship management (Goleman, 1995).
3. **Self-Determination Theory (SDT)**—incorporating key components to one's motivational needs: sense of autonomy, belonging, and positive efficacy (Ryan and Deci, 2000).
4. **Cultural Responsiveness (CR)**—recognition of the importance of including students' cultural references in all aspects of learning (Ladson-Billings, 1994) and becoming a critical educator, but also gaining a better understanding of your own culture and how it affects your success.

Before addressing the IELM, an explanation of each framework will be helpful to ensure understanding. Although you may have been introduced to these motivational theories in other preparation courses, it was most likely in reference to motivating your students. We encourage you to identify how these theories also affect you, the teacher—the human being.

### Maslow's Hierarchy of Needs

Maslow's hierarchy of needs theory was named after Abraham Maslow, a clinical psychologist's of the 20th century (Latham, 2007). The needs are ranked from the most basic of needs at the bottom with tiers that provide additional needs that can be obtained through the meetings of each level, inevitably providing support for one's confidence and life fulfillment. As an important motivational theory applied in the classroom, Maslow's hierarchy of needs (1943) is also important to your development as a leader. Meeting your personal foundational needs is of utmost importance before you can successfully meet those of your students. Without your basic needs met, you cannot be expected to apply exceptional skills in your classrooms. Students cannot successfully learn without their basic needs met. You also cannot expect to be successful without addressing your development and needs.

The model also lends itself to a higher awareness of your stakeholders and their needs. Leaders cannot be successful without being aware of others' motivations to act. Thus, this development will increase your ability to better balance the highly multifaceted needs of the organization. Most would agree that the educational system should meet the needs and enhance the lives of its primary stakeholders, including the students, the parents, the community, as well as the teachers. We will include a description of each level to help you understand the hierarchy of needs according to Maslow.

Beginning at level one, the basic human needs consist of food, clothing, shelter, water, sleep, health, and other essential basics that encourage fundamental survival. These needs, according to the theory, must be met before the door to higher levels of fulfillment and motivation can be opened. If you, or your students, are hungry, do not have warm clothing, experience life instability, or are ill, everything else in your daily life will be affected, including your attitude and performance. Teachers are taught (generally in motivational theory courses) to be on the alert to when students display signs that these needs are not being met and to bring it to the attention of school administrators and counselors. Many schools address this level of Maslow's hierarchy by offering breakfast or lunch programs to ensure the basic nutrition needs of their students are being met. Sadly, some teachers neglect their own basic nutritional needs, which drastically affect their performance in the classroom. Your health is important to you becoming successful and must be taken seriously.

The second level in the needs hierarchy involves safety and security. This level of need can encompass a plethora of things and is often dependent on the individual and his or her environment. It could be the need for physical safety (from weapons in the school or the abuse from others) or it could refer to less visible, but equally important, factors, including job stability, health benefits, a financial savings, or a healthy personal life. It can even include the need for freedom from condemnation, such as religious beliefs (Latham, 2007).

You, as a leader, must feel safe—physically and psychologically—before you can successfully educate groups of diverse learners. Just as it is difficult for your students to concentrate on mathematical concepts if they are worried about being bullied on the playground at recess, it will be difficult for you to be creative, patient, and achievement oriented if you feel as if you may be hurt by a student, a colleague, or a member of your home. As essential as it is to create a safe learning space for your students, it is equally important for you to have this need met. If you as an educator recognize patterns of bullying or other behaviors that may endanger students, or yourself, both physically or psychologically, it is your responsibility to bring it to the attention of school administrators, police, a therapist, or a friend. Be intentional about meeting this need for yourself and your students.

The third level in the hierarchy consists of social acceptance, which includes needs for love and belongingness. This relationally focused level expounds on the idea that humans need to give and receive love, in addition to feeling they belong or fit into a community of family, friends, and/or work peers. An important point about this psychological need is that it encompasses every theory within the Integrated Educational Leadership Model. It is often underestimated or simplified, but the need for social acceptance will touch every area in the development of your teaching and leadership skills. The ways this need is met will be as diverse as the many different people you will meet and your experiences throughout your life. It may take on different faces, but the need to belong is a common thread of the core of all humanity, and without it your motivation can be affected. Parker Palmer (1998) in *Courage to Teach* describes good teachers as those who possess a "capacity for connectedness… connections are held not in their methods, but in their hearts… as the place where intellect, emotion, and spirit converge in the human self" (p. 11).

The fourth and fifth levels in Maslow's theory include the needs for self-esteem and self-actualization. Self-esteem may be defined as being respected, valued, and attaining positive perceptions about one's efficacy. This includes being successful and competent in your career, social circle, and family. The fulfillment of this need opens the door to self-actualization, which may be defined as the act of experiencing purpose, self-realization, joy, and personal acceptance in one's life.

Self-perception or evaluation is crucial at those stages. Taking time to consider yourself, your needs, your strengths, your weaknesses, as well as considering what in your environment hinders this will assist you in meeting these higher level human needs. To become a fully self-actualized person you must intentionally know and establish a vision of where you want to go. The hierarchy of needs is a sequential journey that sometimes zigs and zags and moves backward and forward during the refinement and fulfillment that takes place within each level. To become an integrated leader, you must constantly remind yourself that it is a journey, not a destination. Author Kurt Vonnegut Jr. once said, "We are what we imagine ourselves to be." Your perception of who you are and what you want to accomplish is an important key to your development.

Maslow's hierarchy of needs is easily intertwined with the IELM to create an effective tool for the development of leadership skills necessary for your success. By examining whether those five areas of needs are being met in your personal *and* professional lives (personal friendships, family, school, classroom, etc.), you will become more adept at assessing how those needs are being met for your future students. Self-awareness and social awareness are key factors in being conscious, attentive, and purposeful in your role as a leader. We will elaborate on those in the next phase of the IELM.

## Emotional Intelligence

According to researchers (Abraham, 1999; Carmeli & Josman, 2006; Cherniss, 2000; Goleman, 1995; Lopes, Grewall, Kadis, Gall, & Salovey, 2006; Saarni, 2000), emotional intelligence (EI) is an important facet to becoming a successful leader. Goleman, an EI researcher and author, contends that EI accounts for 85 to 90% of the difference between outstanding leaders and their more average peers, as emotions play an imperative role in influencing behavior. Saarni (2000) suggested that "emotions are functional: they serve to goad us into action whereby we initiate, modify, maintain, or terminate our relationship to the particular circumstances we are engaged in" (p. 70). The Harvard Business Review (2003) proposed that EI has become a fundamental leadership competency that can augment professional achievement.

As a future educator, your cognitive abilities to be an effective teacher will likely be well honed, but *how* you implement your knowledge will be equally as important as *what* you know. That is what makes this part of the model vitally important to your success as an educational leader. In most instances, research suggests that people "feel" before they think. At the least, we do them both at the same time (it all happens in milliseconds). The part of your brain that deals with emotions and the part that performs cognitive, rational thought are so closely linked together that emotions often drive your behavior, especially during times of stress or crisis. Stress is an inevitable part of the daily decision-making process and your emotions will play a part in it. Your understanding of EI development will help you attain greater self-awareness in balancing emotions with rational thinking as you navigate the responsibilities in and outside of the classroom.

Goleman's model of EI includes two domains and four competencies. The first domain is personal competence, which relates to how we manage ourselves. The domain includes self-awareness and self-management; it works under the premise that one must understand self before they can understand others. Palmer (1998) states that teaching is more than technique, and if an educator is to improve, he or she must become self-aware before he or she can make a connection with students. The second domain is social competence, which determines how one manages relationships. The domains include social awareness and relationship management. Understanding your own emotions, how they affect relationships, as well as how others' emotions intertwine are vitally important to your development as a leader. Later in this book, you will have the opportunity to view Goleman's model using the Strength, Weakness, Opportunity, and Threat (SWOT) analysis, which addresses both internal (strength/weakness) and external (opportunity/threat) factors.

With the challenges we are currently facing in education, it is more important than ever to be "emotionally intelligent," to possess the capability to use both cognitive and emotional aptitudes as a tool. Heightening your self-awareness and self-management will enable you to harness your greatest strengths and manage your life to fulfill passionately your professional and personal goals. Understanding others will help you to be more effective in gaining collaboration, as well as influencing individuals (i.e., your students), classes, organizations, and communities.

> *"The key to successful leadership is influence, not authority."*
> *—Kenneth H. Blanchard, author*

## Self-Determination Theory

Self-determination theory (SDT) was first conceived by Edward L. Deci after studying intrinsic and extrinsic motivation and the effect of control on motivation (Latham, 2007). The theory promotes the idea that allowing people more freedom to govern themselves results in increased empowerment, autonomy, diligence, effort, engagement, responsibility, interest, and commitment—the pure definition of positive motivation. Furthermore, the theory states that three traits—autonomy, belonging, and competency—drive this motivation (Deci & Ryan, 2000). The fortification of these traits can affect the perception of self, the environment, and the achievement of goals. We believe that SDT affects performance in the workplace and in academic achievement.

Additionally, the self-determination framework addresses motivation that not only affects the way prospective teachers prepare for the classroom but also the subsequent performance of future learners. It is a framework that can be applied to all stakeholders, especially the prospective teacher (Rosser-Cox, 2011). SDT suggests different levels of motivation that can be achieved along a continuum, depending on the level of self-determination one achieves that includes amotivation, extrinsic motivational levels, and intrinsic motivational levels.

## SDT Motivational Continuum

**Amotivation** is the lowest level of motivation according to SDT. This is basic and is defined as having absolutely no motivation to perform an activity. **Extrinsic motivation** is defined by "levels": (1) *introjected* (I feel something inside me making me do the activity, e.g., guilt); (2) *identified* (I do the activity because I know what the outcome will get me); and (3) *integrated* (I do this behavior because it defines me as a person); and lastly, **intrinsic motivation**: performing the activity for the sheer joy it brings to the person. Overall, SDT suggests that competency, autonomy, and relatedness (belongingness) all lead to enhanced/more positive motivation and psychological well-being, which in turn encourages better results. Each area is important to the development of a motivated leader.

**Competency.** The need for competence is met when one feels capable. When people feel those needs are satisfactorily met, they internalize positive values and attitudes associated with a behavior. Frequent feelings of internal motivation enhance psychological health and overall well-being. In contrast, when a person feels less competent, his or her intrinsic motivation declines (Deci & Ryan, 1985). Practically speaking, if you as a teacher do not feel capable of working with a classroom filled with diverse groups of students when you begin your career, there is a likelihood that your motivation to work with these students will deteriorate, along with your personal well-being and your success.

**Autonomy.** The need for autonomy reflects the desire of individuals to be the source of their own behavior (Deci & Ryan, 1985; Thomas, 2006) and is experienced when individuals perceive their behavior as self-endorsed (Ryan & La Guardia, 2000). Research suggests that autonomy in relation to any given activity, including teaching, encourages the engagement of said activity (Reeve, Jang, Carrell, Jeon, & Barch, 2004). In contrast, the lack of autonomy discourages attentive engagement, which is an absolute necessity to successfully teach learners. People explore their surroundings for a place that will let them apply their talents and gifts, as well as communicate their beliefs and values. We all need a form of autonomy that leads to self-success. When dealing with issues such as how to decrease teacher attrition rates, it is important to note that job autonomy positively correlates with both positive job satisfaction (Hackman & Oldman, 1980; Parker & Wall, 1998) and commitment (Parker, Axtel, & Turner, 2001).

**Relatedness.** The final component of SDT is relatedness, or belonging. Relatedness refers to the need to be cared for, connected to, related to, or a feeling of belonging in a given social setting (Deci & Ryan, 2000; Ryan & La Guardia, 2000). How well you feel like you "fit in" to your environment can facilitate intrinsic motivation and the internalization of extrinsic motivation, whereas neglecting these needs can adversely affect one's motivation (Vallerand, Fortier, & Guay, 1997). Without a feeling of belonging within a school or your classroom, which can be based on relationships with colleagues, students, parents, and the community, educators can experience decreased motivation and personal wellness. It is important to note that feelings of belongingness can initially be difficult to attain when a person feels overwhelmed by the differences in cultures within a new context. Understanding this variable will be helpful in allowing time for the attainment of relatedness in your new career as you create positive personal and professional relationships.

## Cultural Responsiveness

Cultural responsiveness refers to the ability to understand, gain knowledge of, and demonstrate respect for another's culture (Neuman, 1999). Teachers must respect and recognize the need to build on what children already know about their own language and backgrounds in order to incorporate the new knowledge (Garcia, 1994; Gay, 2002; Irvine, 1992; Ladson-Billings, 1994, 1995, 2001). Additionally a teacher must also understand his or her culture and how it affects this dynamic. "Culture is defined as a system of values, beliefs, and standards that guides people's thoughts, feelings, and behavior" (Yokota, 1995; p 239). Important to the understanding of cultural responsiveness is that all beliefs and customs can be correct in the culture in which they derive and should never be ignored or discounted. Additionally, often our perceptions about one another can be false and the acknowledgment of our inability to be always right is crucial.

As the foundational component of the IELM and your development we have included an entire section on this theory (Chapter 7). Cultural responsiveness, cultural competence, and critical teaching are all necessary parts for successfully developing your leadership abilities.

## The Integrated Educational Leadership Model

By incorporating important facets of cultural competence, human needs, physically, psychologically, and motivationally, we believe IELM promotes the integration of essential leadership skills that will be key factors for becoming a successful teacher. The model, which foundationally builds upon cultural responsiveness integrated with the previously defined theoretical models, encourages a more sustainable educator who brings leadership skills to the classroom and schools to further increase the academic success of learners.

Based on the integration of these frameworks, the first step in development is **self-awareness and assessment**. Mark Zuckerberg once said, "Make your own development a priority." Business leaders invest in themselves, and so should you as educational leaders. Two important facets to this phase of self-development are (1) predispositional belief maturity

(Ladson-Billings, 1994; Rosser-Cox, 2011) and (2) your cultural competence (Ladson-Billings, 1994; NEA Policy Brief, 2008). Acknowledging what "makes you tick" will enable you to process successfully cultural competency in this maturation process. It is invaluable to leadership development to know one's self before having the ability to understand and empathize with others. It is through self-reflection that a learner must question experience and examine "the integrity and assumptions and beliefs based on prior experience," and this act of "reflection is most essential for transformation of our meaning structures" (Taylor, 1998, p. 16).

Ask yourself why you believe what you believe. Consider who and what is important to you. Be honest about what makes you happy, what makes you frustrated, and what brings you passion. Evaluate your strengths and weaknesses. Leaders with well-developed emotional self-awareness are more effective intuitive decision makers (Wharam, 2009). By embarking on a process of personal self-reflection, writing about one's life story can encourage self-definition and meaning, which encourages a transformation in a view of self and the world (Dominice, 2000; Gornick, 2001). Autobiographical narratives are a valuable tool for teachers to explore personal values and connect them to the field of teaching (Gusdorf, 1980).

Learning to self-manage is also important because you must ensure that your needs are met before you can possess the motivation and energy required to effectively help others. Being in a career that demands so much of you will take more than just showing up on time. Similar to being in the health profession, the teaching field induces continual emotional and physical stress. When you actively engage others all day and grade paper and design curriculum during your "off" times, you must be mindful of your needs, which (in alignment with self-determination theory and Maslow's hierarchy) include food, shelter, safety, security, physical health, psychological health, autonomy, competence, self-esteem, respect, and belonging. Without fulfilling your own needs first, you will end up with nothing left to give regardless of what the demands are. Life coach, international strategist, and motivational speaker Adrey Marlene (2013) suggests you ask yourself the following questions:

- Managing your thoughts. Are you critical of self? Do you encourage thoughts that promote your success?
- Managing your words and your ability to communicate them. Do you choose carefully the words you speak to enhance your success?
- Managing your actions and behaviors. How are you perceived by others? How do you want to be perceived?

- Organizing and planning ahead to self-manage more effectively. Do you look at ways to encourage order in your life?
- Maintaining your focus on the task. Do you follow through to completion on goals and projects?
- Managing your time. Do you make this a priority?
- Managing your physical self. What habits do you implement to promote a healthy lifestyle?
- Managing your spiritual self. How do you fill your spiritual need?

Reflect back for a moment on the last time you flew on a commercial airline. The attendant stood at the front of the airplane and asked for your attention. First, the attendant gave detailed instructions on how to use the seat belt (as if you needed directions). Next, the attendant pointed to all the emergency exit doors in case you (and 150 other passengers) had to make a mad scramble to disembark. The attendant then explained about using the cushions as floatation devices on the off chance the plane landed in water and you had to take a swim. Finally, the attendant demonstrated how to put on the oxygen mask should the cabin lose pressure. Remember the key words used: *Put the oxygen mask on yourself first, before trying to help your learners.* This is a prime example of self-management—the realization and practicality that you must attend to self needs, emotional, psychological, and physical, first, before trying to help your students. You cannot give away what you do not have. Self-management and self-control go hand in hand. "A person displays self-control when in the relative absence of immediate external constraints, he engages in behavior whose previous probability has been less than that of alternatively available behaviors" (Thoreson & Mahoney, 1974, p. 12.). Zimmerman and Kitsatas (1997) argue that self-management is something that must be taught, describe the following four-stage process that helps students to become self-regulated learners, and encourage educators that they too must possess these skills:

- Observing the teacher—modeling
- Imitation—attempts with feedback as required
- Self-control—independence
- Self-regulation—adapting to new challenges

If we require that students gain these skills, the importance of teacher development in these areas becomes crucial.

The next phase in the Integrated Educational Leadership Model is becoming **socially aware**.

According to Daniel Goleman (2011) the competencies associated with being socially aware are the following:

- Empathy: understanding the other person's emotions, needs and concerns
- Organizational Awareness: the ability to understand the politics within an organization and how these affect the employees, stakeholders, and, in this case, your learners
- Service: the ability to understand and meet the needs of your learners and their parents/guardians

Social awareness is about considering what people need or desire and communicating with them in a way that meets their needs. It includes a keen understanding by the educator about their learners and respecting their individual cultural backgrounds. Your understanding of the cultural competence and emotional intelligence models is extremely important to becoming successful as a contemporary educator. Your learners will need your empathy, acceptance, and respect in acknowledging their individual differences. Incidentally, those three qualities are probably the most determining factors for the development of trust, which is crucial for creating a productive learning and a positive working environment.

According to research, trust helps build positive relationships and improve student performance (Hoy & Sweetland, 2001; Hoy & Tschannen-Moran, 2001; Tschannen-Moran & Hoy, 1997; Hoy, W. K., & Tschannen-Moran, 1999; 2003). Additionally a teacher's trust of the principal is a likely predictor of the level of trust that person has with students, parents, and colleagues (Brewster & Railsback, 2003). We will discuss how to develop skills for social awareness and trust later in this book.

The final phase of the IELM is that of successfully managing relationships. Building successful relationships requires skilled communications, which requires dedication and practice. Most conflicts occur because misunderstandings arise concerning another person's expectations, values, or cultural norms. Fittingly, one's ability to communicate with sensitivity and empathy is the cornerstone for becoming the integrated educational leader. Mike Myatt (2012), contributing editor of *Forbes* magazine, made an important distinction about what that means: "It is simply impossible to become a great leader without being a great communicator. I hope you noticed the previous sentence didn't refer to being a great talker—big difference." He went on to say, "It is the ability to develop a keen external awareness that separates the truly great communicators from those who muddle through their interactions with others."

Learning how to manage successfully relationships requires deliberate effort and practice. One must also possess certain character qualities, such as respect, empathy, kindness, and caring. Peter Drucker stated that "management is doing things right; leadership is doing the right things." Great leaders are driven to do the right things. Developing greater awareness of yourself and people around you will enrich your life experiences and increase your sphere of influence as a leader. Our two-fold objective for incorporating this multifaceted model of theories is to help you attain a greater understanding of how to become a great leader and increase your success in teaching. We consider it to be a "stone unturned" as no other current writings fully address the needs of both educator and student, both leader and follower. To be a successful educator you must become not only the content specialist but also a leader who shows your students the way to greatness and personal empowerment.

> "If your actions inspire others to dream more, learn more, do more and become more, you are a leader." —John Quincy Adams

*Chapter 3*

# Cultural Competence

> *Education must begin with the solution of the teacher-student
> contradiction, by reconciling the poles of the contradiction
> so that both are simultaneously teachers and students.*
> —Paulo Freire

**CULTURAL COMPETENCE**

**To transform one's self into a leader is no easy task; it requires becoming a learner again and again.** Based on the IELM, cultural competency is the foundation for which all development must occur. Social awareness that develops into cultural competency and culturally responsive pedagogy are both based on knowledge of non-similar cultures, as well as one's own culture

(Ladson-Billings, 1994; Ladson-Billings & Tate, 1995). Beyond that, what is truly most important is not the teacher's actual racial, ethnic, and cultural background, but the knowledge of self and others (Cochran-Smith, 1997; Garcia & Malkin, 1993).

Your past experiences, as well as those of your students, play an integral role in the development your current identity, values, and motivations. Cultural responsiveness is a choice to acknowledge both similarities and differences of all people within a culture. Visionary leaders understand that embracing and managing diversity can only serve to strengthen us. That is the premise for the term *E pluribus unum,* adopted by an Act of Congress in 1782, which was placed on the seal of the United States. It is a Latin term that means "out of many, one."

The key to cultural responsiveness acknowledge it to not ignore it. In his book *Color Blind: The Rise of Post-Racial Politics and the Retreat from Racial Equality,* Tim Wise (2010) cautions about falling into the trap of well intentioned "color blindness," which denotes a pattern of sitting on the fence in the face of social change rather than meeting it head on. Other research publications (Ladson-Billings, 2001,1997; Rosser-Cox, 2011) reiterate how teachers regard themselves as change agents and diversity advocates while sometimes failing to acknowledge that different colors do exist within the culture. Not seeing color implies not seeing differences. Even though a teacher may be trying to be "fair" by treating all students the same, not acknowledging differences may actually invoke more harm than good for the students. If a child is left-handed, should you give him a pair of right-handed scissors because all the other students are right-handed? If you do, he will likely struggle more at cutting pieces of paper than those with scissors that match their physical attributes. While this situation seems obvious, we face others every day that are not so cut and dried. Cultural responsiveness means meeting students where they are with the understanding that if one struggles, ultimately everyone does in some way.

Granted teachers are faced with one of the most diverse jobs in the world. Your students' experiences and identities will vary in a plethora of ways from ethnic to socioeconomic levels, to the neighborhoods they live in, their parental units and home life, religion, peer influences, intellectual capability, personality traits, emotional development, food preferences, and the list goes on. If all this seems complex, it is. In fact, at times it may be overwhelming, but you didn't choose this profession because it is easy, right? By gaining a better understanding and appreciation of diversity (Thomas, 2006), you will strengthen relationships with your students and the community.

## Diversity from a Global Perspective

In the literature on diversity there exists little cross-over between research conducted in the private sector and educational institutions. We are undaunted by that fact because we view classrooms and schools as places for conducting business. Leading learners is a skill that takes the same dedication, skill, and enthusiasm as leading employees. The goal of education, like the private sector, is one of service, although terminologies may vary from one to the other. In educational systems we have teachers and counselors where their counterparts in the private workplace may be referred to as performance coaches and mentors. Regardless of those differences much can be learned from the global workplace and applied to the classroom to achieve success.

In the workplace, research overwhelmingly concludes that performance increases when employees are motivated in ways that meet their individual needs. R. Roosevelt Thomas Jr. (2006) created an effective model for applying diverse management styles in the workplace that we believe can be incorporated by culturally competent educators. Thomas explains that strategic diversity management (SDM) is a tool for improving ways that people make quality decisions in situations where critical differences and tensions exist. Because it is a cognitive process, Thomas maintains that anyone can learn to use it (Thomas, 2006). In *Building on the Promise of Diversity* (Thomas, 2006) he focuses on advancing the field of diversity in the workplace by defining it as more than mere differences in color or creed. First Thomas asserts that we are all distinctively unique and our personal identities are comprised of more than we may realize. Second, tensions can arise from our similarities as much as from our individual differences.

The idea of becoming more diversity mature and culturally competent is not a pass or fail destination. It is a dynamic, ongoing process that requires one to continually examine and look beyond personal paradigms to understand oneself and others. Socrates said, "The unexamined life is not worth living." As you read this book we encourage you to continuously ask yourself questions for self-reflection: What determines your personal identity and makes you, you? Your gender? Your age? Your upbringing? Your educational level? Your religion? Your state of health? How have those factors influenced your beliefs, values, and views of the world? What differences do you have with others that affect your happiness, life balance, or ability to get along with people? How can you learn to accept and appreciate those differences as a catalyst for personal growth? What similarities do you share with others that may be limiting you or keeping you stuck?

Thomas (2006) asserted that the majority of the workforce has "difficulty making quality decisions when differences, similarities, and tensions exist" (p. 108). This is often difficult to evaluate because relationships may appear to be harmonious on the surface, while a simmering state of uneasiness or tension may be brewing underneath. Being personally aware of your beliefs, values, and emotional states will help you to better understand and deal with your needs and frustrations. Being socially aware of others' states will help you recognize their needs to facilitate greater motivation and learning. Teachers must respect and recognize where the learner is coming from to best direct them into new areas of knowledge in the future (Cochran-Smith, 1997; Garcia, 1991, 1994; Gay, 2000; Katz, 1999; .Ladson-Billings, 1994; Rosser-Cox, 2010).

According to research, learning is a socially arbitrated process (Goldstein, 1999; Vygotsky, 1978). Learners develop through interactions with adults, classmates, and peers. Feedback is an important part of this development (Darling-Hammond, 1997) and without the proper tools to address a student's needs, such as an understanding of their background, feedback can be more destructive than constructive. You as a teacher and leader in the classroom have a great opportunity to inspire and promote diversity, as well as facilitate learning, if you are willing to become more culturally responsive.

**Culturally Responsive Pedagogy**

National statistics suggest that the population of the United States is becoming more ethnically and socioeconomically diverse (NCES, 2011). Educators must recognize the certainty that many of their students will come to their classrooms with cultural, ethnic, linguistic, racial, and social class backgrounds that differ from their own. Culturally responsive teaching is a pedagogy that recognizes the importance of including students' cultural references in all aspects of learning (Ladson-Billings, 1994). Research has shown that culturally responsive teachers have been effective in educating diverse student populations, including members of racial, ethnic, economic, lifestyle, and cultural minority groups, as well as creating positive strategies to assist students with differing learner needs. Additionally, creating positive relationships has been suggested as critical to effective leadership in culturally and linguistically diverse schools (Banks, 2004; Gay, 2000; Hofstede, 2003; Ladson-Billings, 1995). Understanding what it is that such teachers do can be beneficial for teacher educators concerned with preparing teachers for the diverse school populations prospective teachers will face. It has also been suggested that teachers who have learned culturally responsive pedagogy are more confident and believe they are more effective in their instruction of diverse children. In other words, they possess positive cultural efficacy (Pang & Sablan, 1998).

Culture refers to the ways of living: shared behaviors, customs, beliefs, values, and perceptions that direct groups of people in their daily life. Culture can be developed from one generation to the next or from the past experiences of the individual. Culture influences how people learn, recall information, react to situations, reason, solve problems, emotionally responses, and communicate; thus, culture is an important variable to consider in the intellectual and social development of students. Understanding how aspects of culture can vary can also shed light on the diverse ways students learn, as well as how teachers use their development to encourage academic success of others (Banks, 2004; Gay, 2000; Hofstede, 2003; Ladson-Billings, 1995).

Culture also incorporates the seen and the unseen. **Surface cultures** are aspects of culture that are explicit, visible, and taught. These can include preferences for types of food, dress, music, crafts, dance, literature, language, and games. **"Hidden" cultures** are the habits, assumptions, understandings, values, judgments, stereotyping, and emotional scars that cannot be seen and are difficult to discern. They can include the nature of friendships, attitude toward elders, concept of cleanliness, beliefs about adolescence, preference for competition or cooperation, tolerance of pain, perception of self, perception of past and future, definition of obscenity, attitude toward dependents, and the importance of learning and performance. These are hidden when the person chooses not to articulate them in a way that would make them explicit to others.

In the middle of these two cultural areas lies **implicit cultures** for which the observer must be more alert to see or understand. They are neither hidden nor obvious but affect a person's diversity, and/or cultural competence, nonetheless. These may include behaviors in the areas of courtesy, contextual conversational patterns, concepts of time, personal space, rules of conduct, facial expressions, nonverbal communication, body language, touching, eye contact, pattern of emotions, notions of modesty, concepts of beauty, courtship practices, and notions of authority and leadership. Although schools are designed to offer equal opportunity, culture can affect one's environment and success in a multitude of ways. It is important to consider these questions: (1) How might a student's culture (gender, SES, race/ethnicity, sexual orientation, etc.) negatively or positively affect the student's opportunities to experience a fair chance in and outside of school? (2) How might a teacher's culture (gender, SES, race/ethnicity, sexual orientation, etc.) negatively or positively affect students' opportunities and performance in the classroom?

In the past, much of the culture and diversity research has focused on the learner: cultural adaptation/assimilation issues (Cummins, 1986, 1992; Reyhner, 2001), cognitive ability (Bowler, Smith, Schwarzer, Perez-Arce, & Kreutzer, 2002), language considerations (Gopaul-McNicol & Thomas-Presswood, 1998; Reyhner, 2001), dropout rates (Carpenter, Ramirez, & Severn, 2006; Darling-Hammond, 2006, 2007), and a learner's parental involvement (Carpenter & Ramirez, 2007; Carpenter et al., 2006; Moll, Amanti, Neff, & Gonzalez, 1992; Niemeyer, Wong, & Westerhaus, 2009). Although the understanding of how diversity plays a role in learning has become an important variable of consideration, often schools are organized in ways that reflect the similarities, rather than differences, of students (Guild, 2001). Additionally, how the culture of self affects the teacher's daily life, reactions in the classroom, and ability to develop positive cultural efficacy has been virtually unstudied. The demand for conformity by both the learner and the teacher is still often regarded as the easiest solution (Stevens, Olivárez, & Hamman, 2006). In a business context, if a manager expected all employees to sell a car in the same way, at the same level, would they all be successful every time? Would they all be motivated by the same rewards? What other variables might affect a salesperson on a daily basis? These are important to consider when productivity is driven by individual motivation. So, too, will your future learners need individually crafted, creative ways to guide and encourage their success.

The specificity of applying culturally responsive pedagogy has been strategically outlined by several researchers (Bohannan, 1995; Foster, 1995; Garcia, 1991; Gay, 2002; Ladson-Billings, 1994; McInerney & Hamilton, 2007). Each component of culturally responsive pedagogy can help you to better understand what it will take to develop this skill. Teachers are encouraged to apply culturally responsive pedagogy in the following ways:

- Integrate cultures into the overall academic framework and focus on the whole child's development rather than just the cognitive growth. This includes encouragement of positive motivation, leadership, and confidence while maintaining high expectations for student achievement.
- Apply a nurturing style of interactions with students that demonstrates "cultural caring," including an understanding about what culture is, how culture changes, and how culture is important in explaining people's actions.
- Encourage individual learner strengths, taking diversity into account.

- Demonstrate enthusiasm about the learning benefits for all students.
- Interact with students outside of the school and in the community through appropriate venues such as school and community events.
- Develop a learning community rather than a competitive one (mastery learning focus in contrast to performance focused).
- Practice functional communication between themselves and their students as well as encourage this communication among students.
- Incorporate integrated and thematically diverse curriculum that is rich in content and experiences and based on culturally mature knowledge structures to ensure good scaffolding of activity learning objectives.
- Prepare collaborative learning activities that are encouraging and inclusive of all types of learners.
- Encourage gradual progression from writing in the native language to writing in English with supportive supplements and feedback for English Language Learners (ELL).
- Acknowledge individual students' academic needs, not merely make them "feel good" (Ladson-Billings, 1995).
- Employ individual student cultures as a successful way to encourage learning (Ladson-Billings, 1995).
- Supply students with a curriculum that builds on their prior knowledge and cultural experiences.
- Encourage a belief in the value of academic success with each learner.
- Hold high expectations of each learner.
- Involve parents, and/or other family members, in their child's learning and academic success without prejudgment of the participation by parents of differing backgrounds and time capabilities.
- Encourage positive professional relationships with students that effectively demonstrate caring, respect, and trust.

Motivational and cultural competence research strongly advocates that educators make students feel safe, both psychologically and physically, in the classroom. While Bryant-Davis and Ocampo (2005) suggest increased efforts for assimilation in classrooms while trying to keep one's ethnic identity may lead to increased stress, creating a culture of community in the classroom is still viewed as an important attribute to meet safety needs. When you as an educator attempt to initiate assimilation in the classroom, consider the learners' cultures of identity first to reduce effects of culture shock. Cultural shock, which we will later discuss in more depth, includes decreased cognitive processing abilities, which affects engagement and performance.

Culturally responsive pedagogy also acknowledges the existence of misaligned policies, practices, and beliefs that need to be addressed within an organization (social awareness of the organization). Ladson-Billings (1994) suggests that the word *equality* has become synonymous with "sameness." Awareness of how your school addresses these issues to encourage the acknowledgment of your learners' needs is important to understand. The Center for Multicultural Education at the University of Washington and the Common Destiny Alliance at the University of Maryland found the following principals that need to be considered for improving education (Banks, 2002).

## Teacher Learning

**Principle 1**: Professional development programs should help teachers understand the complex characteristics of ethnic groups within U.S. society and the ways in which race, ethnicity, language, and social class interact to influence student behavior.

## Student Learning

**Principle 2**: Schools should ensure that all students have equitable opportunities to learn and to meet high standards.

**Principle 3**: The curriculum should help students understand that knowledge is socially constructed and reflects researchers' personal experiences as well as the social, political, and economic contexts in which they live and work.

**Principle 4**: Schools should provide all students with opportunities to participate in extra and co-curricular activities that develop knowledge, skills, and attitudes that increase academic achievement and foster positive interracial relationships.

## Intergroup Relations

**Principle 5**: Schools should create or make salient superordinate crosscutting group in order to improve intergroup relations.

**Principle 6**: Students should learn about stereotyping and other related biases that have negative effects on racial and ethnic relations.

**Principle 7**: Students should learn about the values shared by virtually all cultural groups (e. g., justice, equality, freedom, peace, compassion, and charity).

**Principle 8**: Teachers should help students acquire the social skills needed to interact effectively with students from other racial, ethnic, cultural, and language groups.

**Principle 9**: Schools should provide opportunities for students from different racial, ethnic, cultural, and language groups to interact socially under conditions designed to reduce fear and anxiety.

### School Governance, Organization and Equity

**Principle 10**: A schools organizational strategies should ensure that decision-making is widely shared and that members of the school community learn collaborative skills and dispositions in order to create a caring environment for students.

**Principle 11**: Leaders should develop strategies that ensure that all public schools, regardless of their locations, are funded equitably.

### Assessment

**Principle 12**: Teachers should use multiple culturally sensitive techniques to assess complex cognitive and social skills. (Banks, 2002)

An honest examination of social constructs within our schools, classrooms, and learners is imperative. People are not all the same nor do they learn the same way so we can't expect that they can be effectively taught the same way. Education is not a "one size fits all" proposition.

### Stereotypical Pressure

No one likes the feeling of being judged. That type of behavior will definitely affect one's state of belongingness within a community. Unfortunately research indicates the threat of stereotypical pressure is often a factor that causes teachers to *conform* rather than *perform*. When people fear retribution from a particular action, even if they believe the action is right, they may refrain from it. People want to be accepted and to fit into a group. No one likes to face the pain of being scorned or humiliated because they didn't word something politically correctly or they possess a vastly different view than their peers. Many will avoid issues that make them feel vulnerable.

Stereotyping incidences still occur, but more knowledge and awareness of those will bring light to the subject and equip you as a leader to be a catalyst for change. The *Washington Post* (Reid, 2005) reported that a boy had been suspended in Kansas for saying "no problema" in the hallway and another report claimed that a superintendent was physically threatened after allowing the Spanish class to recite the Pledge of Allegiance in Spanish (Rothschild, 2008). A Midwestern state's local newscast reported that an elementary student's Mexican flag had been thrown in the trash at school on Cinco de Mayo. On further investigation, the student reportedly said he was changing into gym clothes in the locker room when the teacher told him, "Give me the flag." The student asked, "What's the problem?" and the teacher reportedly answered, "The problem is that we are in the United States and not in Mexico."

He grabbed the flag from the student and threw the flag in the garbage can (USA Today, 2008). In Connecticut, a teacher allegedly called a child by the wrong name, and when he pointed it out she responded by saying, "How about black boy? Go sit down, black boy" (NBC News, 2012). Cultural awareness and competence are the keys to eliminating stereotypical behaviors that unfortunately still occur in school. Teachers who understand that diversity strengthens classrooms and communities will be the educational leaders of tomorrow.

### Becoming the "Critical Teacher"

The word critical is often misleading. The general connotation for the word *critical* is negative, but in this case we intend it to be positive. In other words, becoming a "critical teacher" is instrumental in your development as an effective educator and leader. In promoting positive change, we need to teach our students *critically* by encouraging them to ask questions and develop a passion for the pursuit of new knowledge. Future leaders, which include many of your students, should never simply assume information as fact (remember what they say about the word *assume*). Leaders learn to question why things are the way they are. How else can we improve today's problems if we don't rise to higher levels of thinking? Critical teaching prepares students for the real issues they will face in the future. It encourages them to take a stand for their personal convictions and become a force for positive change in their communities. Critical teaching isn't always easy and sometime faces extreme opposition because it challenges the status quo. Galileo was accused of being a heretic and put under house arrest because he had the audacity to claim the earth revolved around the sun. Columbus was ridiculed because he believed the world wasn't flat. If we as educational leaders don't challenge the status quo and encourage inquiry, who will?

Becoming a critical teacher is an important link to becoming more culturally competent and preparing learners to be successful in the future. This is about global sustainability, which will require making well-informed decisions and finding creative solutions to tomorrow's problems. We must view the world through a larger lens that includes self first, then others, if we want to prepare learners for the future. You must become a fully integrated "whole" leader to become an effective agent for positive change. First, focus on self-awareness, which incites you to examine your own beliefs, values, and motives. Then develop social awareness by becoming informed about the beliefs, values, and motives of others. Finally, practice effective relationship management/

leadership skills by teaching and encouraging others to rise to greater levels of self-awareness and social awareness. Interestingly, research shows that 80% of continuing professional development is focused on the development of the "professional" skills of teaching, that is, the broadening of subject knowledge, teaching techniques or the structure of the curriculum (Gray, 2005). We believe that is vitally important, but no more so than the ideology of self-knowledge, the most important piece of the IELM.

## Section I Review

### Section Activities

**Activity 1:** Individually, make a list of events you feel may have had the most impact on education. Beside each of these events clearly explain what consequences they may have had. Next, form groups and see if you all chose the same events. Discuss why and what in your own experiences might have led to your belief that your list was the most important. Listen to others and their reasoning. Also see what events may be similar. Talk about why each of you chose these items. Do you have similar past experiences with these people. How does your background affect what you consider to be most important?

Lastly, reflect in writing how you believe your past experiences, memories, and life affect how you see events and consequences. Do you think you need to be more open to realities? Are you very sensitive to realities? Do your reactions make it difficult for others to hear how you feel?

**Activity 2:** How culturally competent are you? Answer the following Diversity Self-Assessment questions:
- What is my definition of diversity?
- Do the children in my classroom and school come from diverse cultural backgrounds?
- What are my perceptions of students from different racial or ethnic groups? With language or dialects different from mine? With special needs?
- What are the sources of these perceptions (e.g., friends, relatives, television, movies)?
- How do I respond to my students, based on these perceptions?
- Have I experienced others' making assumptions about me based on my membership in a specific group? How did I feel?
- What steps do I need to take to learn about the students from diverse backgrounds in my school and classroom?
- How often do social relationships develop among students from different racial or ethnic backgrounds in my classroom and in the school? What is the nature of these relationships?

- In what ways do I make my instructional program responsive to the needs of the diverse groups in my classroom?
- What kinds of information, skills, and resources do I need to acquire to effectively teach from a multicultural perspective?
- In what ways do I collaborate with other educators, family members, and community groups to address the needs of all my students?

Source: Adapted from Bromley (1998).

# SECTION II

## Integration Through Self-Awareness

*Taking charge of your own learning is a part of taking charge of your life, which is the sine qua non in becoming an integrated person.*
—Warren G Bennis

Self-awareness and management can be the most difficult part of growing and being prepared for all that life has for you. But being honest with one's self is not easy. It may sound easy, but we all like to believe we are right. We will all make wrong decisions. We will all lose focus at times. Feeling, loving, and caring for others can be hard on a person but we should never give up hope that it matters. Discover yourself. Make the time. Accept the things, like your past, that you cannot change. Dedicate yourself to today and tomorrow to be better and to become the leader that your future students will need. What you do and how you prepare yourself starts now. Be aware of how you open yourself to growth, to becoming everything this career choice has to offer you.

Knowing what you believe will affect all of the other pieces of the puzzle. Asking yourself how this affects your mental health, choice in relationships, stress level, and ability to be more than you ever thought you could be rides on this truism. We encourage you to skim over the chapters in this section and identify what makes you who you are and how this affects your teaching life. Again, knowing yourself will help you with the continual process of becoming who your future learners need to also be successful in their futures. You will be affecting others, developing others. This is an honor and a responsibility. Never take its importance for granted.

### Something to Think About

A former student sent me this story. The names have been changed but the event is too often true. Learning to manage your responses can affect lives.

Veronica was new to the United States. She spoke little English and her experiences in her home country had been brutal. She trusted few. She knew no one. Her first days in a U.S. high school were overwhelming. Although there were many students who spoke her native language, it was very different here. Her mother had found work cleaning homes, and their small apartment was a mansion compared to her memories of what home had been. She saw many kids with much more than she had ever had and she felt alone and was frightened.

Within a week at school, Veronica had tried to "hide" in the back of classrooms, trying to talk to no one, but one day, a classmate turned around in class and said, "¿Quieres almorzar conmigo?" (Do you want to have lunch with me?) Her heart was so happy.

On their way to lunch, the girls were chatting in their native language and they were stopped by a teacher who reprimanded them for not talking in English. Veronica's friend told her to ignore the teacher and that everyone in that school was like that, but Veronica was hurt. She began acting out in her classes, being quite rude to the teachers, and although there was never a severe disciplinary incident involving Veronica, she began to hang out with others who, for lack of a better word, were rough. Her grades suffered and her motivation was to survive, and she felt that attaching herself to others who hated these teachers was the best way. After barely making it through, and often not making it through, Veronica had set her sights on quitting school as soon as possible, but her *madre* would not hear of it.

Three years later, Veronica walked into a remedial math class and it changed her life forever. Ms. P was kind and seemed to care. Even when Veronica tried to "cop an attitude" Ms. P just patted her on the back and continued to help her. When she arrived on her third day of class small pieces of paper were attached to items all over the room, such as a chair, a cabinet, a folder. Each piece of paper had a Spanish word on it: *silla, gabinete, carpeta*, and many more. One of the white students in the class immediately asked what they were for and Ms. P simply said, "I have decided I need to brush up on my Spanish." She started using Spanish as she explained her lessons. It was not good Spanish, but it was Spanish.

Little did she know that she, over the year, had changed the life of Veronica. Veronica felt like she was cared about and that she belonged and that she did not have to hide who she was in Ms. P's classroom. Her grades got better and she often went to Ms. P when she was struggling. Ms. P was always encouraging and always believing in Veronica's ability to learn math as well as unbeknown to Veronica at the time, that she could be successful in her new school and her new life.

We are not sure where Veronica is today, but our source says she is happy, a great mother, a wonderful and loyal employee, and a good citizen to her community. This is what teaching is about: encouraging all of your students. We do not always understand what they have been through or why they respond the way they do. However, we can model empathy, encourage hope, and teach them our content in ways that may change their lives in ways we could never predict. The Integrated Educational Leadership Model can encourage us to become the teacher who makes the choice to change lives for the better, not to change the child.

*Chapter 4*

# Beliefs, Personality, and Knowing Yourself

*There is only one corner of the universe you can be
certain of improving, and that's your own self.*
—Aldous Huxley

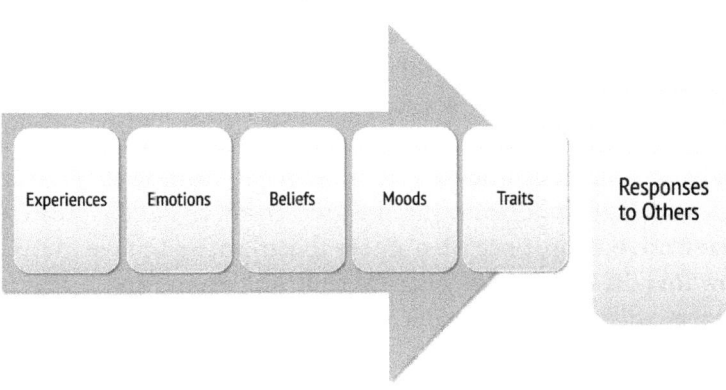

Gnothi Seauton is an aphorism attributed to a host of ancient Greek sages, including Heraclitus, Pythagoras, Socrates, and Plato. The aphorism, translated into English, "Know Thyself," has a variety of meanings attributed to it in literature. The question we pose to you is: If you don't know yourself, how can you truly know your students? Gold and Roth (1993) defined self-awareness as "a process of getting in touch with your feelings and behaviors" (p. 141). Increasing self-awareness involves an in-depth awakening of how people and events affect our emotional processes and behaviors, as well as how we affect others, especially our students. Self-awareness is the cornerstone of your success as an educator. Inc. Magazine (2007) reported, "Although it is probably one of the least discussed leadership competencies; self-awareness is possibly one of the most valuable. To be self-aware is the state of being conscious about your strengths and your weaknesses. It is a product of knowing what you are good at while acknowledging what you still have yet to learn." (Musselwhite, 2007, p. 1)

Your effectiveness as a teacher also depends on your willingness to manage your behaviors and needs, especially since you will have those same expectations of your students. If you are remiss is identifying and meeting your own needs, how can you lead others to do so? Simply being aware and acknowledging whether you are at a healthy positive place in life or a fragile one can have a great effect on how you manage your classroom and lead others. Throughout your career, you will experience varying levels of challenges to your psychological, emotional, and physical health, in addition to those pertaining to finances, economic security, and putting your kids through college. Those are all normal. The key is to acknowledge where you are and manage each situation as a piece of the larger puzzle.

Becoming self-aware takes personal discipline and practice. A great place to start is to simply sit quietly and listen. If you were to do that, what would your intuitive voice say? Perhaps your classes are stressing you to the max, or your boss is driving you crazy, or your significant other is being insensitive. By acknowledging your difficulties, it will be easier to manage them. Author M. Scott Peck said, "Life is difficult. This is a great truth, one of the greatest truths. It is a great truth because once we truly see this truth, we transcend it. Once we truly know that life is difficult—once we truly understand and accept it—then life is no longer difficult. Because once it is accepted, the fact that life is difficult no longer matters."

If you do not identify your emotional rough spots, how will you negotiate them without getting bruised and beaten along the way? According to Long (1996), "As teachers we have a room, a group, equipment, materials, a curriculum, instructional methods, and grades, but most of all, we have ourselves. What happens to us emotionally in the process of teaching . . . is the critical factor in determining our effectiveness" (p. 444).

In light of focusing first on self, it is important to address what that exactly means. Our psychological self is driven by our past and vicarious experiences, which affect our beliefs about self and others, sometimes unconsciously. Through gaining a greater awareness of your preprogrammed beliefs, values, and emotional triggers, you will be more able to effectively manage yourself and your students. These qualities are absolutely essential for becoming an integrated educator.

What were the significant events that molded you into the person you are today? Who influenced your beliefs about yourself and the world? Did a past event inspire you to become a teacher? Was it a good experience or a bad one? Do you want to become the teacher you never had or aspire to be like a particular teacher who made a meaningful difference in your life? What was your home life like? Did you have supportive parents and family members? What about friends? Were you a social butterfly or a loner in school? Were you picked on or did you pick on others—or do you believe this does not really happen? What about grades? Did you get good grades or bad? Were you involved in extracurricular activities or did you work to help support your family? Did you attend a large school or a small one? Was your school racially integrated or more homogeneous? Did you attend an urban, suburban, or rural school? All of those events (and these are only the tip of the iceberg) affected your beliefs, efficacy, responses, behaviors, emotions, psychological development, diversity competence, physical health, and overall psychological preparedness for the classroom.

## Assessing Your Beliefs

Research suggests that personal beliefs may be one of the most important constructs in the educational development of a teacher (Mertz & McNeely, 1992; Tiezzi & Cross, 1997). A belief is the psychological state in which an individual holds a proposition or premise to be true (*Stanford Psychological Encyclopedia*)(2013); it also may be evident as an opinion or conviction. According to Kagan (1992), beliefs are "principles of practice, personal epistemologies, perspectives, practical knowledge, or orientations" (p. 66) that are integrated into every individual. We choose to believe something based on "ethnic and socioeconomic background, gender, geographic location, religious upbringing, and life events" (Richardson, 1996, p. 105) as well as what we deem to be politically correct (Rosser-Cox, 2011; Weyrich, 1999).

Paul Weyrich (1999), the president of the Free Congress Foundation, sent a letter to the National Center for Public Policy Research expressing the intolerance of political correctness. The following is an excerpt:

> The United States is very close to becoming a state totally dominated by an alien ideology, an ideology bitterly hostile to Western culture. Even now, for the first time

in their lives, people have to be afraid of what they say. This has never been true in the history of our country. Yet today, if you say the "wrong thing", you suddenly have legal problems, political problems . . . you might even lose your job or be expelled from college. Certain topics are forbidden. You can't approach the truth about a lot of different subjects. If you do, you are immediately branded as "racist", "sexist", "homophobic", "insensitive", or "judgmental."

In the context of education, it is critical that we question beliefs, both conscious and unconscious, because they are based primarily on our experiences filtered through the eyes of a student (Kagan, 1992; Lortie, 1975; Pajares, 1992). You were a student most of your life, and still are today. Those experiences shaped your beliefs about learning, teaching, and the discipline it takes to be an "educator." Research suggests that prospective teachers bring firmly held beliefs about teaching and learning to their preparatory programs (Mertz & McNeely, 1992; Zeichner & Gore, 1990): beliefs developed primarily through an "apprenticeship of observation" (Lortie, 1975) or "teacher watching" (Barnes, 1992).

Do your beliefs enhance your abilities to be an effective educator or make them more difficult? Teacher preparation researchers report that belief systems developed through life experiences strongly influence yet often constrain what prospective teachers are willing and able to learn about the educational process (Ball, 1988; Mertz & McNeely, 1992; Rosser & Nelson, 2012). These predispositional beliefs may remain consistent during preservice teachers' academic preparation (Murphy, Delli, & Edwards, 2004) and continue into the teaching profession (McNeely & Mertz, 1990; Mertz & McNeely, 1991). This is a cause for great concern, because preparation is highly important to one's success. In all areas of academia critical inquiry is essential, meaning that all beliefs should be questioned to let go of old paradigms and be open to the limitless depths of knowledge. The following are some examples of limiting beliefs about education, according to research:

- My teaching personality is more important than that of content knowledge or cognitive skill. Teachers are simply born to be teachers (Whitbeck, 2000).
- I just "knew" I would be good at it [teaching] (Richards & Killen, 1994).
- Low socioeconomic status (SES), poverty, and minority students have more difficulty learning than do other students (Alexander, Entwisle, & Horsey, 1997; Alexander, Entwisle, & Thompson, 1987; Dietrich, 1998; Katz, 1999; Olmedo, 1997; Rist, 1970).
- Schools with higher numbers of African American learners tend to be

lower-income, more dangerous, and inner-city (Rosser-Cox, 2011).
- Most hispanic [sic] children speak Spanish [sic] (Rosser-Cox, 2011).
- 7 out of 10 pre-service teachers believed that they were prepared to begin teaching without participation in a preparation program (Mertz & McNeely, 1991).
- [African American] parents generally have little education, leading to school apathy (Rosser-Cox, 2011).
- Minority students are harder to motivate (Rosser-Cox, 2011).
- Creating relationships with the minority parents will be difficult (Rosser-Cox, 2011; Rosser & Nelson, 2012).
- Teaching is more difficult in minority schools and white schools are more "ideal" (Rosser-Cox, 2011).

Personal awareness of what you believe and why you believe it will serve as a useful tool for navigating the vast sea of the teaching profession. You won't be expected to know everything, but you will be expected to learn and adapt as you encounter a constant flow of challenges involving an array of cultural facts, myths, and history. You must also be aware that humans are hardwired for homeostasis, which sometimes ensnares us into a trap of old thinking patterns. Research indicates the disregarding of new information that differs from one's current beliefs has been found to have a neurologically physiological reaction in our brains that makes us feel "good" (Rilling, Gutman, Zeh, Pagnoni, Berns, & Kilts, 2002). Much like an addict who gets a "fix," the area in the brain that responds to rewards lights up (releases dopamine) when a person discounts evidence that challenges his or her own beliefs (Westen, Blagov, Harenski, Kilts, & Hamann, 2006).

Additionally, emotional triggers and hot-buttons have a similar physiological reaction. These triggers can be defined as "situations, events, or subjects that elicit strong emotional responses," referred to as "Amygdala Hijacking" (Goleman, 1996). In layperson's terms: the emotional center of the brain overrides rational thinking capabilities (Nadler, 2009). Anatomically speaking, the amygdala, located at the center of the limbic system, takes over the neocortex, the frontal part of the brain responsible for rational thinking. The amygdala is the emotional part of the brain that controls the "fight or flight" response in each of us. When one feels endangered or vulnerable, the amygdala is triggered and stress hormones inundate the body (Nadler, 2009). This often leads to irrational behavior based on a physiological reaction. Interestingly, a person can much better control a response once he or she understands what is happening internally.

Emotional hijacking rarely occurs solely because of the current situation at hand. The amygdala is triggered when an event resembles a traumatic experience of the past, which incites a reactionary "hot button" in varying degrees (Amunts et al, 2005). Irrational responses can surface as feelings of anger, rage, anxiety, worry, depression, guilt, or other moods. Sometimes the neocortex (the rational thinking part of the brain) will even join in as an "accomplice" to rationalize such feelings and the ensuing behaviors linked to them. Have you ever justified your anger with an air of self-righteousness? If so, you are normal. Take comfort in knowing that all human beings do at one time or another.

The danger with emotional hijacking is that it can take place in an instant and cause lasting irreparable damage, especially if it occurs repeatedly. Irrational emotional episodes will drastically affect your ability to lead your students and build collaborative relationships with your peers. Additionally the resulting stress can be detrimental to your health by causing high blood pressure, heart disease, and a plethora of other medical conditions. Remember, you must put the oxygen mask on yourself first.

Past experiences, emotional triggers, beliefs, moods, and personality traits can all affect our perception, which we interpret as "reality." Consequently our responses to others and our environment are based on those variables. Some serve us better than others, to be sure.

## Personality Traits

A person's personality is the distinctive pattern of behavior, thoughts, opinions, and emotions shown by individuals (Furnham, 1999; Hinton & Stockburger, 1991; Mehta, 2012; Rusting & DeHart, 2000). It is inclusive of all the variables we discussed above. Personality is often considered in the discussion of what makes a good teacher. Personality traits can lend themselves positively or negatively in any given situation, as it drastically affects one's style of thinking, feeling, and acting (Costa & McCrae, 1992; Mehta, 2012). According to Mehta (2012), "Most classroom problems are people problems: hence, one requires insights into human behavior in order to teach successfully. There is a clash of personalities many a times" (p. 1). Additionally, studies suggest that personality traits affect personal satisfaction in various situations, especially with one's job (Connolly & Viswesvaran, 2000; Hart, 1999).

An "ideal" or "natural" teacher's personality is difficult to characterize because differing environments require a diversity of skills. However, effective teachers are perceived as personable by their students, with a willingness to become involved and create caring relationships (Ladson-Billings, 1994; Marbley, Bonner, McKisick, Henfield, Watts, & Shen, 2007). Their intuition tends to be well-developed and their insight into themselves and others is acute. They are aware of what is going on inside them, and they have excellent acuity, or "with-it-ness" about their surroundings and those in it (Kounin, 1971/1977). They also possess high expectations for their learners (Good, 2012).

Successful teachers also display the ability to apply multiple, simultaneous decision-making skills related to content delivery, appropriate pedagogy, student relationships, praise and student feedback, successful classroom discipline, creative and universally supportive materials of instruction, and maintenance of positive relationships and interactions with students and colleagues (Griffin, 1999). Mehta (2012) concludes that successful teachers are also "energetic, passionate and empathetic."

In another study conducted by Dr. Susan Thompson and colleagues at the University of Memphis, the most common characteristics for successful teachers are (1) the ability to be fair and to exhibit a positive attitude; (2) to start each day prepared for all the day might offer; (3) the ability to develop a personal connection with students; (4) to radiate a sense of humor, creativity, and forgiveness of others; (5) a willingness to admit mistakes; (6) a respect for everyone in the environment that includes high standards/expectations for *all* students; and (7) compassion and encouragement of the learner community where all learners have a sense of belonging (2004).

Although these "ideal" teacher characteristics can be more natural for some than others they are skills all teachers can perfect over time. According to Maddocks (2007) how you attain skills and succeed in personal development "is largely determined by your attitude." The development of your emotional intelligence (EI) includes managing your behaviors, emotions, and personality traits. Although you may not be able to completely rescript your personality or emotions, you can manage them.

Developing the interpersonal skills to be a great teacher is a choice you will make based on your willingness to become:

- Self-aware in tending to your own needs before attempting to meet the needs of others
- Cognizant of your emotional triggers and identify whether they support or undermine your goal to become a successful teacher
- Aware of personal behaviors and attitudes that are adversely affected by past experiences and limiting beliefs

- Empathetic to others and appreciate individual differences

## Belief in Self

Self-efficacy is defined as one's beliefs about his or her abilities to perform at specific levels in specific contexts (Bandura, 1997). You may be a confident person overall, but when you walk into a classroom of students and suddenly face the complexity of the situation you may find it to be rather daunting. Efficacy for teaching diverse learners (Pang & Sablan, 1998) is often more difficult than one imagines and can be especially overwhelming for new teachers.

Stress and anxiety, which have become epidemic, affect levels of confidence. According to the 2010 report by the American Psychological Association, we live in an overstressed nation.

> Feeling the effects of prolonged financial and other recession-related difficulties, Americans are struggling to balance work and home life and make time to engage in healthy behaviors, with stress not only taking a toll on their personal physical health, but also affecting the emotional and physical well-being of their families. (p. 1)

If you want to improve your response to stress, boost your belief in self. According to Gaur, Salanova, and Peiró (2001), "One's beliefs about oneself can act as moderating variables in the stress-strain relationship." Additionally, the stress-efficacy cycle is a continuum as stressors reportedly have a decreased negative effect when an individual's self-efficacy is more positive (Mossholder, Bedein, & Armenakis, 1982). Having confidence in what you are doing is vital to being successful and maintaining a healthy psychological self.

Supporting this stress–self-efficacy continuum, research suggests that teachers in the past have referred to their training to work with diverse learners as "baptism by fire" (White-Clark, 2005), and according to a national staffing survey by the National Center for Education Statistics, 54% of reporting teachers said they were teaching culturally diverse students, but only 20% felt prepared and capable to meet their learners' needs (U.S. Department of Education, 1999). This stressor continues to evolve as it is linked to motivation (Deci & Ryan, 1985, 2000; Deci, Ryan, Gagné, Leone, Usunov, & Kornazheva, 2001; Grant & Secada, 1990; Ladson-Billings, 1994) and student achievement outcomes (Bandura, 1997; Goddard, 2001; Goddard, Hoy, & Woolfolk Hoy, 2000; Tschannen-Moran, Woolfolk Hoy, & Hoy, 1998). Therefore, your level of confidence in your ability to perform affects your learners, which in turn affects your psychological health and feelings of competence, which in turn affects the students, and the cycle goes on and on. The subject of stress is extensive and learning to manage it vital. Chapter 5 will be dedicated to helping you better understand stress and how to create work/life balance in your profession.

Taking risks and engaging in creative thinking requires courage and self-confidence. Teachers with a strong sense of perceived self-efficacy exhibit greater levels of planning and organization (Allinder, 1994), are more open to new ideas and methods to better meet the needs of their students (Guskey, 1988; Stein & Wang, 1988), exhibit greater enthusiasm for teaching (Allinder, 1994), have greater commitment to teaching (Ashton & Webb, 1986; Podell & Soodak, 1993), demonstrate a positive influence on students' achievement (Ashton & Webb, 1986; Podell & Soodak, 1993), choose more challenging goals, are more likely to take responsibility for student outcomes, and persist in the face of difficulty (Ashton & Webb, 1986; Bandura, 1997; Gibson & Dembo, 1984). Additionally self-confidence affects job satisfaction (Caprara, Barbaranelli, Borgogni, & Steca, 2003). Self-examination is essential for becoming a successful educator, both personally and professionally. The following are tips for building self-confidence and developing positive self-efficacy:

- Define your own life purpose and core values—To thine own self be true (Hamlet). Stop trying to please everyone else and march to the beat of your own drum. Decide what is important to you and do it.
- Be mindful not to take things personally. Everyone has room to grow. Another's criticism does not make you a failure nor does someone's praise make you a success. You must take ownership of where you want to go and who you want to become.
- Associate with positive people. "You are the average of the five people you spend the most time with" (Jim Rohn, author).
- Do not compare your life with others. Your life is neither better nor worse than anyone else's life. It is simply your life, to do with whatever you choose.
- Make daily deposits into your self-esteem account. Establish a daily practice of positive affirmations, inspirational reading, and positive visual imagery that promotes and supports a healthy self-esteem. Be willing to take time to develop your teaching skill set.
- Be a learner. Never be afraid that not knowing an answer makes you incapable.
- Be willing to learn and creatively restructure your behaviors, whether in your personal life or in the classroom. Continual development of self is

vital to developing positive efficacy.

Letting go of old limiting beliefs and heightening your self-worth will help you to be a more successful teacher. You will walk into your classroom feeling confident and competent. This is one of the most vital areas in teacher preparation (Feiman-Nemser, McDiarmid, Melnick, & Parker, 1989; Joram & Gabriele, 1998; Mertz & McNeely, 1991, Rosser & Nelson, 2012; Rosser-Cox, 2011; Whitbeck, 2000). It is absolutely crucial to develop positive belief structures and chart your path based on the person you aspire to become as an educator and a leader.

> *"What lies behind us and what lies ahead of us are tiny matters compared to what lives within us."*
> —*Henry David Thoreau*

*Chapter 5*

# Evaluating and Managing Stress

> *The mind can go either direction under stress—toward positive or toward negative: on or off. Think of it as a spectrum whose extremes are unconsciousness at the negative end and hyperconsciousness at the positive end. The way the mind will lean under stress is strongly influenced by training.*
> —Frank Herbert

Even though it is sometimes overlooked as a component of teacher training, stress plays a significant role in physical and mental well-being (International Labour Organization (ILO), 1986, 1992). According to the American Psychological Association, two-thirds of Americans report that work is their main source of stress and 30% of workers noted "extreme" stress levels from work circumstances (American Psychological Association, 2007, 2008). Managing stress is important to your overall success as an educator, as on any given day, you will play a number of different roles: counselor, administrator, parent, nurse, paper pusher, teacher, and mentor. Wearing many hats can be challenging and stressful to your entire well-being. Hans Selye (1974), considered by many to be the father of modern-day stress research, found that it is caused by physiological, psychological, and environmental demands. The Merriam-Webster Dictionary defines *stress* as a force exerted when one body or body part presses on, pulls on, pushes against, or tends to compress or twist another body or body part; a physical, chemical, or emotional factor that causes bodily or mental tension. In essence, stress is a change that causes physical, emotional, or psychological strain. In his book *Mind as Healer, Mind as Slayer*, Kenneth Pelletier (1977) summarized, "Generalized, and unabated stress places a person in a state of disequilibrium, which increases his susceptibility to a wide range of diseases and disorders" (p. 76).

According to the former National Institute for Occupational Safety and Health (NIOSH) Director Linda Rosenstock, "Work stress imposes enormous and far-reaching costs on workers' wellbeing." (Centers for Disease Control and Prevention, 1999, p. 1) The relationship between the body and mind is fascinating. When we fully grasp the integration between the two we will understand how our health affects motivation and the ability to perform. Managing stress is essentially about managing one's needs for self-care. That varies from person to person and only you can assess what you need to stay healthy.

The choices you make to maintain good health will affect your family, students, parents, peers, and above all yourself. You will not be performing mundane tasks each day nor will you clock out when you go home with no thoughts about work until the next day. Whether preparing lessons, grading papers, dealing with a struggling student, or working a school event after hours, your career is a 24-hour-a-day proposition. Teaching is a lifestyle, not a job. Teaching is personal. Teaching is all-encompassing. Teaching is multifaceted. Teaching is who you are.

As a leader you must remain calm and confident. Be aware that stress not only diminishes your productivity, patience, energy, and personal fulfillment. It can also affect how others perceive you. This can create a vicious downward spiral because as others' respect and esteem for you declines, it can produce a mirroring effect where you begin to lose respect and esteem for yourself as well. The less confident and worthy that you feel, the more susceptible to harmful stress you will become. Additionally, the likelihood for additional stresses in other areas of your life increases, thus repeating the stress cycle that affects your physical and emotional health (U.S. Department of Health and Human Services, 1999).

The Department of Human Services (1999) reports that 70–80% of all illnesses that accompany visits to a physician are stress-related/induced. They also report that the cost of job stress in the United States is estimated at $200 billion annually. If you better understand yourself and your needs, you will gain the skills that will help you identify what increases your stress as an educator, allowing you to become more proactive in managing the stress variables. This in turn can positively boost your overall physical and psychological health, self-confidence, personal relationships, and success with your future students. However, not all types of stress are harmful or even negative, and it is important to identify in yourself the type of stress you are experiencing, because everyone has "stress." There are a few different types of stress we wish to differentiate:

- **Eustress:** a type of stress that is fun and exciting and keeps us vital (e.g., riding a rollercoaster or watching your favorite sports team win a close game). Eustress is a term coined by endocrinologist Hans Selye. The word consists of two parts. The prefix eu- derives from the Greek word meaning either "well" or "good." When attached to the word stress, it literally means "good stress." Eustress is the positive cognitive response to stress that is healthy, or gives one a feeling of fulfillment or other positive feelings (Nelson & Simmons, 2004).
- **Acute Stress:** This is a short-term type of stress that can either be perceived as positive (eustress) or more distressing (what we normally think of when we think of "stress"); this is the type of stress we most often encounter in day-to-day life (e.g., facing a deadline or dealing with a thoughtless driver on the road). It is the most common form of stress. It comes from demands and pressures of the recent past and anticipated demands and pressures of the near future. According to the American Psychological Association the most common symptoms are (1) emotional distress, which includes some combination of anger or irritability, anxiety, and depression; (2) muscular problems such as tension headaches, back pain, jaw pain, and the muscular tensions that lead to pulled muscles and tendon and ligament problems; (3) stomach, gut, and bowel problems such as heartburn, acid stomach, flatulence, diarrhea, constipation, and irritable bowel syndrome; and (4) elevations in blood pressure, rapid heartbeat, sweaty palms, heart palpitations, dizziness, migraine headaches, cold hands or feet, shortness of breath, and chest pain (Miller, Smith, & Rothstein, 1994).
- **Episodic Acute Stress:** This happens when acute stress seems to run out of control and become a way of life, creating a life of relative chaos or drama that can feel never-ending. The most common symptoms include over-arousal, short-temperedness, irritability, feelings of anxiousness, nervous energy, persistent tension headaches, migraines, hypertension, chest pain, and tension (Miller, Smith, & Rothstein, 1994). The workplace can develop into a very unhealthy place for someone experiencing this stress.

Those who have a tendency toward this type of stress include Type As who have an "excessive competitive drive, aggressiveness, impatience, and a harrying sense of time urgency" (not to be confused with the "Type A" personality; Friedman & Rosenman, 1974). Cardiologists Friedman and Rosenman also note this type exhibits a "free-floating, but well-rationalized form of hostility, and almost always a deep-seated insecurity." Frequent episodes of acute stress for the Type A individual is not uncommon, as well as a higher likelihood of coronary heart disease (in comparison to Type Bs, who exhibit an opposite pattern of behavior).

Another form of episodic acute stress derives from persistent worry (American Psychological Association, 2013; Miller, Smith, & Rothstein, 1994). Worriers find possible disasters in most situations and have a tendency toward pessimism. The workplace for them becomes an unrewarding, negative place where something awful predictably happens. Symptoms of chronic worry include overstimulation and tension with a tendency toward depression rather than anger and hostility (American Psychological Association, 2000; Miller, Smith, & Rothstein, 1994). With the worrier, lifestyle and personality problems become so normal that they rarely notice anything wrong with their behavior. These individuals take little self-ownership of their situation and often blame their anguish on other people or situations they feel are out of their control. They typically rationalize their worry obsession by claiming, "This is just who I am."

- **Acute Stress Reaction:** Also called acute stress disorder, psychological shock, mental shock, or simply shock, acute stress reaction is a psychological condition arising in response to a frightening or traumatic event (American Psychological Association, 2000; Miller, Smith, & Rothstein, 1994). Symptoms include severe anxiety, feelings of guilt, difficulty sleeping, irritability, poor concentration, hyper alertness, an exaggerated startle response, motor restlessness, feelings of detachment from the self and the world (almost as if in a dream), memory and concentration difficulties, or increasing difficulty recalling details of the traumatic event (also called dissociative amnesia), which may occur within a month after the experience. Other symptoms can include death, accidents, divorce, abuse, intense fear, helplessness, and more (American Psychological Association, 2000; Miller, Smith, & Rothstein, 1994).

It is essential to have a support system in place to deal with stressful situations in a healthy way. To share or not to share is the question (Dimaggio, Lysaker, Carcione, Nicolò, & Semerari, 2008). Talking to family members and friends about the situation can be helpful, even though they may not completely understand or identify with your behaviors and emotions. Understanding your own as well as another's feelings is a cultivated skill that not all people possess (Dimaggio et al., 2008). It is vitally important that you learn as an educator to identify and take action to respond to the chronic stressors in your life, as well as your students'.

- **Chronic Stress:** This the most taxing type of stress because it seems never-ending and inescapable, like the stress of being in an unhappy marriage or an extremely unfulfilling job. This type of stress can lead to burnout or a sense of emotional hopelessness, which is not healthy to submit children to. Many medical conditions begin with chronic stress. The effects of excess cortisol and glucocorticoids suppress immunity, increasing risk of infection, disease, and inflammation. Stress-related medical conditions include gastrointestinal, cardiovascular, respiratory, musculoskeletal, skin, psychological, and reproductive disorders.

There are medical situations that can also increase your likelihood for harmful stress, which can lead to all of the mentioned physical and emotional reactions. Chronic pain, insomnia, Addison's disease, adrenal fatigue, eating disorders, autoimmune disorders, hormonal imbalance, and menopause are a few that can cause chronic stress symptoms. Being in tune with what's going on in your own body and mind will help you manage your stress as well as others'. It is important to realize that this is not shameful or a character flaw to admit that you need help in dealing with these life situations. If you have a "silver bullet" complex, get over it. No one is indestructible or exempt from the storms of life.

So when does stress become chronic? It occurs when you shift from having the ability to focus on a goal or circumstance in your life to focusing on the alleviation of the stress in any way you can, regardless of the negative consequences it might cause. Rather than proactively preventing problems that may create undue stress, you begin to react to the circumstances around you in ways that don't adequately meet your current needs. Physiologically the body reacts by evoking the fight-or-flight response (also called the fight-or-flight-or-freeze response, hyper-arousal, or the acute stress response; Jansen, Nguyen, Karpitsky, & Mettenleiter, 1995). During this reaction, certain hormones such as adrenalin and cortisol are released into the bloodstream, causing the heart to race, changing various autonomic nervous functions, and slowing digestion by shifting blood flow from the abdominal area to the arms and legs. Thus the response was originally named for its ability to enable us to physically fight or run away when faced with danger (Gleitman, Fridlund, & Reisberg, 2004). Today, fight-or-flight is activated in situations where neither response is appropriate, such as in traffic or during a stressful day at work. When the perceived threat is gone, normally, systems are designed to return to a standard function, but in cases of chronic stress, a lingering effect continues in the body.

So what should you be aware of in your daily self-management? In the case of chronic stress, the first symptoms are relatively mild, such as persistent headaches and increased susceptibility to illness. However, with continued exposure to chronic stress, more serious health problems may develop. These stress-influenced conditions may include the following:

- Depression
- Diabetes
- Heart disease
- Cancer (possibly)
- Hyperthyroidism
- Ulcers
- Obesity
- Obsessive-compulsive or anxiety disorders
- Eating disorders
- Sexual dysfunction
- Tooth and gum disease
- Hair loss

## Managing and Coping with Stress

Once stress gets out of control, it is like trying to stop a 747 taxiing down the runway. It is much easier to stop it before it starts. It is easy to address stress when we are at a heightened level, but during those times, we have a tendency to react in non-healthy ways: outbursts, turning inward, and becoming angry, to name a few. These hasty, impulsive actions can often exacerbate the stress, making the cycle increase rather than decrease. When stressful events occur, remember to stop, take a deep breath, and engage your self-talk to resist the temptation of overreacting or blaming yourself. Consider what you might tell your student if he or she was experiencing this stress. What would you tell a colleague or family member? Now, tell yourself and take your own advice!

You may not change reactionary behavior overnight, but you will eventually by simply being aware and evaluating your options to respond in healthy ways.

When you begin to evaluate, rather than react to, a situation such as student behavior problems and personal relationship difficulties in a more constructive way, you will begin to feel the difference and the positive feelings that will continue to help you to maintain control of your stressful situations—which, as a reminder, you cannot avoid, especially as an educator. Over time you will discover that the best antidote to stress and prevention of distress is your self-awareness and emotional self-discipline. The following are some additional effective ways to combat stress:

**Learn Relaxation Techniques:** Relaxation techniques include practices such as progressive relaxation, guided imagery, self-hypnosis, and deep breathing exercises. The goal of all these techniques is to consciously produce the body's natural relaxation response, characterized by slower breathing, lower blood pressure, and a feeling of calm. Relaxation is more than a state of mind; it physically changes the way your body functions. When your body is relaxed your breathing slows down, blood pressure and oxygen consumption decrease, and people often report an increased sense of well-being. This is commonly referred to as the relaxation response, which serves to counteract the effects of long-term stress.

The relaxation response was developed by Dr. Herbert Benson of Harvard University from a series of experiments on reducing stress and controlling the fight-or-flight response. Here is a simple technique you can try:

- Sit quietly and comfortably.
- Close your eyes.
- Start by relaxing the muscles of your feet and work up your body relaxing muscles.
- Focus your attention on your breathing.
- Breathe in deeply and then let your breath out. Count your breaths, and say the number of the breaths as you let it out (this gives you something to do with your mind, helping you to avoid distraction).

If you practice this technique for 10 or 20 minutes three to four times per week, you will begin to gain an increased awareness of whether you are tense or relaxed as you become more in touch with your physical body. You will also be better able to relax when you become stressed-out by putting your body in a calm state. Your concentration may improve as well because you will be strengthening the part of your mind that decides what to think about.

## Preventing Excess Stress and Avoiding Burnout

If you are like many people, you chose to become a teacher because you wanted to make a difference with your students. You can already feel the exhilaration of seeing the expression on their faces when they fully understand a new concept. That passion will make you a great teacher, but overzealousness can also lead to burnout. You must continually engage in self-care. Remember our earlier admonition: "put the oxygen mask on yourself first before trying to help others." You can care for others best when you make it a priority to take care of yourself.

Sometimes you may feel a sense of helplessness with the continuous onslaught of stress. The bills won't stop coming, there are always more papers to grade and not enough hours in your day, and your family responsibilities keep piling up. However, you do have more control than you might think. In fact, the simple realization that you are in control of your life is the foundation of healthy stress management. Take charge of your thoughts, emotions, and the way you deal with problems. Acute stress may be unavoidable, but much of the episodic acute stress and chronic stress—the kind that damages your health— can be minimized by keeping your life organized and reducing chaos. Manage your time and establish clear priorities. Engage in healthy relationships, set firm personal boundaries, and adopt a healthy lifestyle.

Some people adapt to stress better than others. Dr. Suzanne Kobasa of the City University of New York graduate psychology program conducted research to examine why some people simply don't let stress "get to them" (Stockdale, 2012). She and her colleagues identified more than 700 high-profile executives who were facing personal and career upheavals. Although hundreds of executives showed physical symptoms of stress, a smaller group did not experience the same symptoms of stress. On further analysis of this small group, specific personality traits were identified that suggested how/why the individuals better managed the stress situation. A person exhibiting the following traits understands that he or she is not totally in control but yet is not a victim:

- **Commitment.** Commitment is the tendency to involve oneself in whatever one is doing. This includes a deep and enduring commitment to yourself, your family, your work, your community, and other important values. Individuals who are committed to their values believe that their life has meaning and purpose.
- **Control.** Control involves the tendency to believe that and act as if one can influence the course of events. It is a belief that you can change the

impact of a situation by the way you view and react to it. This kind of control is the opposite of helplessness. It is a belief that you can control yourself and your reactions to what life hands you. It is the refusal to be victimized. When faced with difficulties, people with this trait use active strategies to either change the way they think about a problem or attempt to resolve the problem directly. The healthiest students approach problem-solving with a sense of control instead of passivity.

**Challenge.** Challenge involves the expectation that it is normal for life to change and that change will stimulate personal growth. People with this trait embrace change as an exciting opportunity to grow. This excitement is in direct opposition to boredom. They are highly aware that boredom is not the key to happiness.

There is no surefire way to avoid stress, but you do have options and tools to help yourself and others. You won't be the first educator to look in the mirror and ask yourself, "Can I really do this?" And you definitely won't be the last. The key is to listen, learn, and apply your skills to respond to the stressful issues that arise in your life. Create positive relationships with fellow teachers who are committed to supporting each other and the students. Your physical and emotional health will have a drastic impact on your happiness and the longevity in your profession. You will inspire, motivate, and cultivate learning better in your students when you consider yourself in the equation. How can you be effective if you are surviving on four hours of sleep each night and on the verge of physical or emotional exhaustion? You matter.

Keep in mind it is all about balance. Learn to work smarter, not harder. Harry K. Wong (Wong and Wong, 2001) suggests that by delegating certain tasks to your students, you will actually increase their learning. For example, try breaking your class into small groups and instruct them to compile a list of study questions that will appear on the next test. They can then swap their lists with other groups and discuss key topics. This will free you up to guide and facilitate discussions on learning instead of constantly carrying the ball. You may not be able to do this for every topic, but keep in mind that the more you put the onus on the students to learn, the more responsibility they will take to do it.

Make time to have a positive life outside the classroom. Setting clear boundaries between your professional and personal life is one of the most powerful things you can do for yourself. By doing so, you will be able to be more fully present in each moment of your life and spend more quality time with people who are important to you. Plan evenings out with family or friends.

Set aside adequate time for nurturing yourself and your personal relationships, and do not feel guilty that you are not home grading papers.

Listed below are some questions that are designed to assist you in making choices to manage work/life balance and avoid burnout:

- How would you rate your current state of balance on a scale of 1 to 10, where 1 is completely unfulfilled and 10 means completely fulfilled in life?
- What values or qualities of living would need to be present for you to increase your personal fulfillment?
- What three actions could you take right now that would create the greatest impact on your well-being?
- What are three things you do in daily life that have no relevance to work or life fulfillment?
- What are you willing to give up?
- What actions are you committed to take, or do more of, that would create greater personal fulfillment and strengthen work/life balance?
- When will you begin?
- Who will you ask to become an accountability partner?

Work/life balance will not happen by accident. You must be intentional and vigilant about it. First, evaluate where you currently are and what personal needs must be addressed or eliminated to experience more fulfillment in your life. Make a firm commitment to your health. Managing work/life balance and preventing burnout will be beneficial for you personally and professionally. When you establish healthy boundaries between your work life and personal life, you will be more relaxed and clear-headed. As a result, you will be more productive, more effective, and more resilient. With an enhanced sense of well-being you will also be a much more effective teacher. Be proactive in the management of you! Recharging your batteries daily with the appropriate amount of good sleep, exercise, and nutrition does make a difference. You owe it to yourself and your students.

*Chapter 6*

# Awareness and Your Mental Health

> *It's up to you today to start making healthy choices. Not choices that are just healthy for your body, but healthy for your mind.*
> —Steve Maraboli *(from* Life, the Truth, and Being Free*)*

Obviously mental health is of great importance to your future success, even though the topic of mental health is sometimes avoided during teacher training for being too "messy." You must develop an understanding of the signs, symptoms, and challenges of mental health issues that can occur with you, your students, parents, and stakeholders to become a fully integrated educator. People often avoid the topic of mental health issues because of stigma attached to them. Depression, anxiety, and other disorders affect millions of people each day and this is something that people should not be ashamed of or avoid, regardless of erroneous public perceptions.

You may face numerous mental health issues during your life either directly or indirectly, and they can affect your attitude, motivation, and sometimes your ability to empathize with others. Understanding how you feel about issues such as depression, mental illness, mental deficits, and deviant behaviors will prepare you to adapt if they penetrate your environment. For instance, you may despise people who use drugs to self-medicate, while showing a great deal of empathy for people who use other behaviors for coping mechanisms. Your reactions toward mental health are based on stereotypical beliefs stemming from your personal experiences.

Do you have any personal experiences with mental health issues? Sadly, either ignorance or naiveté sometimes makes it difficult to empathize or effectively deal with it, even though the U.S. Department of Health and

Human Services (1999) reports that only about 17% of U.S. adults are in a state of optimal mental health. There are hundreds of conditions and it would be impossible to address all of them in one book, but understanding some of the more common mental disorders may help you to better manage your classroom environment.

### Recognizing Mental Health Issues and Symptoms

According to the World Health Organization (2001) mental health is "a state of well-being in which the individual realizes his or her own abilities, can cope with the normal stresses of life, can work productively and fruitfully, and is able to make a contribution to his or her community." Mental illness is defined as "collectively all diagnosable mental disorders" or "health conditions that are characterized by alterations in thinking, mood, or behavior (or some combination thereof) associated with distress and/or impaired functioning" (U.S. Department of Health and Human Services, 1999). Research has indicated that mental disorders, especially depressive disorders, are strongly associated with chronic diseases including diabetes, cancer, cardiovascular disease, asthma, and obesity (Chapman, Perry, & Strine, 2005).

One of the most common mental health issues is depression (Kessler, Chiu, Demler, & Walters, 2005), which can be caused by stress as well as one's physical health such as fatigue, illness, and hormonal imbalance. Depression affects more than 26% of the U.S. adult population (Kessler, Chiu, Demler, & Walters, 2005) while approximately 8% of adolescents meet the criteria for major depression (National Alliance on Mental Illness, 2013). It has been estimated that by the year 2020, depression will be the second leading cause of disability throughout the world—the first being heart disease (Murray & Lopez, 1996).

### Facts About Depression

According to research, 30% of women at some time in their life will suffer from a form of depression. The rate for men is approximately 15%, but we should take into account men are less likely to report the issue of depression (Murray & Fortinberry, 2005). Why do some people, especially men, tend to neglect or ignore such common psychological issues? Because 54% of the population believes that depression is a weakness, not an illness (Murray & Fortenberry, 2005).

It is important to understand that depression is not a weakness. It is a common human condition that is complicated and it cannot be simply dismissed by telling someone to "just get better." Read the following passages that we have included from public sources. Although this subject is not intended to be a prime focus of this text, its importance to your self-awareness is valid. The following is an excerpt from a public online blog by a teacher suffering depression:

### Teaching with Depression: Is There Any Way Out?
Written by Jesse Scaccia

As a teacher, you are not allowed to get depressed.

There is too much work to be done. The kids feast on any perceived weakness, especially in a new teacher. Or, the kids take it personally, and think you're upset with them. Being depressed can make it seem like you don't believe in the lesson, the school, the education system itself, and if you don't believe in these things, there's no way the students will.

But teachers are only human. I'd even go a step further than human. In many cases they are the most human, with naturally flowing sympathy and an innate desire to shepherd their younger brothers and sisters. But it's this extra-humanness that, unfortunately, makes teachers more susceptible to depression.

It's a horrible catch-22: being a teacher you're not allowed to be depressed, but the emotional output required by the job makes you more likely to be depressed. Is there any way out of this mess?

I am a man who has battled depression since early childhood. I was still in primary school when I first held a knife and wondered just what I could do to myself with it. So I know depression, and it is something I've had to deal with at some point at every step of my teaching career. What I can tell you is, first of all, you can't wish depression away. So for those of you reading who are thinking right now, "Well, why not just not be depressed?" that solution is a ghost. It doesn't exist.

So until the depression is mitigated by drugs or therapy, what is a teacher to do? I've tried everything. I've drank a Coke before each class and kept a drawer full of Kit-Kats. I've faked it, pretending to be happy, hoping the kids weren't savvy enough to see through my mask. I've taught for me first, worrying more about making sure I enjoyed teaching my lessons then whether my students did (because, hey, if I like it they'll probably like it too). I have even been honest with my students. I've told them flat out, "Hey, I'm kinda of depressed today. Take it easy on Mr. S, will yah?"

Sometimes these solutions worked, and sometimes they didn't. By now, at 30, I know myself well enough to mix my own happiness smoothies on the fly. Sometimes it takes a Kit-Kat with a dash of Radiohead in-between classes. Sometimes I use a life line, and text a friend mid-class. I have figured out what works for me.

So for those of you teachers reading who battle depression—and I know you're there—my only advice is the advice you give yourself. Be reflective and recognize your triggers. Know yourself well enough to be aware of what can pull you out of that dark blue pool. If all else fails, channel your inner Michael Jordan. Someone once asked him why he played so hard every night, even against teams the Bulls were blowing out. His answer was that there might be one fan out there who will only see him play that one time, so he had to give his best. As a teacher, you never know if this is the only time in a student's life they'll hear a certain lesson. So you have to play hard every period.

As always, never forget this handy cliché: This too shall pass.

I feel the need to add some "real talk" here at the end. For some depressed people, teaching just won't be right for you. There will be too many expectations and pressures from a myriad of sources. Your life will be too rigid, the negative reinforcement will outweigh the positive. You might care too much or be too sensitive, making your small, everyday failures (of which there are a million a week) into a million potential depression triggers a week.

Blog response #1:
Thank you so much for this post. I also suffer from depression, and right now, I am going through a tough time. But it's not just me, one of my colleagues is having marital problems and another just "can't get happy." It's nice to know that we are not alone. Don't get me wrong, I love my job, and my students. Many times, a kind word, or hug, from a student is exactly what I need to get through the day. But our jobs are SO HARD!!! We have to be everything to everyone, and right now, I am tired, wore out and don't even know who I am anymore. I know my triggers (perfection). I am very reflective of what I could do better to make myself less depressed. But like you said, you can't just wake up and "be happy," even if you wanted to. Thank you for allowing me to be me, and letting me be myself, which ultimately, will make me a better teacher.

Blog response #2:
WOW! Thank you for posting. I feel like I'm the only teacher out there with Depression and perfection… I had a meltdown the other day before my first graders came into my class and I couldn't stop crying. I have been in bed almost all weekend, crying. Thankfully I have a super supportive coworker who had gone through this in a different school and told me what to do. She took my students for the morning, told our principal I needed to go home, and made my lesson plans for next week. My struggle now is, when do I go back to school? When I can get through the day without crying? I have a super tough class of first graders and at home, a 4yr old and 7yr old, and a husband who also teaches but isn't very nurturing and ignores my depression probably because he doesn't know what to do. I can't keep up with my home (due to my perfection) and I'm not emotionally stable to handle the demands of my needy students. HELP!

Blog Response #3
My fiancé whom I had been with for the last seven years just passed away. This is my first year teaching and I have been so ashamed that I've let depression grab a hold of me as strong as it has… .It is good to know that this doesn't mean that my teaching career is over (we worked so hard to get here). And that I am not the first person to realize that depression and teaching are a hard combo to manage. Thanks for the words :)

Blog response #4
… I had to leave school today because I could not stop crying—in front of 11th graders. My classes are overloaded—30 plus. I work in a very poor, mixed ethnic school where the kids are pregnant, abused, and can barely function in English on a 6th grade level. But I've been told to "RAISE EXPECTATIONS!" Are you… kidding me?… I'm a single mom of 2 (5 & 10)… I'll lose my house if I can't pay the mortgage. I'm

sorry, but a coke and some chocolate or breathing are not going to get me anywhere with this internal battle… I spend so much time preparing lesson plans and grading papers that I rarely have a moment…. And when I get home from work, I snap at my own kids because work has left me so angry and frustrated…

Experiences may vary, but the management of stress and mental health is often difficult, especially for new teachers. The Association of Teachers and Lecturers in the United Kingdom reported that nearly half of their country's secondary school teachers have suffered mental health problems. The main cause for this is thought to be increased behavior problems in the classroom, which are apparent in U.S. classrooms as well. Studies indicate that as many as 46% of educators have admitted to taking antidepressants rather than facing long layoffs as an alternative for coping with the stress they were experiencing (Garner, 2005).

Becoming aware of the signs of distress is important. Changes in mood or the presence of erratic emotions are all warning signs that you need to stop and slip the oxygen mask on. Perhaps the feelings are normal, such as sadness in the case of a loss, but if chronic signs begin to appear, seek help. According to the National Institute of Mental Health, symptoms of depression may include the following:

- Difficulty concentrating, remembering details, and making decisions
- Fatigue and decreased energy
- Feelings of guilt, worthlessness, and/or helplessness
- Feelings of hopelessness and/or pessimism
- Insomnia, early-morning wakefulness, or excessive sleeping
- Irritability, restlessness
- Loss of interest in activities or hobbies once pleasurable, including sex
- Overeating or appetite loss
- Persistent aches or pains, headaches, cramps, or digestive problems that do not ease even with treatment
- Persistent sad, anxious, or "empty" feelings
- Thoughts of suicide, suicide attempts

We have included a list of mental help services that may assist you if you are ever in need of sources for yourself, a colleague, a family member, or a friend (see Appendix A). Mental health issues are real and affect children, both in their homes and at school. To be successful it is necessary to maintain awareness of all issues that may negatively affect your learning environment.

*Chapter 7*

# Self-Motivation

> *Be miserable. Or motivate yourself.*
> *Whatever has to be done, it's always your choice.*
> —Wayne Dyer *(American self-help author and motivational speaker)*

Although you will spend much time in the future studying how to motivate your students, your own motivation will play a key role in their success both in and outside of the classroom. It is important to ask yourself, "What motivates me to do what I do?" Your answer may vary depending on what topic currently has your attention. What are your motivations to become a parent or not? What motivates you to do well in school? What motivates you to be more or less social? What motivates you to be active, or not, in the community? What motivated you to become a teacher?

Studies based on the altruism and beliefs of prospective teachers give insight into the motivation of teachers. Most teachers choose the profession because they want to make a difference with their students and their personal motivation is tied into the expectancy that they will. When educators are disappointed with the fit between their expectations and the realities of the job it can lead to a more stressful work environment (Cherniss, 1980; Eaton, 1980; Leiter & Schaufeli, 1996; Pines, 1993; Stevens & O'Neill, 1983).

With that unexpected reality also comes frustration that sometimes fuels the fire for blame: teachers blame their preparation; preparation programs blame the ideological beliefs of the incoming future teachers; lawmakers blame districts and administrators; districts blame lack of training; administrators blame communities and programs; communities/parents blame whoever is the closest to their sword. Be careful not to be caught in the never-ending circle of blame and stay focused on why you chose to teach in the first place.

You are here to make a difference. Right? So, what happens the first time you experience a student who simply doesn't care or won't respond regardless of how hard you try to help him or her? What if you encounter several students like that for days, weeks, or months on end? The reality is, you may. You must hold on to the belief that you are making a difference regardless of the immediate feedback and stay motivated by intrinsic factors much like those who work with the homeless, feed the poor, aid the ill, and counsel the hopeless. You are here to serve, but don't neglect to engage in self-care.

What really motivates you? It is okay to be driven by multiple factors. We all are, but the desire to "make a difference" is really what will make you feel astounded when you watch a child's eyes beam from the illumination of a new idea you introduced to her. If you are motivated by money this is probably not the profession for you. In fact it will seem downright unfair. The equity theory, first developed in 1963 by John Stacey Adams, states: if a person is receiving low pay that does not match the time he or she puts into the work (e.g., teaching, grading, attending school functions, etc.) then the person's motivation will decrease. Can this theory realistically apply to teachers? You must know that you are walking into this web (low pay and lots of hours), so there aren't any surprises here. Remember that decreased motivation may not affect your lecture style, but it can affect you in more subtle ways, such as your attitude toward parents, coworkers, family, and the standards of your work performance, not to mention your overall personal fulfillment toward your job.

How do you maintain personal motivation? We believe it is through the continual self-awareness and management of physiological, social, emotional, and psychological needs, which involves a delicate balance. Daniel Goleman (2011) refers to these as the keystone for emotional intelligence and cultural competence. In essence, becoming consciously self-aware means to be fully awake and attentive of your own needs, so you do not allow your performance to be affected by frustration, anger, or fear.

## Managing Your Self-Identified Motivators

The following suggestions will assist you in the management of personal motivation:

- **Stay in Control.** Be active in managing your surroundings, both personally and professionally, through planning, observation, and assessment. Create small attainable goals that you can work toward to meet larger, big-picture goals.

- **Manage Your Time.** The truth is that we have no control over time—only ourselves. Consider your own behaviors: Do you overcommit; do you neglect to finish projects; do you feel guilty when others need you when you are busy? It is important to again consider what we can and cannot do. If you do not manage your time well, as if a valuable gem, your motivation and energy cannot be fully given to your learners, or even your personal relationships. If your first attempt is unsuccessful, go back to your plan, review your progress, and design a new plan. Practice making your time valuable.
- **Recognize Your Successes.** In the face of challenge, never neglect to use positive reinforcement and self-talk to remind yourself that you are worthy and you are making positive progress. Take time to notice the little things that you have accomplished, in your classrooms, with your relationships, in attainment of your goals. It is often difficult for persons to tell each other that they have succeeded, so make it a practice to tell yourself.
- **Ask for Feedback.** From your students, from your colleagues, from your closest friends, but be prepared to be a learner. It is difficult sometimes to see what we are doing from outside of our busy world. It never hurts to ask your students: "Do you think that the way I explained this equation makes sense for you?" We cannot be successful unless others are also succeeding.
- **Use Your Support Network.** Friends, family, colleagues, or even a counselor. Dealing with the emotions of children and youth can be tough. Don't be a gossip, but recognize when you just need to share how you are feeling: good and bad.
- **Stay Healthy.** For this we will go into more detail later, as your health and wellness are vital to your success.

### A Cycle of De-motivators

The disabling cycle of de-motivators that currently exists in education must be addressed to take our educational system to a new level. This cycle focuses on you, the educator, and the realities of educating youth. It is based on understanding of self and how to maintain a healthy self, even in a climate of negativity, which is not going to change soon. *The educator and future educator must discover a means by which to find the power within the self—to meet the challenge at hand—without losing one's true self. There is but one irrefutable fact that few will argue with: our country has a difficult yet important job to do—educate and prepare our youth to succeed—and we must find a way to do this successfully.*

Today's teachers and leaders face unprecedented challenges resulting in a vicious cycle of stress and sacrifice, with little or no recovery time to continue any positive momentum. Consequently, even the most dedicated teachers—who deftly manage their personal issues as well as those of others—can spiral into frustration and despair. The good news is that it does not have to be that way.

To counter the inevitable "cycle of stress" in the teaching role, educators must consciously step out of destructive patterns that have been developing since the history of education in this nation began and renew the self: physically, mentally, and emotionally. This is paramount in maintaining your effectiveness as an integrated leader in education who is successful and fulfilled. Right now you may be thinking that this won't be you, and that's great—most new teachers do. However, you must recognize that teaching is one of the most important careers that a person can choose, and we encourage you to take steps now to protect your mind, your body, and your heart, so that you maintain your excitement and love for the field of education.

## Chapter 8

## Importance of Self-Care

> *Those who think they have not time for bodily exercise*
> *will sooner or later have to find time for illness.*
> —Edward Stanley

It is especially important for new teachers to practice self-care. New teachers are often expected to assume a full schedule of classes, create lesson plans, develop teaching techniques, and manage their classroom in relative isolation. They are also expected to quickly learn administrative responsibilities, from communicating with parents to navigating the school's computer network, taking attendance, and locating the faculty bathrooms. New teachers have to weather an exhausting first year that most veterans come to view as a rite of passage. Consequently attrition rates for beginning teachers who have not had strong teacher-preparation programs are double those who have been involved in such programs (Ingersoll, 2003).

Meeting our physical needs, including being physically healthy, is our most basic need. Being physically healthy means not only doing different kinds of activities but also includes how regularly you do those and the intensity level you are maintaining. In other words, if you say you exercise regularly, it does not mean that you are physically healthy. There are multiple elements that comprise physical health and they must work in tandem to make a person overall physically fit. Three of those elements are the following:

1. **Cardio Respiratory Endurance.** Cardio respiratory endurance is actually a combination of the respiratory system and circulatory system working together to supply necessary fuel required during physical activities such as exercise or any kind of physical task. To improve or maintain cardio respiratory endurance, you need to engage in exercises that keep the heart rate elevated and sustained for 30 minutes or longer with physical activities such as brisk walking, bicycling, jogging, or swimming. Remember not to exercise too hard and strenuously. We suggest you use the Borg rating of perceived exertion (RPE) as a way of measuring physical activity intensity level. Perceived exertion is how hard you feel like your body is working. It is based on the physical sensations a person experiences during physical activity, including increased heart rate, increased respiration or breathing rate, increased sweating, and muscle fatigue. Although this is a subjective measure, a person's exertion rating may provide a fairly good estimate of the actual heart rate during physical activity (Borg, 1998). This is also the preferred method to assess intensity among individuals who take medications that affect heart rate or pulse rate. The Borg RPE method is based on a 20-point scale, where a perceived exertion rate of 18–19 would be considered "extremely hard." Cardio respiratory exercise is suggested at a perceived level of 12–14. Begin with slow activities that you enjoy and then gradually increase your level of strain. By doing this, you will hopefully experience what it means to be physically healthy.

2. **Eating a Balanced Diet.** The National Institutes of Health define a balanced diet as eating a variety of foods in the proper amounts to provide enough energy and nutrients to support growth and sustain a healthy body. That means getting just enough, but not too much, of any particular type of food or individual nutrient. A balanced diet is different for everyone because the foods selected from within each food group will vary with individual taste, and sometimes with individual health concerns.

3. **Muscular Strength, Endurance, and Flexibility.** Your muscles provide the ability to engage in any physical activities that require the force of strength. Performing weight-bearing or resistance exercises is the best way to make your muscles fit and stronger. To strengthen your muscles and build a healthy body try exercises such as light lifting weights, calisthenics, or even climbing stairs. Muscular strength and endurance is the ability of the body to work regularly for a long time without getting fatigued. Flexibility is the ability of joints to move in all directions. Activities such as walking, swimming, bicycling, jogging, dancing in various forms, and yoga can be used to improve muscle strength, endurance, and flexibility.

**4. Body Composition.** Body composition is a blend of different elements such as muscles, bones, fat, and other vital parts of the body. It might be possible that bathroom scale body weight may not change over time but the proportion of all the elements should stay balanced. Body composition is a strong indicator of the state of your health and it is important in managing your body weight, specifically the fat content. Obesity, which has become an epidemic in our society, can drastically increase your risk for health problems, especially heart-related disease and diabetes.

The annual healthcare cost of obesity in the United States has doubled in less than a decade and may be as high as $147 billion a year, says new government-sponsored research. Because women have a higher level of necessary fat than men do, obesity levels are different depending on one's gender. The American Council on Exercise reports that women are considered to be obese when their body fat percentage reaches 32%. For men, however, the obesity level is only 25%. If weight management is a challenge for you, we recommend Weight Watchers or any plan that offers healthy eating guidelines in addition to a support group for weight loss, and regular exercise such as that suggested above.

**5. Sleep.** If you have small children you are aware of how important it is for them to get enough sleep. If they do not, they can become irritable and lethargic. The same is true for you. Most healthy adults tend to require between 7.5 to 9 hours of sleep per night to function at their best. Sleeping well is essential to your physical health and emotional well-being. Persons who have incurred sleep interruptions for as little as 3 weeks have reportedly become sick more frequently, increased concentration problems, and were more easily agitated. Many physicians also consider sleep to be a barometer of a person's health, much like taking a temperature. And sleep is something that we tend to take for granted, which can lead to numerous health issues before we even realize its effects.

Sleep disorders are more common than people think and they do affect your ability to educate, create relationships, and manage time. If you now, or during your teaching career, experience any of the following, you need to take it seriously, if you are serious about being and staying at your best for the children you serve.

- Have trouble falling asleep even though you feel tired
- Have trouble getting back to sleep when awakened
- Don't feel refreshed after a night's sleep
- Feel irritable or sleepy during the day

- Have difficulty staying awake when sitting still, watching television, or driving
- Have difficulty concentrating during the day
- Rely on sleeping pills or alcohol to fall asleep
- Have trouble controlling your emotions

If you begin to suffer from insomnia, become self-aware. Ask yourself:

- Am I experiencing a lot of stress?
- Am I depressed? Do I feel emotionally flat or hopeless?
- Do I struggle with chronic feelings of anxiety or worry?
- Have I recently experienced a traumatic experience?
- Am I taking any medications that might be affecting my sleep?
- Do I have any health problems/symptoms that may be interfering with my sleep?

Common causes of insomnia and sleep problems include the following:

- Poor sleep habits and sleep environment
  - Examples of poor sleep habits are irregular sleep hours, consumption of alcohol before bedtime, and falling asleep with the TV on.
- Pain or medical illness
  - Pain can keep you from sleeping well. In addition, many health conditions such as a frequent need to urinate, arthritis, asthma, diabetes mellitus, osteoporosis, nighttime heartburn, menopause, and Alzheimer's disease can interfere with sleep.
- Medications
  - Combinations of drugs, as well as the side effects of individual drugs, can impair sleep or even stimulate wakefulness.
- Lack of exercise
  - If you are too sedentary, you may not feel sleepy or feel sleepy all of the time. Regular aerobic exercise during the day, at least 3 hours before bedtime, can promote good sleep.
- Psychological stress
  - Significant life changes can cause stress, anxiety, or depression, which may also affect sleep patterns.
- Sleep disorders
  - Restless legs syndrome (RLS) and sleep-disordered breathing such as snoring and sleep apnea can occur as you age and should be considered during your career.

Seek out ways to better sleep. Here are some suggestions:

**Naturally boost your melatonin levels.** Artificial lights at night can suppress your body's production of melatonin, the hormone that makes you sleepy. Turn off the TV and computer at least one hour before bed. Don't read from a backlit device at night (such as an iPad). If you use a portable electronic device to read, use an eReader that is not backlit, that is, one that requires an additional light source such as a soft bedside lamp.

**Provide a peaceful environment.** Make sure your bedroom is quiet, dark, and cool, and your bed should be comfortable. Noise, light, and heat can cause sleep problems. If you cannot avoid a highly lit environment, try using an eye mask to help block out light.

**Move bedroom clocks out of view.** Watching the minutes tick by when you are having difficulty sleeping is a guaranteed way to stay awake.

**Keep a regular bedtime routine for better sleep.** Although busy schedules and grading and ballgames and raising a family can make time an issue, dedicate yourself to maintaining a consistent sleep schedule. Make this a priority. Remember that you will be more productive to complete tasks if you are well rested, getting more completed in shorter amounts of time.

**Block out noise.** If noise, such as snoring or traffic, is keeping you awake, try ear plugs or a white-noise machine.

**Develop bedtime rituals.** It is important to tell your body that it is preparing for sleep. Taking a bath, playing music, relaxation and stress management techniques, and deep breathing may be of help for obtaining optimum sleep.

**Limit your use of sleeping aids and sleeping pills.** Many sleep aids have side effects and are not meant for long-term use and can often make insomnia worse in the long run. Therefore, it's best to limit sleeping pills to situations where a person's health or safety is threatened.

### Managing Chronic Pain

If you suffer from chronic pain, it may be hard to imagine life without stress or anxiety. Being in constant pain can lead to feelings of fear, helplessness, and despair. If you feel disheartened about the future of your chronic pain condition there is hope. There are coping strategies you can learn that will give you a sense of control over your pain, even when it is intense. Anxiety can intensify feelings of pain and disability, so first it is important to come to terms with your condition. Regaining control of your situation can help lower your stress level by putting you back in the driver's seat.

While coping strategies may not completely eliminate your pain, they can help you get it to a level that you can deal with. At the least, you can keep your pain from getting worse due to pain anxiety. One potentially effective coping strategy is acceptance that you have a chronic pain condition. You may be in pain for a long time. It could even last the rest of your life. How could this not cause anxiety? The bigger question is: How can you learn to live with your chronic pain? Accepting it is not easy. It may even feel like giving in. Learning to accept your chronic pain condition may take time, especially if you are still in the grieving stage. However, it is the first step in letting your anxieties go. Here are some other tips for coping with chronic pain:

**Keep a pain journal.** The written word is powerful. Writing about how you feel, including your anxieties, can give you a greater sense of control over your pain condition. Regardless of what is going through your head, write it down. Get it on paper and out of your system.

**Discuss your pain.** When you are in chronic pain, it helps to talk about it. One of the worst things you can do is pretend you aren't in pain. Don't worry about what other people will think. Be honest about your pain with others and be honest with yourself.

**Let go of your grief.** Grieving is a natural part of being diagnosed with chronic pain. Do what you need to do to get it out and let it go. Scream. Get angry. Hit a pillow. Cry. Be sad. Then when you are done, move on. Yes, you have chronic pain. Yes, it stinks. No, it isn't fair. But staying stuck in the grief stage won't help your pain, and it could cause even more anxiety.

**Practice guided imagery.** This strategy helps you to bring your mental attention to a state that is detached from the physical sensations of pain. There are three stages to guided imagery: relaxation, visualization, and positive mental suggestion. Lie down, close your eyes, and simply become aware of your breathing. With each exhalation, allow the tension in your body to release, as you become increasingly relaxed and comfortable. Bring your awareness to your toes and let go of any tension you may feel there. Then move to your ankles and release all the pressure as you continue to become more relaxed with each breath. Continue progressing up your legs, gently relaxing the muscles in your calves, thighs, hips, lower back, and upward throughout your body to the top of your head. You may wish to listen to soothing music as a background.

In the visualization stage, imagine that you are transported to the most beautiful, serene place that you can remember. It may be a pristine tropical beach with crystal azure water, white sands, and swaying palms; or a beautiful clearing in a rainforest with lush ferns, a bubbling stream, and the calls of wild birds in the air; or it may be a pine-covered mountain plateau overlooking a lush valley. Wherever you are, imagine the sounds, feel the sensations, inhale the aromas of this beautiful, safe, comfortable setting. Once you have created your safe space, offer the mental suggestion that when you are in this place, you are free from pain, anxiety, and discomfort of any kind. Whenever you need to return to this place, you need only to close your eyes, take a few deep breaths, and simply re-create it in your mind.

Being aware of what physical needs you have and practicing self-care is basic but often ignored and the list of physical needs that a person, including yourself, may have is lengthy, but awareness of what your needs are is the first step. Throughout your development, you will find it necessary to address how, or if, you are being affected by your physical needs. When these needs such as adequate shelter, food, safety from physical and psychological harm, security (such as a paycheck), and pain are ignored, the consequences decrease your likelihood of you not only being a successful educator but also a happy individual who is at peace and content in your life as a whole.

Additionally, our behaviors often influence many of our choices such as eating habits, exercise, leisure time, perfectionism, and rigidity. It is hard to argue that if the previous are in check, one's health should be better, and one's physical needs more satisfied. A new body of research indicates that personality may actually be a major determinant in how you manage the things in your life that have the potential to increase your stress and by understanding how your own actions may potentially "put gas on the fire" is another important step to self-awareness development.

### Managing Your Personal Life and Relationships

Becoming aware of your personal life and how it affects your overall health and success in your professional life is often ignored. We contend that it is in this area that you may need to work the most. As a person who desires to be a service helper, it is important that you evaluate your personal social arena. Is it healthy? Are the people in your life healthy? Do they make you better or do they increase the amount of stress you have in your life? Is it helping or hurting your development in becoming a healthy and whole adult? The following are important for you to consider in your personal life, if you plan on truly becoming an integrated educational leader:

**Set healthy boundaries.** Know when to say yes and when to say no. Before saying yes to anyone, evaluate if it is the best decision for you. Acknowledge your limitations and don't try to leap tall buildings in a single bound. Ask for help. Trying to be a super-teacher has its consequences (usually negative).

**Recognize your threshold for stress.** The first signs of stress usually include increased heart rate, change in appetite, fatigue, or irritability. Pay attention to the situations that trigger stress for you and either avoid them or learn relaxation techniques, such as focused breathing.

**Begin your day on a positive note.** Start your day by doing something that raises your state of well-being and puts you in a positive frame of mind. It may be enjoying quiet time in meditation or prayer, thinking about the people or things you are grateful for, taking a walk, or sharing a cup of coffee with family or friends.

**Take frequent breaks.** You will be amazed at the impact even a five-minute break can have on your stress levels. Whether you spend it simply relaxing your brain and body or eating a healthy snack, you will feel rejuvenated. The work you do will be more efficient, too. Set a goal to take a five-minute break at least every hour and encourage your students to do so as well.

**Exercise regularly.** Exercise can decrease stress hormones, such as cortisol, and increase endorphins, the body's "feel good" chemicals that give your mood a natural boost. Research indicates that even moderate amounts of exercise help improve concentration, increase energy, and decrease the risk of stress-induced illnesses. Three of the best exercises for stress are yoga, walking, and swimming. Set a goal to exercise at least 30 minutes a day. If you have a busy schedule, you may find it easier to split your workout into smaller chunks. Try doing 10 minutes of yoga before your morning shower—you can even do it in your pajamas. Breaking up the work day with several 10-minute workouts can wake you up and make you more productive. We suggest that you find an exercise partner to help you stay motivated.

**Eat healthy.** Remember the old adage: "You are what you eat." Good nutrition is an essential part of being an effective educator. If you are a first-year teacher, it may be challenging to find the time and energy to prepare nutritious meals because you will likely be busy setting up your classroom and getting to know your students. A grueling schedule makes it even more important to eat a nutritious diet to maintain high energy levels. Get in the practice of eating a high-fiber breakfast and packing a healthy lunch to take to work. Schools often lack easy access to healthy foods for teachers. To avoid eating fatty foods full of empty calories, keep a stash of healthy food on hand. Whole fruit keeps well without refrigeration, which makes it ideal to store in your desk drawers. Whole wheat crackers, nuts, fresh vegetables such as carrots and celery, air-popped popcorn, and energy bars are also easy to store. We recommend that you "graze" several times a day on healthy snacks to keep your energy levels high.

**Get adequate amounts of rest and sleep.** We all need rest and sleep. Without it we increasingly run the risk of suffering ill health and burnout. One way to get rest is to take up an enjoyable hobby. If you spend your work day performing in the classroom, slow physical activities such as walking can help you unwind. Reading novels, watching television, listening to music, or socializing can also be restful. Most of us need an average of six to eight hours of sleep a night. If you are regularly deprived of adequate sleep, your concentration and energy levels will decline. That will cause you to lose your effectiveness on your job and you will be more susceptible to illness because of a weakened immune system. If you have become used to being tired all the time, you will be amazed at how sharp and energetic you will feel once you start sleeping normally.

**Identify toxic relationships.** When a person is in the middle of a toxic relationship, it can be hard to see how damaging the relationship is to self-esteem. Although your partner may be a good provider, a good father, and at times loving and kind to you, at other times, you may feel alone, frightened, or in distress. Dr. Lillian Glass, author of *Toxic People*, describes a toxic person as "anyone who manages to drag you down, make you feel angry, worn out, deflated, belittled or confused." It is important as an educator to protect yourself from these types of relationships, as they will drain you of confidence and energy and affect your ability to successfully educate.

1. Your partner puts you down verbally, in private or in front of others
2. Your partner tells you he or she loves you but behavior shows otherwise.
3. Your partner doesn't want you to see or talk to friends or family.
4. Your partner is jealous of the time you spend with your kids.
5. Your partner shows up often at your work unexpectedly or opens your mail.
6. Your partner calls you often to see what you are doing.
7. You cry often or feel depressed over your relationship.
8. Your partner says you would have the perfect relationship if only you would change.
9. Your partner wants you to be dependent on him or her.
10. Your partner does things for you and then uses them to make you feel obligated.
11. Your thoughts, opinions, accomplishments, or words are devalued.
12. You don't know who you are anymore without him or her, or how you would survive.

13. Your friends/family do not like your partner or do not think that you are good together.
14. You have changed things about yourself to suit your partner.
15. You always go where your partner wants to, such as movies, restaurants, etc.
16. Your partner has made you feel afraid or unsafe, and you have been afraid to speak the truth at times for fear of upsetting him or her (walking on eggshells).
17. You don't feel you have control of your life anymore.
18. Your self-esteem is lower since you've been with your partner.
19. You think it's up to you to make the relationship work.
20. You keep secrets about your relationship from others who love you because they wouldn't understand.
21. Your partner makes you feel unattractive or stupid.
22. Your partner accuses you of cheating and is overly jealous.
23. Your partner can be sweet to you one minute and mean the next.
24. Your partner seems sweet/loving to you when he or she thinks you are about to leave the relationship, or after he or she has been mean to you.
25. You can't remember the last time you felt happy for more than a few days straight.

Being honest with yourself about what variables are healthy and what are not in your life will not be easy. However, your desire to become a leader in education has obvious consequences. You hold the esteem and future lives of young learners in your hands. You could enter a field that is much less demanding—much less affective to others—but you chose education. What an honor, but remember that you will only be as good as you want to be. Pick your social circles carefully. You need positive reinforcement to help meet your needs before you can meet the needs of your students. Be aware.

Keeping in mind that you cannot change the world, you can, however, be aware of the social variables that affect your goal to pave the way for your students to be academically successful and psychologically fulfilled. Although you cannot make others believe in your students as much as you do, you can make a difference, but it will take a huge amount of dedication to being aware of the many social effectors, which are often unpredictable, that have the potential to affect your goal as an educator.

# Section II Review

### Section Activities

**Activity 1:** Body language is very important for how you manage and present yourself. Up to 93% of what we say is said through body language. Take the following body language survey developed by Catherine A. Martin.

1. **When you approach someone or they approach you are you aware of the space created between you and the other person?**
   Yes, I am fully aware of my distance and others' distance.
   No, I do not notice such things.
2. **Do you feel tense or uneasy if someone is staring at you?** Y or N
3. **When someone you are talking to starts looking away or fidgeting do you:**
   Continue to talk or stop talking and/or change the subject.
4. **Do you keep comfortable eye contact while conversing without staring?**
   Yes, I keep eye contact while talking and occasionally look away.
   No, eye contact makes me uncomfortable.
5. **Do you consciously smile when you greet another person?**
   No, I am not aware of my facial expressions when greeting someone.
   Yes, I make sure I have a pleasant look on my face when I greet.
6. **Are you aware of your tone of voice during a conversation?**
   No, I just talk and don't think about it.
   Yes, my tone of voice is important and I am aware of it.
7. **Are you aware of your facial expressions while someone is talking to you?**
   Yes, I make sure my facial expression shows interest.
   No, I just listen without any awareness of my facial expression.
8. **Do you nervously play with objects or fiddle with things during a conversation?** Y or N
9. **If someone is hesitating a lot during a conversation and not maintaining good eye contact do you:**
   Trust what the person is saying or have doubts about what is being said.
10. **I find it easy to tell someone's mood just by being with them for a short while.** Y or N

Scoring:
Question 1: Y=1 N=0
Question 2: Y=0 N=1
Question 3: Continue to talk or stop talking =0 change the subject =1
Question 4: Y=1 N=0
Question 5: Y=1 N=0
Question 6: Y=1 N=0
Question 7: Y=1 N=0
Question 8: Y=0 N=1
Question 9: Y=0 N=1
Question 10: Y=1 N=0

If you scored 9 or 10 you are very aware of your body language and that of others. You usually read people well and are a pretty good judge of character. You are very aware of people's motives and usually accurate in your assessment of them.

If you scored 7 or 8 you may be missing important clues when it comes to communicating with others in a positive way. You may find that you are often mistaken when it comes to reading people and that may interfere with your ability to make good friends and attract others to you.

If you scored 6 or less then it is recommended that you read up on communication and body language. You have the opportunity to improve. You may not be giving a good first impression and that may make it more difficult to make good friends and have good relationships in general. You may find it difficult to interview well and therefore you may not get the job offers you are looking for. You may find you are not very popular and may get rejected by others more often than you want.

Consider the following:

- One's proximity is important.
  - Personal space is needed and if invaded can cause an individual to feel uncomfortable or threatened. The distance between you and the person you are meeting should be on average an arm's length.
- How you look at someone can mean many things to many differing cultures.
  - In general, however, staring intimidates and can cause great anxiety in most people. Gang wars have been started over someone just staring.
- What you have to say should not always take priority.
  - Sometimes it is also important to stop talking and/or change the

subject. Who you are speaking to may be losing interest and it is important to identify why. It may be time to reconnect. It may be time for you to just listen.
- Eye contact is important.
  - People tend not to trust others who cannot keep good eye contact. Make your eye contact comfortable without staring.
  - If encountering a person who cannot keep contact, do not always assume this means they are being untruthful. Cultures differ. You may have doubts about what is being said because often a lot of hesitation and lack of eye contact can suggest the person is not being truthful, in a majority of cultures, but not all.
  - In North America, it is often a sign of respect or caring when one makes direct eye contact when talking to a superior person such as a boss or the president or a friend, while in Japan or China, it would be a sign of disrespect if one were to directly look a superior in the eye such as the emperor or, even, in some common cases, an elderly person. It could also be based on personality or past experiences. Learn to not judge before you know.
- Facial expressions can elevate or deflate any meeting or discussion.
  - Make sure to have a pleasant look on your face when you greet or assist someone, even if that person may have you frustrated. Facial expressions can make or break a chance at meeting and encouraging a positive relationship with someone. A pleasant look and smile will go a long way.
- Your tone of voice is important.
  - If the tone is right, then people are more receptive to what is being said. Listen to others in conversation and you will learn what tone is best. If you start out with a tome that is accusatory or deflating, you are much less likely to make successful progress in helping the matter.
- Show interest.
  - Try to mirror the other person's facial expressions. This makes them feel that you are listening to them.
  - Being distracted (e.g., talking on the phone, grading, playing with objects) can tell a person you do not really care about what he or she has to say.
- Learn to pay attention to others' body language.
  - If you are not in tune to others you may misinterpret situations, motivations, and opportunities. Take a moment to try to see what others' faces and bodies might be saying.

# SECTION III

## Integration Through Social Awareness and Management

*Let us not look back in anger, nor forward in fear, but around in awareness.* —James Thurber

**CULTURAL COMPETENCE**

Managing your social awareness is vital to becoming a successful integrated educational leader. Whether you are evaluating the climate of your community and classroom, managing discipline, discussing learning with parents, identifying safety issues, or creating relationships that encourage learning authenticity and goal attainment, you must be aware and take responsibility for your part of this dynamic with your learners.

Many of these students will have few relationships that bring positive outcomes to their lives. This is not negotiated by socioeconomics or ethnicity. There are abusive people, parents, and significant others in every "group" of people. Learning to not stereotype and be empathetic, real, and highly expectant from your students will help you to become the one who gave them vision, even hope.

### Something to Think About

It is important to find common ground with your students and with your colleagues. A first-year teacher from the Midwest posted the following "great day" in a social networking site. We do not suggest that everyone needs to become a "gamer," as we certainly are not, but for this teacher, her common ground in this area is successfully encouraging buy-in from her students (names have been changed):

> **Boy 1:** Mrs. Richter, have you played the new Halo?
> **Mrs. Richter:** Of course I have! You know, I actually completed the campaign last night.
> **Boy 2:** WHAT??? Already?? It JUST came out like, last week!
> **Mrs. Richter:** Guys, I wasn't lying when I said I was an intense gamer.
> **Boy 1:** Psh, whatever I bet you played it on easy.
> **Mrs. Richter:** Nope . . . heroic. (insert gasps from about 6 different kids)
> **Boy 1 whispering to Boy 3:** Dude, our teacher is so awesome.

# Chapter 9

# Your Learners

> *I know there is strength in the differences between us.*
> *I know there is comfort, where we overlap.*
> —Ani DiFranco

Your awareness of the social environment you live and work in is highly important to your success as a teacher, a leader, and a human being. Understanding you learners is foundational. You will not only be a teacher when you graduate from your program. You will be mothers, fathers, community leaders, significant partners, researchers, and friends. You will not only grade papers and guide children who are not your own, but you will balance life full of joys, pains, hardships, and rewards. Although the most poignant to your career will be social awareness in the learning environment, to become an integrated leader it will be necessary for you to be aware of all of your daily contexts and how to manage them positively.

Dr. Roosevelt Thomas Jr. (2006) defines diversity as "the differences, similarities, and related tensions that exist in any mixture" (p. xi). Limiting ourselves to the thought that diversity only encompasses race and gender inhibits our ability to understand diversity in a broader sense. It is important that you gain the social awareness to address these differences with tolerance and an understanding that your way is not the only way. And lastly, that diversity is a good, but complicated, dynamic. Willingness to learn from each other is what sets us apart globally. Understanding that many things make us diverse is a huge step toward being culturally competent and aware.

Often the things that hold us back from positively developing a better understanding of those around us is our ability to believe myths or assume something about another culture. Rather than be open to the reality about what we *know*, we assume we are right and, often, we adamantly oppose anyone or anything that puts our beliefs into question. When we choose to develop our cultural competence, it is not only important to know ourselves as we have discussed, but it is also important to be aware of the social norms and myths that we easily accept without basis.

Myths about what being culturally competent is—and is not:

- **If I do not see color, I am being equal.** UNTRUE
  Ladson-Billings (1994, 1995) and Ladson-Billings and Tate (1995) suggest race does matter in the context of education. Ladson-Billings (1994) suggests a "disconnect" with racial issues and practical strategies. It is important to see color; it is important to see differences to make the necessary changes in our own understandings to best serve *all* learners.
- **I do not stereotype; that would be wrong. I like every child and treat every child the same.** UNTRUE (Even though it is hard to admit it.)
  Several investigations indicate that many typical teachers and preservice teachers have lower expectations of and predispositions about achievement toward low socioeconomic status (SES), poverty, and minority students (Alexander, Entwisle, & Horsey, 1997; Alexander, Entwisle, & Thompson, 1987; Katz, 1999; Olmedo, 1997; Rist, 1970) (although these may be unconscious) including levels of motivation, levels of intelligence, behaviors, dress, and potential to succeed (Rosser-Cox, 2011).
  Preservice teacher bias/stereotyping tendencies are common (Olmedo, 1997; Rosser-Cox, 2011) and often the behaviors and actions of teachers set the stage for stereotyping, even when unintended. The stereotyping of students' comments of preservice teachers has also been suggested to be more profound with those who also passionately and emphatically believe that they have *never* stereotyped, suggesting a disconnect with what stereotyping is and is not (Rosser-Cox, 2011).
- **I do not discriminate. That would not be right.** UNTRUE
  *Discrimination*, according to the Webster Dictionary, has two definitions:
  1. The unjust or prejudicial treatment of different categories of people or things, esp. on the grounds of race, age, or sex.

2. Recognition and understanding of the difference between one thing and another.

The latter—recognition—is as important as *not* being colorblind. Understanding our differences and learning how to manage them and create an exceptional learning environment actually applies "discrimination" in this form (Rosser-Cox, 2011; Thomas, 2006). However, the unfair form can be just as common and is not acceptable.

In 2000, the National Conference for Community and Justice (NCCJ) conducted a nationwide survey called *Taking America's Pulse II* (Smith, 2000). They found that:

1. Gays and lesbians are the most discriminated against group in America, followed by African Americans
2. 31% of Asians reported affliction and unfair treatment/discrimination
3. 16% of Hispanics and 13% of whites also reported having experienced at least one occurrence of discrimination during the prior month

In 2008, according to a study at Yale University published in the *International Journal of Obesity*, research suggested that discrimination against people who are overweight is as common as racial discrimination. The study suggested that bias against people who are considered "fat" is common—in employment, education, public accommodations, and virtually all aspects of our society.

In regards to gender, the sociological analysis of gender is the identification between biological sex and gender. In other words, sex is a property of the biological characteristics of a "being" and gender is a socially constructed idea of what "female" or "male" is supposed to look like. Thus, in its simplest form, it has been suggested that teachers use gender expectations as a means of maintaining classroom control: seating undisciplined boys next to girls as a strategy and encouraging girls to "mother" students who have fallen behind, and often those students are male (Scantlebury, 2009).

So where do these conscious and/or unconscious stereotyping and negatively discriminating behaviors derive from? Sociologists have pointed at many variables that may affect this. (For this text, the most pertinent to learning environments have been listed.) It is important that as educators, we consider each of these variables and if, perhaps, we have things from our lives/past experiences that could affect the way we teach learners, we must identify them and successfully manage these conditions.

1. **Social Experiences**. Many prejudices can be passed along from grandparents and parents to children. The media—including television, movies, and advertising—also perpetuate demeaning images and stereotypes about assorted groups, such as ethnic minorities, women, gays and lesbians, the disabled, and the elderly.
2. **Stereotype Threat.** Stereotype threat is the sense of threat that can arise when one knows that he or she can possibly be judged or treated negatively on the basis of a negative stereotype about one's group (Steele, 1997; Steele & Aronson, 1995). For instance, white teachers say they don't see color because they fear if they say they do, they might be categorized as a racist. In this case, the fear itself has lead to a disparity of actually being culturally responsible based on what the teacher feels is the majority belief of the "group."
3. **Peer Pressures**. Prejudices may bring support from significant others (e.g., fellow teachers, coaching staff, and administrators), so rejecting prejudices may lead to losing social support, and in teaching we *need* the support of our peers. The pressures to conform to the views of families, friends, and associates can be overwhelming.
4. **Unconscious Fears and Authoritarianism.** As addressed in the historical section of this book, fears can drive many biases and racist actions. People who favor an authoritarian personality, in particular, can display rigid "ideological" conformity and express intolerant sexual, ethnic, political, and religious opinions (Altemeyer, 1988; Mockabee, 2007; Stenner, 2005). Fears associated with social exclusion and group dissolution have been suggested as a primary explanation of the developed fears (Eigenberger, 1998). This suggestion aligns well with the increase in racial tension during competitive job markets, too.
5. **Ethnocentrism.** Ethnocentrism is the tendency to evaluate others' cultures by one's cultural norms and values. This can be blatant or subconscious. For instance, if your background and beliefs are strongly embedded in the idea that children should be automatically respectful to teachers and to the rules, children who do not behave in this "norm" may be easily categorized as "trouble makers." However, this may not at all be what is happening. We will continue the discussion of behaviors later in this book.

Discrimination is real, and although sometimes unintended, it is painful to those who reap its results. Learners are all different and it is an incorrect assumption by many that if we ignore the differences, we are being culturally mature. This is not the case, and it is important to learn about the skills it will take to be culturally responsive. On the same note, although parents and adult stakeholders do generally have a more developed ability to self-assess at a higher level than many K–12 learners, the same is true for these groups. Any person can react to another, initially based on their own past experiences and myths within their own culture.

### Racism

The target of racism has also continued, and will continue, to grow out of fear when we, as educators, do not understand those who do not match predefined norms of what we as individuals know and understand. Members of vulnerable groups, often racial, religious, or ethnic minorities or disempowered majorities, are still experiencing abuse and violent acts that violate their human rights. In many countries this pattern of discrimination extends to women; children; persons with disabilities; indigenous; lesbian, gay, bisexual, and transgender (LGBT) persons; and members of other vulnerable groups who lack the political power to defend their own interests. Often members of these groups are denied economic opportunity or the ability to abide by their social or cultural traditions or practices as they are oppressed and even restricted in their ability to speak freely, to assemble peacefully, or to form associations or organizations. Social justice and injustices have become paramount in our media and in our everyday lives. Hate crimes bathed in racism are still occurring. Hispanics currently constitute the largest group of reported hate crimes by racist antagonists and African Americans compose the second-largest minority group still today. Hate crimes against minority sectors of this nation still psychologically affect those who identify with the group, which has its own obvious effects within classrooms across the country.

Diversity acceptance and tolerance have dominated our concerns in education, and to a point the nation, whether it agrees or not, gets it. Bullying, male/female stereotyping, dropout rates, and propaganda built on fear still hurt our forward movement. As a competitive nation, none of its participants want to come in second. We have been given tools to address with great confidence the issues of teaching learners who differ cognitively, ethnically, socially, physically, spiritually, and mentally. Ask yourself: **What stone has been left unturned when developing an educational system that is meeting the needs of its stakeholders?** We contend again that it is you. No one has considered the traumas our teachers have endured throughout the growth process. So, now it is time to address *you*!

You, as a teacher, with the power to make a difference each day with a child, hold the key. We contend that it is you who has the passion and ability to change what has been broken—not legislators—not communities—YOU. The number of applicants to the Teach for America program, a highly competitive program that recruits recent college graduates to teach for two years in low-income areas, increased from 35,177 applicants in 2009 to 46,359 in 2010 (Carpenter, 2010). It is obvious that teachers desire to be or to become excellent. However, you as a preparing teacher may be focusing on what everyone else needs but it is essential that you also consider your own needs to maintain balance and wholeness so that you have yourself to give. We assert that wanting better educational progress is an inherent need of those that claim the career of teacher. However, unless the outcome balances with the input, no one wins. Understanding how to secure your motivation and be psychologically healthy is vital. You are not only a servant to your learners, communities, and to the state and nation, but also a person with daily needs that must be met for you to function at your best.

It is not only our students who are more diverse in today's society; our teachers are as well. You have differing needs, belief systems, and values. Society will not simply give you what you need to succeed in this career—you must take it, own it, and hold on for the journey of your life. America is still the number one exporter of innovation, creativity, and freedom in the world and you are the key to securing this standing. *You are important and you are valued.*

## Students Need to Belong

The need to belong is another social area with which you must learn to be actively aware. Students must feel they belong and are accepted members of a group if they are to reach higher, more positive, levels of development. The feeling of not belonging and isolation is one of the biggest causes of stress in the body and can be painful, and sometimes crippling. Maslow (1971) suggested that most maladjustment and emotional illness in our society could actually be traced to the failure to gratify the basic human need for belonging. And we wonder why gangs have become so popular?

Research suggests that the need to belong can affect a child's motivation, mental health, and academic performance (Crandall, 1981; Deci & Ryan, 1985, 2000; Goodenow, 1993). If you recall, the need to belong also affects adults in this way. This feeling of detachment and alienation can breed inner feelings filled with rejection and loss of self-efficacy. Even more difficult for you, the educator, is how to spot a child who feels alone even in a group. Children, experiencing this, can react in different ways: internalization that creates a sense of self-loathing or externalization that creates a sense of loathing for others (Beck & Malley, 1998), both of which decrease their likelihood of creating meaningful bonds with others.

An additional concern is that research also suggests that supervising adults (including educators) rarely intervene (Craig & Pepler, 1997; Frey, Hirschstein, Snell, Edstrom, MacKenzie, & Broderick, 2005). However, is that because bullies disguise it so well, or because educators have their attentions in so many other places besides the social activity going on in the environment? Whatever the reasoning, this apathy increases concern about the motivation and readiness of teachers. Safety for students and for teachers is of much greater concern than ever before. Gangs, access to weapons and drugs, poverty, complicated and abusive home environments, and many other changing environmental factors have steadily increased. Being socially aware to combat bullying is difficult but possible.

### Importance of Tolerance and Acceptance

Tolerance and acceptance go hand in hand in building strong relationships and encouraging belonging for your students. We are all attracted to people who have similar qualities to us. In the forming stages of building relationships, whether on a personal or professional level, it may seem as if everything is fine, or at least we are not too bothered by the other's idiosyncrasies (something we all have, by the way). As the relationship matures, we enter the inevitable chaotic stage, even with people we like, where all of a sudden our differences become glaringly obvious and we don't like the person nearly as much as we had previously thought. That is where real growth begins for us and our relationships.

Unlike assimilation—where everyone's differences are lost in a giant melting pot—multiculturalism advocates the idea that maintaining our different cultural identities can enrich us and our communities. Multiculturalism does not promote ethnocentrism or seek to elevate one cultural identity above another. Instead, it celebrates diversity by allowing us to value our individual heritages and beliefs while respecting those of others. Respect for each others' cultural values and belief systems is an intrinsic part of cultural diversity. Lack of respect is often based on ignorance or misinformation. If you do not understand another's values, lifestyle, or beliefs, it is much easier to belittle them. And so the seeds of prejudice and intolerance are sown.

Humans are not clones. We all have differences and we will not always agree with every person we encounter. That is what makes life interesting and exciting. "Interesting and exciting?" you say. "How about frustrating and stress-inducing?" Although the latter seems more probable, once we become good at building and understanding the dynamics of functional relationships the "interesting and exciting" will be more prominent.

Building relationships does not mean that we are "besties" with everyone and think that our students and parents are perfect. Building relationships takes many forms and requires empathy, which is the capacity to recognize feelings that are being experienced by another. You may not agree with another person's political views or religious beliefs. You may not see eye to eye with someone who has different generational or cultural values than yours. And you may be thoroughly put off by the kid with the purple hair, tattoos covering both arms, and 27 body piercings who parked a car next to yours in the school lot. But everyone has feelings and we all want to be respected. If you want respect you must first give it.

Clarity about what empathy is and is not is also important. Being empathetic does not mean we adopt everyone and all of their hurts, ideas, and experiences as our own, but we do communicate in ways that show respect. Respect in this form is understanding that whatever this person feels is real to the person and should not be discounted as wrong. Empathy is the key to tolerance and acceptance, but what is the difference between them? Tolerance is an action. More precisely, it is a restraint from action. In the case of diversity, tolerance is treating people with respect whether you like them or not, or whether you accept them or not. Acceptance, on the other hand, is an emotional or mental state. In the case of diversity, acceptance is actually embracing another's differences as a possible option in society.

For example, you may not agree with someone's chosen lifestyle. If you go 24 hours without criticizing or condemning that person, you have practiced a basic level of tolerance. More precisely, you have restrained yourself from making negative judgments about someone with whose lifestyle you do not agree. If you treat a person like this as politely as you would any other stranger, you are said to have practiced a high level of tolerance. While you may disagree with his or her lifestyle, you have not been disagreeable. Your view of the person's lifestyle has not changed, but you have risen above the need to act out on your opinion. That is tolerance.

As an educator, sometimes it is difficult to be tolerant as we get caught up in the business of the classroom. Reports are numerous that cite teachers for calling certain lifestyles or parental actions wrong in the classroom. It is difficult not to throw your two cents out there, but you must ask yourself if it is worth losing the relationship or not. In our personal life this is an important question as we choose to not be a part of certain groups of people, but in education, you do not have a choice of who to be academically successful with and who you do not. You must control your emotions. You must control your tongue. You must see the bigger picture and remember that your job, although multifaceted, although complicated, can be simple. You are to successfully educate young children and youth and this takes positive relationships, trust, and tolerance.

In the case of acceptance, what would it take for you to *accept* their lifestyle as it is? First you would have to agree with it. Doing so may require you to change your core beliefs about what is right or what is wrong, and research is abundant that this is difficult. If you believe a particular lifestyle or behavior is immoral, against your religion, harmful to others, or ultimately self-destructive, it will likely be impossible or too objectionable for you to accept it. Therein rests the dilemma with unrestricted acceptance. It is not something that can just happen and remembering this will help you to understand how important tolerance becomes and why it is important.

This distinction between tolerance and acceptance is also significant because it creates a natural boundary of what the general population can ask of any individual or group. Can we ask an individual to practice a basic level of tolerance of diversity? Yes, because people do have the right to act on their opinion. Can we ask an individual to accept diversity? No, because people do have the right to act on their opinion. Both cases are covered by the First Amendment, which implicitly protects the freedom of thought, without which the freedoms of speech, the press, and religion are meaningless.

The significance of this distinction is enormous between tolerance and acceptance. To tolerate something is simply to put up with it; as shallow as it may sound, to "deal with it." It does not mean you have to like it or approve of it. To force you to accept it is as wrong as you forcing others to accept your beliefs and values. Unfortunately societal decrees in education often have not been to impart the children with tolerance, but rather to mandate acceptance, forcing assimilation to said values of the majority. The distinction is sometimes lost. We should seriously encourage social toleration, meaning the willingness to coexist with those of different opinions, lifestyles, religions, ethnicities, and so forth. However, not everyone is going to like everyone else or want to associate with them, because to impose acceptance on people is an act of intolerance.

If you as a future educator will help your students to become more informed about our world with the vast diversity of people in it, then maybe, just maybe, your students will broaden their views and make a decision to not only tolerate but also accept people who are different from them. And as you practice this, you too may become better at fighting our natural reactions (remember the amygdala) to things you do not understand. What better place for that to happen than in our schools—where the highest levels of learning about tolerance and acceptance should take place—but it will take your acknowledgment of its importance to make it a reality.

It is important to become aware of the children in your classroom. They arrive with the same predisposition to preexisting beliefs as you do. Some of your learners will have experienced "burned out" teachers, or worse, teachers who have become so tainted with frustration and lack of belief in their abilities that they are ineffective and sometimes abusive. These so-called bad eggs, which have become helpless based on the expectations and labeling of a society and system that have cultivated their hardened hearts and deflated self beliefs, may have decreased the trust that your learners have for you. They may even have embedded attitudes of disrespect for and anger against authority figures such as yourself—the teacher.

This can be frustrating, especially to a new teacher who simply wants to do a great job, but being aware that the behaviors are not personal, but real to the student, based on past experiences will help you to reach them. Remember that many times negative behaviors are a result of fear—fear of an abusive teacher, fear of disappointing a teacher, fear of making a fool of themselves. The students' negative responses to you could be triggered by almost anything: your race, religious differences, socioeconomic differences, family-value differences, or even your teaching style and demeanor. This does not mean that you cannot teach them.

You must choose to understand and consciously process that these students walk into your classroom with a predisposed opinion about the importance of learning, the proper social behaviors given the setting, or even the level of cooperation that they should be required to offer in your classroom. You cannot take a child's predisposition personally. Although this text may be the first time you have considered your preparation to be this multifaceted, that you recognize its reality will prepare you greatly for unanticipated events. Your students, whether in kindergarten or in 12th grade, do not have the same developmental maturity as you do. The skills of understanding their past and how it affects their present are doubtfully even a thought to them. You must be the proactive agent in the relationship, but to be this agent you must see and hear before you declare judgment.

Consider your own needs. If you have had little sleep, how will you respond to others? If a family member is in trauma, does it affect your attitude? Your behaviors? Human nature dictates we protect ourselves and as much as life events affect us as adults, for children without the necessary and more mature coping skills that adults gain through life, the outcome can be more complicated. Granted, children are resilient, but sometimes life can be too much for anyone. So the important variable you must consider every day when you walk into your classroom is that your life may not have been disrupted since the day before, but one of your learner's lives may have been turned upside down. It is important to not take behaviors of your learners personally, or to judge. Take time to listen, to watch, to hear *before* you react.

# Chapter 10

# Awareness and Learner Safety

Safety is an important need for you and your students. Without this need being met, students are unable to achieve successful learning. Fear of a loss of safety can come from multiple environments: family, peers, and school. Being aware of what threatens your learners takes listening and cultural competence, since often safety is also defined by culture.

### Awareness of Bullies

Being aware of bullies in your school will be a mandatory part of the job. Approximately half of U.S. students are affected by traditional bullying each school day. It happens on buses, in the cafeteria, gym, hallways, playground, and in classrooms. The most frequent form of bullying is the use of words (teasing, taunting, ridiculing, name-calling, and gossip), not blows. This type of bullying happens in the "physical" world such as between classes, in the back of the room, and at recess. Part of being socially aware is also to understand the possible, and in some situations probable, social environment threats. One of the most profound in education is bullying.

Research suggests an average of 2.4 bullying episodes occur every hour within classrooms (Craig, Pepler, & Atlas, 2000). In *classrooms*. So many times the teacher has no idea that it is even happening. Additionally, the students who observe bullying can be traumatized (Charach, Pepler, & Ziegler, 1995), which then encourages a support system for retaliation (Musher-Eizenman, Holub, Miller, Goldstein, & Edwards-Leeper, 2004). Additionally, there is rising apprehension that bullying also increases the possibility of students bringing weapons to school to protect themselves (DeVoe & Kaffenberger, 2005).

If you are a preparing teacher, you may be questioning how spotting these interactions could be difficult; however, bullies take many forms and use many techniques (e.g., being feared or avoided, or sometimes overly uplifted by others), often based on their insecurities and needs. Fortunately, there are behaviors and reactions that typically occur between the bully and their victims. A profile of a bully may include the following and in many cases these clues are well hidden:

- A need to overpower or be in control
- Choosing victims who shy away from conflict
- Deriving satisfaction from inflicting duress on another
- Lacking empathy for their victims
- Justification of their actions by blaming others for provoking them
- May be unhappy, angry, or impulsive or the opposite—uncomfortably jovial and social with certain groups
- Possess a low self-esteem or deteriorated sense of belonging or the opposite—make others feel bad about themselves and makes them feel like they do not belong

In addition to being alert for bully behaviors, teachers should be aware of victim behaviors in students, such as reluctance to attend school, complaints of frequent illnesses, drops in grades and academic performance, torn clothing, bruises, sensitivity to criticism, less positive social development and reactions to peers, or reports of lost possessions. Victims may react passively or assertively, which complicates evaluation of what is actually happening.

Passive victims usually have a difficult time asserting themselves in a group and react to bullying by withdrawing. These students may seem disengaged and sometimes indignant at times. In contrast, assertive victims tend to be hot-tempered and aggressive. They provoke incidents only to become victimized by their own actions and in some cases blamed for the incident blindly, with no empathy by those in charge for the previous actions that have taken place. Subsequently, these students are then mistaken for bullies because they frequently seem to be in the middle of fights and arguments. To complicate this, some bullies also "befriend" teachers, creating an innocent looking barrier to disguise the actual pain he or she is causing others.

This is where our past experiences also need to be considered. The term *bullying* may bring to mind visions of a hulking kid taunting a scrawny one on the playground, but bullies come in all shapes, sizes, and ages. Bullying may even occur by a principal toward a teacher. According to the Workplace

Bullying Institute (WBI) (see www.workplacebullying.org/), an estimated 54 million people in the U.S. workforce (37%) have reported being bullied at work, and teachers are no exception to this statistic. If you are a teacher or become a teacher who is being harassed or mistreated by your principal, document the incidents, corroborate with peers who may be experiencing the same treatment, and discuss the issue with your human resources department or union representative. However, be cautious and protect yourself. Most bullies are very good at turning the tables. You will need to be aware of your responses and actions, but you can beat a bully.

**Cyberbullying**

There is now a new type of bullying that is familiar to most of us: cyberbullying. Cyberbullying is using the Internet, smartphones, video game systems, or other technology to send or post text or images intended to hurt or embarrass another person. Cyberbullies persecute teens in an assortment of ways: by pretending to be someone else to get them to reveal personal information, by lying about them online, by pretending to be them while communicating with someone else, and by posting unflattering pictures or videos of them. This new, more difficult to "see" type of bullying is making the environment of your classroom more difficult and injuring to teachers and students. Bullying in cyberspace can be accomplished almost 24 hours a day and is not bound by school hours. And now, the bully may not even have to come face-to-face with the victim. Unfortunately, the Internet often shields the bully from the consequences of his or her hurtful actions.

With close to 100 million cell phones owned in this country and Internet in homes now the norm, cyberbullying in the form of text messages, emails, photos, website postings, or videos on Youtube can go viral in minutes. Defamatory information about peers can be sent out quickly and anonymously. Myspace and Facebook are popular places for this information to be posted. And unfortunately a reported 81% of youth who use this method said that cyberbullying is funny. As an increasing number of youths have access to computers and cell phones, the incidences of cyberbullying are likely to climb.

Studies indicate that cyberbullying incidents have quadrupled in five years. In 2000, 6% of young people reported they had experienced some form of cyberbullying (Crimes Against Children Research Center at the University of New Hampshire, 2000). In 2004, of 1,556 youth, 42% had been bullied online (i-Safe America, 2004). And in 2005, a study by National Children's Home Charity revealed that 20% of students had been cyberbullying victims. (Ross, n.d.). But a study performed by Patchin & Hinduja (2011), that included only

Internet-using adolescents, found that over one-third had been cyberbullied. Half of these victims also admitted, however, to cyberbullying others. Being aware of how this is happening and who are likely predators and victims can assist you in being aware of what is going on with your learners, because the unfortunate truth is that many cases do not get reported.

Getting kids to report this behavior is also difficult. Middle school and high school girls are twice as likely as boys to report receiving email, text messages. or chat room messages that teased, mocked, and ridiculed them (Kamaron Institute, School Surveys, 2007–2009). Sixty-two percent said that they had been cyberbullied by another student at school, and 46% had been cyberbullied by a friend (Kowalski et al, 2005). Sadly, only 20% of cyberbullying victims tell their parents about the incident, and most victims are more likely to tell a friend (42%).

Behaviors you can watch for include the following:
- Signs of emotional distress during or after using the Internet or phone
- Being very protective or secretive of their digital life
- Withdrawal from friends and activities
- Avoidance of peer gatherings
- Slipping grades and "acting out" in anger
- Changes in mood and behaviors

Many teens report that cyberbullying is simply a joke, not foreseeing the negative consequences it could have on the wounded. Some report that cyberbullying occurs through peer pressure from others who think the practice is just part of growing up. And cyberbullying can increase the violence in and outside of school. Close to 30% of teens who have been bullied report wanting to seek revenge on those who cyberbullied them. Ninety-two percent of teens who were cyberbullied report knowing the bully and half of those adolescents knew the cyberbullies from their school. Remember that cyberbullying incidents sometimes end violently.

How cyberbulling messages are communicated:
- Text or digital imaging messages sent on cell phones
- Emails
- Instant messaging
- Web pages
- Web blogs
- Chat rooms or discussion groups
- Other information communication technologies

How can you help by being aware?
- Talk specifically about cyberbullying. Explain that it is harmful and unacceptable behavior.
- Encourage your classroom of learners to report to an adult immediately if they are victims of cyberbullying.
- Advise students to not respond to a bully.
- Tell your students to save the bullying messages or photos.
- Let teens know that they can report bullying incidents to Internet service providers (ISPs) and website moderators.
- Remind teens to keep their passwords a secret from everyone except their parents.
- Explain to teens that it is not their fault if they become victims of cyberbullying, but it is important for them to tell a parent or their school counselor if they are victimized.
- If asked, speak openly with teens about cyberbullying.
- Create a way for kids to anonymously report cyberbullying.
- Be proactive in your school about cyberbullying.
- Request that children and youth sign an Internet safety pledge promising they will not cyberbully or share their personal information.
- Establish acceptable Internet use and anti-cyberbullying policies.
- Inform parents that they should establish Internet use rules for their kids.
- Sponsor an Internet safety awareness day for kids and parents to learn about safe Internet use.

Cyberbullying can leave victims at greater risk for anxiety, depression, and other stress-related disorders. In some rare but highly publicized cases, some kids have turned to suicide. It is greatly important that you be aware.

## Adaption to Context Threats

Cultural or environmental adaptation is the ability to fit into a context that differs from one's own background, and the research has predominantly focused on minorities and/or immigrants who have entered environments (countries) and not felt "a part" of said environment. These learners struggle with psychological and sometimes physiological problems/consequences due to this displacement. However, based on the National Education Association's definition of what diversity is, this is not simply a minority/immigrant issue:

> the sum of the ways that people are both alike and different. The dimensions of diversity include race, ethnicity, gender, sexual orientation, language, culture, religion, mental and physical ability, class, and immigration status. While diversity itself is not

a value-laden term, the way that people react to diversity is driven by values, attitudes, beliefs, and so on. Full acceptance of diversity is a major principle of social justice. (http://www.nea.org)

With the increase of migration/relocation throughout this country by many Americans, as well as the increase in poverty and the current political and economical instability, a crisis in a student's cultural adaptation is prudent as the demand to process change and adapt to a new school can be difficult. You are also susceptible to crisis and cultural (or transitional) shock, as changes are rapid in our present world and it is important to identify adaptation difficulties both in yourself and in your students if you wish to be a leader in such a volatile and multifaceted career.

Consider the cultural adaptation process, as reported by the University of Illinois Counseling Center, which helps to better understand the process of adaptation and the possible reactions to high degrees of change. Often these stages have only been applied to transitions between countries, but if the United States is as diverse as we claim we are, each town, city, state, and area establishes a variety of cultural norms that are relevant to possible declines in academic performance of students and attrition in teachers.

**The Honeymoon Stage.** This is usually the first stage experienced when you are changing your cultural environment. This could be a school or community that differs greatly from what you know, not just what we typically think of as culture change (i.e., country to country). In this stage everything seems exciting and new. Many in this phase experience increased curiosity and interest in the newness of the surroundings and eagerness to begin new opportunities that may be found.

**The Transitional or Culture Shock Stage.** In this stage, the primary focus is on the differences between one's foundational culture and the new culture and the conflicts that are taking place due to these differences, including the following:

- Not being sure how to interact with people
- Not having a clear idea of how to make friends or create relationships with people who differ from yourself
- Not being understood when you express yourself in your usual way
- Finding that food and eating customs are different (e.g., moving from a rural Midwestern state would lend many differences in this area in comparison to a highly populated west coast culture)
- Finding that religious practices are different
- Finding large differences in the educational system

- Finding that some people in the new culture are impatient when you don't understand things right away
- Finding out that some people are prejudiced against others from different cultures (and sometimes being the victim of said stereotyping/racism)

The conflicts may be with other people or internal, as one's own values, habits, and preferences may differ greatly from the norms and expectations of those from the new environment. Students and teachers alike may experience many of the following symptoms that accompany culture shock, which in turn affects the academic success of your students and your success as an educator:

- Anxiety
- Homesickness
- Anger
- Loneliness
- Helplessness
- Uncontrollably overwhelmed
- Fearful for your safety, both physical and psychological
- Uncertainty of self
- Shaken beliefs in one's own competency
- Lack of belonging
- Fear of the unknown and unfamiliar
- Confusion about which values you should actually have and apply
- Cognitive fatigue
- Physical fatigue or excessive sleep
- Feelings of helplessness and withdrawal
- Irritability and negative behaviors
- Depression
- Compulsive eating/drinking/weight gain
- Stereotyping of people in the new culture
  - "The teachers are mean here," "the kids are snobby," "the students don't care"—we could all add a few
- Hostility toward people in the new culture
  - Bullying, fighting, threatening behaviors

**The Recovery Stage.** After having spent some time in the new culture, people begin to resolve some of the conflicts they may have experienced and also begin to regain a sense of appreciation that they might have experienced in the first stage. They have learned more about the new culture and are able to have a better understanding of external and internal resources that help in managing demands and conflicts that might arise. Feelings typical of this stage are a mixture of the first two stages.

**The Adaptation Stage.** This stage consists of people developing a realistic understanding of the similarities and differences between their own culture and the new culture. They begin to differentiate between what they agree with and what they do not. In some cases, natural assimilation,[1] or acculturation,[2] of the new culture is accepted with ease and a value and appreciation of both cultures develops. This stage may be characterized by a sense of confidence, maturity, flexibility, and tolerance.

The problem lies in the cultural shock stage where students as well as teachers can be stuck for long periods of time, affecting behaviors and healthy motivation. Culture shock is considered the psychological state of loss and/or disorientation that can occur through a change in one's familiar environment, which requires adjustment.

If a student that has experienced a school where violence and low performance are the norm moves into a high-performing school with highly academic and motivated learners who demonstrate compliance to the order of the learning environment with oppositional norms than he was accustomed to, chaos can result. Although this example may not be the most volatile of examples, it still reminds us that response to change in our environments is difficult and does affect how we will perform as an educator without the knowledge and skills to address it. It is plausible that culture shock is negatively affecting classrooms and academic performance as never in our history. With rapid migration of families, the idea that students and teachers are greatly affected by this should be more thoroughly addressed. We are no longer a village raising a child. We are a mixture of often oppositional experiences that can collide when cultural competence and appropriate diversity management is not applied.

We reiterate the following concerns that may attribute to the support of this idea:

- 39% of youth suffer from mild to severe depression and 9% of high school students report being severely depressed (Garfinkel, Hoberman, Parsons, & Walker, 1986).
- The proportion of 15/16-year-olds reporting that they frequently feel anxious or depressed has doubled in the last 30 years (Hagell, 2012).
- The proportion of 15/16-year-olds with behavior problems (as rated by parents) also increased, from approximately 7% in 1974 to approximately 15% in 1999 (Hagell, 2012).

- Youth delinquency and in-class behavior concerns are rising at astronomical rates.
- Teachers "losing it" at school is now commonly reported and even publically posted (e.g., YouTube, Facebook, Myspace, etc.).
- Teachers are currently reporting feelings of increased depression and increased rates of anxiety related to their chosen careers.
- Ability for families to relocate is easier than ever, increasing the diversity of our classrooms.
- Violent crime rates across the United States increased by about 18%, and property crimes increased by 11% between 2010 and 2011 (Bureau of Justice Statistics, 2012).
- Poverty is at the highest level since 1965 (Associated Press, 2012).
- Violence in schools is not limited to the inner city as often assumed: a large number of schools indicated as a "violent crime" group were located in rural areas (36%) (U.S. Department of Education, 2002)

In history there was probably a time that a teacher could assume that a child's glazed stare was apathy; however, this is no longer the world we live in. Cognitive fatigue, excessive sleepiness, and hostility (with a host of other symptoms) prevent learners from processing what you need them to process. Physiological stress reactions including outbursts, crying spells, alcohol or drug abuse are all warning signs that the change being experienced by our students, and often their parents, may be overwhelming and one thing that will not change is that there will always be change.

Adjusting to a new culture and environment is a normal process and can generate a wide variety of reactions and feelings. Even though the adjustment process is described as a number of successive stages, remember that not all people experience each stage and not necessarily in the order listed. Also, the stages can last different lengths of time for different people, and sometimes people cycle through these stages more than once. This is real. It is not a simple over-dramatization. Your students are often not adjusting to their surroundings, the pressures from peers and parents, and their own, normal, development of self. Understanding the reality that it is tougher to successfully teach is valid and can help you better understand why it is necessary to not only teach, but to be a leader.

The conflicts one feels during the shock stage may be with aligned to others or may be internally based on one's negotiation of the new values, habits, and preferences, especially when contrasted with the norms and expectations of those one is most conditioned to have. The following suggests ways you can help a student to better adjust if he or she is not able to break the cultural shock cycle. Encourage a student who seems to be having difficulty in adjusting to his environment to:

- become involved in an interesting extracurricular activity;
- attend community events;
- keep a journal about what they are feeling; or
- talk to the school counselor.

**Traumatic Events**

One goal of teaching is to also help children grow and thrive to the best of their potential. This includes creating a safe environment, which is fundamental in increasing a learner's potential to learn and develop (Maslow's hierarchy of needs). Children are not immune from dangers within and outside the school, but often we forget with our busy and demanding duties and schedules that our learners may be going through potentially deflating circumstances. Sometimes these issues can be serious. Psychological trauma may occur during a single traumatic event (acute) or as a result of repeated (chronic) exposure to overpowering stress (Terr, 1992). Causes for trauma include, but are not limited to:

- Exposure to domestic violence
- Abuse, including sexual, physical, emotional
- Natural disasters, such as a flood or earthquake
- War or other military actions
- Abandonment
- Witness to violence in the neighborhood or school setting, including fights, drive-by shootings, and law enforcement actions
- Personal attack by another person or an animal
- Kidnapping
- Severe bullying
- Medical procedures such as a surgery, an accident, or serious illness.

Additionally, family changes such as divorce and death can cause trauma for a learner. When a danger or significant change is something that a child cannot process, such as an event that threatens injury, is life-threatening, or even psychologically scarring, it can be traumatic for a child or adolescent.

Rarely do teachers, parents, and other outsiders realize that trauma affects basic regulatory processes in the brain stem, the limbic brain (emotion, memory, regulation of arousal and affect), the neocortex (perception of self and the world), as well as integrative functioning across various systems in the central nervous system (Moroz, 2005). It is a physical and real outcome of some negative events that a child may experience.

According to Moroz (2005) and other health professionals, children and youth who experience overpowering psychological stress are susceptible to changes in brain neurophysiology. Trauma-based response patterns (e.g., dissociation, numbing, freezing, hyper vigilance, and hyper-arousal) can affect behaviors and learning as well as normal child development, self-esteem, and immune system functioning. "Traumatic experiences are stored in the child's body/mind, and fear, arousal and dissociation associated with the original trauma may continue after the threat of danger and arousal has subsided" (p. 10).

Understanding and being aware of how children experience traumatic events and how these children express their grief can assist schools in responding to the learners and assist them through challenging situations. You may not feel sometimes like you are helping, but simply by knowing the signs you are able to adjust your reactions and classroom management techniques to encourage rather than further demoralize the learner. The goal is to give a safe place to these children so that they can not only learn but also in some cases heal. If their personal environment is in disarray, it should be obvious that unconsciously, behaviors can also be traumatic to your classroom balance and safety, preventing you from being a successful educator and, thus, increasing the stress not only for you but also for your other learners.

Most educators actively recognize that a child's age affects how he or she experiences traumatic events; however, the level of development often is dismissed. It is important to be aware that both psychological and social development is just as important to how your learner will cope. Age may not always be the prime indicator, but your awareness of both is vital.

The National Child Traumatic Stress Network (http://www.nctsnet.org/) reports the following age-based behaviors in reaction to trauma to be aware of:

- Preschool and young school-age children
  - Feelings of helplessness and uncertainty about whether there will be continued danger
  - Experiencing a general fear of non-related life experiences
  - Difficulty describing in words what is bothering them or what they are experiencing emotionally
  - Decrease in previously acquired developmental skills

- Sleepiness
- New parental separation anxiety
- Unwillingness to participate in what was previously normal activities, such as playing with other children
- Loss of some speech/verbal skills
- Loss of toileting skills
- Fear of going to sleep during naptime
- Play that focuses on or reenacts the traumatic event, possibly with an attempt to change the negative result of the traumatic event

- School-age children
  - Feelings of persistent concern over their own safety and the safety of others in their school or family
  - Increased ego preoccupation that may include reliving their own actions during the traumatic event
  - Difficulty focusing
  - Heightened startle response and hyper alertness
  - Agitation
  - Over-arousal or under-arousal
  - Withdrawal or dissociation
  - Avoidance of eye contact and/or physical contact
  - Terrified responses to sights, sounds, or other sensory input that remind the child of the traumatic experience(s)
  - Guilt or shame over what they did or did not do during the traumatic event
  - Constant retelling of the traumatic event
  - Constant verbal descriptions that indicate overwhelming feelings of fear or sadness
  - Sleepiness
  - Greater difficulties concentrating and learning
  - Uncommon complaints of headaches and stomachaches
  - Unusually reckless or aggressive behaviors
  - In the case of divorce, clinging behaviors, loss of confidence, and displays of sadness

- Adolescents
  - Self-conscious worry about their emotional responses to the event
  - Feelings of fear, vulnerability, and concern over being labeled "abnormal" or different from their peers
  - Withdrawal from family and friends
  - Feelings of shame and guilt about the traumatic event

- Fantasies about revenge and retribution to those who they feel instigated the traumatic event
- Radical shifts in the way these children think about the world
- Self-destructive or accident-prone behaviors
- Displays of unusual hostility toward others
- In the case of divorce, because the adolescent is at a more rebellious stage, grievances can be intensified. Adolescents tend to pull away and often feel betrayed as well as become angrier and less communicative than younger children.

Most teachers teach because they care so greatly about children; the emotional and physical challenges children in trauma face after exposure to a traumatic event are significant and can be difficult on your environment and your own stress level. It is helpful for parents and teachers to work together to help children negotiate their feelings during trauma but often teachers, and other outsiders, separate themselves from the situation in hopes that it will take care of itself, often believing that it is not their business or that they do not want to increase their own stress. Your job mandates you provide the best learning environment possible for all students. No one said this would be easy.

One difficult area for a teacher is how to balance and tolerate regression and aggression in developmental tasks by a learner. Remember that tolerance, according to the National Child Traumatic Stress Network, is important to the child's healing process. If children feel at fault or like they have no control, being disciplined for what they are having difficulty controlling can encourage their continued feelings of victimization, confusion, and anger. How long regression should be tolerated is difficult to determine. Work closely with your counselor and the child's parents who will be more qualified to assist in this decision.

It is also important to acknowledge the normality of your learner's feelings and to be careful not to discount what the child remembers or believes about the situation. Even if distorted, the child's accounts may be real to him or her. Parents can be invaluable in supporting you and their children, but they are often left out of the equation. Additionally, in the case of a traumatic divorce, one parent can often be left out based on non-valid rumors or manipulations. Include both. When children experience a traumatic event, the entire family is affected. This awareness is vital to the health of the child, unless otherwise indicated by a health professional or court.

Also remember that when dealing with family members, each may have different experiences associated with the event and multifaceted emotional responses that differ greatly. Recognize that these differences in recall are not unusual.

Teaching children is emotional. If you are aware of this, you will be one step ahead in taking care of your well-being. Remember that there are sources of information that you can access to help you decide what steps you can take to help, and although you are not certified in "counseling," you are not helpless. Use your resources. And in the case of abuse, remember that you are legally bound to report it so that it can be investigated.

Social awareness is an important part of becoming a successfully integrated educational leader. As noted, this is not an easy feat and your continued openness to grow in this area is imperative. Cultures will continue to change. Classrooms will continue to offer challenges and it is up to the healthy teacher to balance these challenges to provide the best opportunity for learners to develop in a positive manner and to gain knowledge at their highest potential. With this attentiveness to social realities you will then be able to become a better manager of your relationships, both personally and professionally.

Notes

1. Assimilation involves a gradual change and takes place in varying degrees; full assimilation occurs when new members of a society become indistinguishable from older members. New customs and attitudes are acquired through participation with the new culture.
2. Acculturation is a merging of cultures as a result of prolonged contact.

## Chapter 11

## Managing Social Relationships

> *Remember, we all stumble, every one of us.*
> *That's why it's a comfort to go hand in hand.*
> —Emily Kimbrough (1899–1988),
> an American author and journalist

Managing relationships, both personally and professionally, can at times be difficult. This social component supports both the hierarchy of needs information we have supplied as well as the Integrated Educational Leadership Model we have proposed. Finding "belonging" is an important need that, as we have also noted, is a part of every dimension of the model. You, your learners, your colleagues, and your parents all have this need, and when managing your relationships, this is an important variable to remember. Managing diverse relationships and workplaces is, in the words of Dr. R. Roosevelt Thomas Jr. (2006), a leader in diversity management, reminds us that not all people have a natural ability to be good managers, but it is a skill that can be learned and refined over time. Although his ideas have been mostly applied in the business workplace, the concept is one that educators can apply as it lends to the necessity of being culturally competent and a successful educational leader.

As a teacher, you are a manager; you are a leader. You did not get to choose your "clients" but you must successfully serve them. Thomas (2006) suggests to us that each of our journeys to mastering the "craft" of managing diversity, also called strategic diversity management (SDM), are different. There is not a picture-perfect road map about how to manage the circle of social interactions that includes your personal and professional relationships. It is about applying *everything* you have learned, whether through theory, field experiences, past experiences, or self-reflection, that will make this process of successfully managing relationships successful.

Additionally, diversity includes all differences between us and encourages a multifaceted amount of factors for you to consider continually in your learning environment. Being culturally competent and creative can be important to your success. Often educators have a desire to control the learning environment rather than being open to exploring the most positive way to increase learner engagement and growth in their classroom. When it comes to your learners there are many "best practices" and they do not all apply to every situation. The key is to be culturally attentive and apply practices that suit your classroom of learners. This is where (and why) this becomes so difficult for you as a "new" teacher.

Teachers are generally passionate about learning and their learners. As an autonomous educator, you may feel adamantly about what teaching practices you believe will work best, but having the maturity and development to know that every class of learners you will teach will bring a new dynamic and creative restructuring by you may be a constant factor in being successful. Learning about your classroom participants and applying awareness will be a key in managing these relationships to their fullest potential. There are several areas of visible differences/similarities that can be considered from the onset of a relationship, whether with colleagues, parents, or learners, to assist you in creating a positive environment for both you and your learners. It has been said that true leaders inspire others, and so does an educator, but understanding each of your learners is key to your success.

Building healthy relationships will make the management of your classroom much more enjoyable and efficient. When students believe their teachers truly care about them as individuals, they are much more likely to cooperate in class and work more diligently to be the best students they can be. Approval, affirmation, and admiration go a long way toward building classroom success for students and the teacher. As an integrated educational leader it is fully your responsibility to create an environment where this dynamic is possible. Listed below are some ideas for forming healthy relationships with your students, as well as others who are significant to you.

Finding multiple commonalities is important. You do not have to actually share someone's interests to know about what the person is interested in.

Knowing what people enjoy is critical when having meaningful conversations, especially in the classroom. Find as many communication channels as possible with others and they will want to connect with you as well. At the same time, it is also important to reveal your own interests. Remember, all successful relationships are mutual.

Research and experience tells us that youth especially appreciate when teachers are knowledgeable about things that interest them such as:

- Sports
- Hobbies
- Clubs
- Popular movies
- Music
- Artistic interests

Many times the most influential and respected teachers are familiar with the names of the popular bands in town, the latest funny movies, and which students are active in which sports or clubs. Additionally, if you actually attend one of those events, it doesn't take long for students to learn that you, too, have something in common with them. However, just guessing at what interests your students (or any person with whom you desire a relationship) will not lead to successful relationship building or learning. Get to know your students. Ask questions. Learn about their backgrounds.

Knowing your students' family and economic backgrounds will help you develop a better understanding about individual behaviors in the classroom, which in turn helps you to build better relationships. An only child will most likely exhibit different behaviors than children/teens from large families. Students from affluent families sometimes (but not always) behave differently than those from poverty. It is important to know as much as possible about each learner and sometimes it is as simple as being attentive. Leaders pay attention. Apply the social awareness skills you learned about in the previous section.

You can also learn about your students through actual writing assignments and gain knowledge about their abilities to express themselves in written form. For older students, one of the first assignments of the year should encourage an honest, revealing autobiography. Make sure they include details about parents, siblings, their neighborhood, how many times they have moved, where they have lived, special interests, favorite meals, and so on. This will give you a better frame of reference for knowing how to respond to certain situations in the classroom, as well as what not to say or what might be motivating an outburst or their lack of effort. With younger students, drawings can say a lot about your learners.

Educational leaders often stress the importance of establishing and tracking students' goals and their success in meeting these goals. To be an effective teacher you must also be accountable for the goals and commitments you create. Not being accountable can counteract any progressions you have made to building a trusting learning environment. When you make verbal and written agreements with others, demonstrate the willingness to follow-through and consistently keep your word. Being consistent in this area will help develop credibility and trust in all of your relationships.

Also, remember to be ethical. Never publicly discuss the failings of others, even in the teacher's lounge. Granted, people like hearing a little gossip, especially the dirt about others. But in actuality, people never respect those who dish that dirt. This includes allowing students to talk badly about fellow colleagues. If you hear a concern, stop the public discussion, but follow up with a student or your administrator, privately, if you think there is a problem.

Additionally, if you are having problems with a student, you may naturally want someone to make you feel validated in your frustration. Be aware that this can do more harm than good and, in some cases, your opinion of a student could get back to the parent or the child—something that you never intended. If you talk about anyone's failing, talk about your own. Be humble. Admit your mistakes. Laugh at yourself. While you should not laugh at other people, you should always laugh at yourself. People will laugh with you and they will be better for it.

Being an effective listener is also important to your success in building healthy relationships and becoming an integrated educational leader. Students, and most parents, hold more respect for the teachers who really listen to them. Whether it pertains to their most challenging problems or their funniest stories, teachers who listen to their students create lasting, meaningful bonds. If you want others to listen to you, make it a practice to listen to them first. Ask questions. Maintain eye contact. Smile. Frown. Nod. Respond verbally and nonverbally. Don't check your phone. Don't glance at your computer monitor. Don't focus on anything else, even for a moment. If your student believes that you are only there to get your paycheck and not be their teacher, you will soon find out that they have little time to be one of your success stories.

As we have discussed throughout this text, times have changed. We are all going many directions, balancing many things, and technology has made the world much smaller. However, you must apply simple rules to this truism, when building relationships, although they are often forgotten by busy teachers, as well as others. Essentially, this is why you must become a leader. In this chaotic world, the students of tomorrow need you to be willing to take the time to grow them and to believe in them.

**You Cannot Connect With Others If You are Too Busy Connecting With Your Stuff at the Same Time**

Disconnecting gestures when a person is sharing personal ideas and information can suggest to others that they are unimportant to you. When you are speaking with another person, do not offer advice until he or she asks. Listening shows you care much more than offering advice. When you do offer advice the conversation often becomes about you. Speak when you have something important to say for the other person, not you.

When you are purposeful in how you engage with others, including your students, observe how the other person begins to become more engaged with you. People take notice when their words are heard. Additionally, when students are given a voice, a multitude of fantastic lessons can arise from their vocalization—creative ideas, debates, persuasive writing assignments, and compelling essay topics abound. We all want to be heard. Youth often are dismissed due to age and cultural norms. When they feel like they matter, they acquire "belonging" and their efficacy as a person can positively develop. By modeling good relationship building strategies you also assist your students in their social development. This is all part of being a successful teacher and an integrated leader.

Building healthy relationships with students may be the most important skill teachers possess. Once students trust a teacher and know their voice actually matters, they are much more likely to flourish in the classroom. It sounds simple but it works. Students want their teachers to care for them. Parents want you to educate and nurture their child. These relationships will be some of the most powerful self-esteem builders you possess as a leader.

**Relating to Parents**

Understanding how to create relationships with learners and parents is not an easy task. Like us all, parents have diverse past experiences that affect what they believe should or should not be happening with their child in schools, and it can be overwhelming to determine exactly how to please them all. Additionally, media discrepancies and misconstrued actions can fuel emotions with parents. Most importantly, remember that parenting is not easy. Parents, many times, just need to be heard.

Here are some examples:

- Parents who have children who do not present low academic ability may be concerned that their children are not receiving the individual attention they need due to the attention they perceive is being extended to "slower" learners.
- Parents who have struggling children may not feel like their child is getting the education they need to catch up with their peers.
- Parents who move often may compare schools and programs, but with little understanding of the possible societal norms that create these differences.
- Parents who are living in poverty are busy trying to survive, working multiple jobs, while trying to have a relationship with their child. They are not apathetic or uncaring. They may not know exactly how to communicate with you or may feel intimidated or embarrassed.
- Parents who do not speak English struggle to communicate with educators, and thus many times do not.
- Parents who were raised in the community may perceive students who move into the classroom as outsiders.
- Parents (outsiders) who have moved see these communities as closed-minded.

Creating good communications with parents is vital. Parents are the most important teachers children will ever have, and it is important that there is mutual support between the teacher/school and the parent. The variables listed above make it difficult to actively get parental involvement, and in many cases teachers and administrators fear having parents in the classrooms. Often teachers complain about parents who interfere and then about those who never participate. Additionally, many parents say that educators only say they want their help because they are made to feel like intruders and often their ideas are ignored. This is true at both ends of the economic spectrum. One mother when asked about her experiences in volunteering to help with her child's high school marching band made the following statement:

> I was asked if I would mind helping. It was tough to work it into my work and mommy schedule but said I would. At the first practice I walked to the field to help the students check their alignments and the next thing I knew a loud speaker was shouting at me from the top of the stands. It was the band director. He, in front of the students said I was not to help with anything until he instructed me how to help and exactly what to say. I was embarrassed for myself and my child. That night I cried for hours. I was never active with the band or band parents again. It was a horrible experience.

This type of story is not unusual. Be cautious to not berate parents when they give up their time to assist you. One's pride can be a significant wall to many positive parental and student relationships.

The following are seven recommendations for better relations with parents.

- Educational buzzwords should be avoided. Many times this makes you look like you are trying to be better and smarter than the parent. Terms such as taxonomy, small learning communities, meta-cognition, cooperative learning, discovery learning, constructivism, emergent literacy, authentic assessment, and block scheduling are not familiar to people who did not specialize in education. Do not expect them to know your lingo when you may not know theirs either. Do you just off the cuff know what dye sublimation is? Just checking.
- Visit parents where it is convenient for them. This can sound difficult but sometimes one visit can make all the difference in them feeling comfortable meeting with you at school or being a part of activities. They need to know you care. Visitation sites may include their home, church, activity center, or even at a local diner next to their work. It may also be helpful to recruit active parents to invite others to meetings. This creates a less intimidating environment when other parents solicit one another as a friend.
- Ask parents to share their backgrounds and expertise. Assign special days that parents can give presentations in several classrooms on the cultures and customs of their home countries. Children could travel from room to room to visit each "new" area.
- Listen to your parents. School leaders know how to listen and communicate with parents. Control your emotions when a parent suggests something with which you are unfamiliar. Listen. It may be easier to add to your activities than you think.
- Ask parents to volunteer. By allowing parents to assist in jobs such as copying homework packets; answering phones; hanging student work on the walls; raising money for extracurricular activities; translating flyers, newsletters, and school information; assisting in a weekly classroom newsletter for parents, and monitoring hallways, teachers will have more time to complete their other duties, reducing stress and time management issues.
- Create a community of care. Parents want what is best for their children. Seek out ways to promote your school as one that cares about the students and about their well-being.

- Use whatever is needed to communicate. With all of the technology today, find ways to communicate with busy parents. Mass texting and emailing about activities takes little time and can make a big difference to your students and parents.

It can also be said that even a teacher, possibly you someday, who has struggled teaching in one type of environment may react to another similar environment based on past or vicarious experiences. As an educator, ready to arm your students with knowledge, this can be difficult, especially if your past experiences are positive and the environment you walk into is hostile or biased to you.

For instance, if you have been teaching successfully in a school where you are the minority, but were accepted and supported by parents and students, and you enter a new school where you are the minority, but they have had negative experiences with someone of a different race and treat you with animosity, you may feel shattered, even angry that they would judge you based on your skin color. This is a prime example of how two experiences, without understanding and awareness, can collide. Unintentional biases in both cases are real and the ability for a person to adjust maturity to address how past experiences may be affecting emotions and reactions may be more difficult for one person than for another. Teachers and students and parents are different. They have differing experiences. All have beliefs stored within, some of which you may not even realize. Remember the signs of an amygdala hijack discussed earlier. Be aware of your emotional reactions.

When a person feels passionate about something, it is not abnormal to respond or react, but making sure that you have the skills to respond appropriately is key, and this is something people often forget—it *is* a skill that can be practiced and perfected. However, others may not know what you now know, so it is up to you to be aware if you wish to become an educational advocate.

### Success and Parents

Inconsistencies are also still profound within education as this nation explores how to define "superior learning" and the goals of what learning should be. In one arena, parental involvement in the education of a child is considered an absolute must to make advancing strides (Carpenter & Ramirez, 2007; Carpenter et al., 2006; Garcia, 1991; Niemeyer, Wong, & Westerhaus, 2009; Reynolds, 1992). However, how this is defined within communities can almost be seen as a value based in fear as well. A recent survey of American teachers revealed that 20% of new teachers and nearly 25% of principals identified their relationships with parents as a cause of significant stress in their jobs (MetLife, 2005). "Parents believe that they are not welcome, based much on their own educational experiences . . . they don't feel like [being involved] is guaranteed to be a good experience." These parents are often stereotyped by educational professionals as not caring about their child's education, but this is not always true and should never be assumed.

A parent's separation from the child's school crosses socioeconomic cultural barriers: the lower educated and the higher educated. It is profound to consider that schools that contain a well-cited majority of parents who feel unable to question or participate in their child's education based on low socioeconomics and lower educational attainment are much more likely to encourage participation by way of cookouts and parent-teacher meetings. However, although not often reported in the media and research, communities consisting of more educated and higher-socioeconomic backgrounds have also been blatantly denied access to volunteer or participate, even when volunteering, and the perseverance of such parents has encouraged educators to further segregate these parents through labeling and over-dramatizations based on stereotyping and fear.

Like it not, attitudes toward parent involvement are real. One personal example includes a junior high school that could not afford to serve all of its gifted students because of limited staffing, so it chose the ones it wanted to serve. When the parents of the excluded students were made aware that their children were not being served, they volunteered to bring and assist with programs for these learners. They volunteered free time and expertise. Amazingly, however, the school cancelled the entire gifted program within 24 hours of this offer, lending professional parents within the community a heightened awareness that this school did not want them in its environment. The parents later were told by a source that the school did not have time to deal with parents who wanted to invade their rights to educate. None of these parents have volunteered to assist the school district again.

Over-parenting, as it has been labeled by some, has deterred many parents who desire to be involved (Gibbs, 2005). Often community members and parents are purposefully excommunicated by those inside the educational facility based on a fear of diversity. Diversity of thoughts and actions? Whatever it is, this constant tug-of-war only exasperates the current strides to move forward and to teach better. It has been suggested that parental involvement positively affects achievement (since the 1970s). But how that looks in the eyes of a school can be different, based on where you live, the socioeconomics of the community, and the fortitude and self-perceived competence of school leaders. Unfortunately, the administrators, teachers, and parents all become a part of the stress equation. Additionally, this dysfunctional relationship fuels distaste for the educational system by some and continues the cycle of dissatisfaction and concern that affect educators across the country.

Without acknowledging the truth in where we have walked, whether it is our fathers, our grandfathers, or great-grandfathers, we now carry the burden to make it right. The age of technology has made blatant the abuses of our past and made accessible the many that still exist today. Our educational goals have made progress but with our ever-changing dynamics, there may never be a clear-cut teaching practice for every classroom, since the shape of the puzzle piece keeps transforming. But one profound variable is that the U.S. educational system has been pummeled with negative campaigns discussing how "poor" the educational system is. Media and researchers retort that the "white value system" (indicative of years of segregation) is not working for the masses of minorities and our country's suppressed people, which now includes teachers. And in reality, is our current negative campaign against educators working for anyone? It decreases the motivation of everyone involved.

**Generational Gaps**

Understanding the changes that occur between generations of society is also important as an educational leader. These differences are essential in building successful multigenerational relationships. Although we cautiously warn you that any information that labels a person as "this" or "that" is obviously unfair (it would be the same to say all "whites" are like this, all "Republicans" like that), importantly, the generalizations of experiences that occurred to specific groups affect the group members' belief systems and behaviors. Better understanding the changes that have occurred and subsequent disparities that may exist between generations assists us in better communications and tolerance of the differences we have. Each generation has had experiences that have occurred during differing developmental periods in their lives. These generalizations can help to prepare us as we understand that change also affects us in personal and subtle ways.

There are various ways to distinguish generational differences to counteract the negative responses in our relationships. Each of the major generations (generations = generalizations and not absolutes), Traditionalists (born 1925–1945), Baby Boomers (born 1946–1964), Gen X (born 1965–1980), Gen Y (born 1981–1999), and Gen Z-Nexters (born after 2000) have set their own trends and had their own cultural impact.

One of the ways generations distinguish their differences is through the use of language. Thus a generation gap creates a parallel gap in language, which causes complications in daily communication within schools. As each new generation seeks to define itself as something apart from the old, it adopts new lingo or slang, a set of colloquial words or phrases used to reinforce social identity within a particular group. As each successive generation strives to establish its own unique identity, slang provides a quick and readily available dialect that causes generational gaps in a societal context.

Every generation develops new slang, but with the advancement of new technology, gaps have widened between the older and younger generations. Students today have private conversations in a crowded room due to the advances of cellular phones and text messaging. Among that group a form of slang or texting lingo has developed, which often leaves those not as tech savvy out of the loop. Students increasingly rely on technological mediums such as smartphones, instant messaging, and email to create inventive, quirky, and private written language, which often enables them to hide in plain sight. It has perhaps become this generation's version of Pig Latin.

Another generational gap with language occurs within families in which different generations speak different primary languages. In immigrant families the first generation usually speaks primarily in the native tongue. In the second generation family members often speak primarily in the language of the country they currently live in while still retaining fluency in their parent's dominant language. The third generation, and thereafter, tends to speak entirely in the language of their current country, retaining no conversational fluency in their grandparent's native tongue. In this case, the second-generation family members serve as interpreters, further propelling generational differences through linguistic gaps.

Another phenomenon the current generation of youth faces is the incessant use of the Internet. Students today will be global citizens the rest of their lives because of the advancement of the World Wide Web. Many have the perception that the computer is a tool that helps make kids smarter, and there is no disputing the advantages this technology affords. However, teachers and parents should not be lulled into the misconception that nothing harmful can happen from using the Internet. As we discussed earlier, cyberbullying is on the rise. Additionally, with the accessibility of the Internet there is an increased risk of child abductions, online identity theft, and lawsuits from all types of intellectual property, including music and movies.

Unfortunately, the proliferation of Internet use among children, which constitutes a large and highly influential segment of our population, has exposed a dark side of the World Wide Web. The anonymity of the Internet and the ease of creating a plethora of identities have opened up new avenues for online predators, identity thieves, hackers, and other conniving individuals. Since children are typically unaware of the tricks and techniques these predators use, they are at a higher risk level than other Internet users. Teachers today must be cognizant of these risks and educate their students about how to avoid them.

According to a report by the United Nations Joint Staff Pension Fund, *Overcoming Generational Gap in the Workplace*, there are distinct differences between generations and your knowledge of them can continue to assist you in building positive relationships with others. Each of you may fit into differing groups, so understanding a bit more about the generations can help to guide you.

Traditionalists tend to be:
- Team players
- Indirect when communicating
- Loyal to organizations
- Respect authority
- Be dedicated and sacrificial
- Believe in duty before pleasure
- Obedient
- Responsive to directives
- Leaders
- Believe in their seniority that comes with age
- Adhere to rules

Traditionalists experienced World War II, and the economic and political uncertainty of the times created a generation that is hard working, financially conservative, cautious, and loyal. They may have difficulty with change, as they are not generally risk takers or tolerant. Due to their experiences they have a tendency to respect authority and obey rules. As such a command and control style of leadership seems appropriate in their view.

Baby Boomers tend to:
- See the big picture
- Introduce fresh perspectives
- Not respect titles
- Disapprove of absolutes

- Like structure
- Be optimistic
- Be team oriented
- Be uncomfortable with conflict
- Be sensitive to feedback
- Be attentive to health and wellness

The Baby Boomers were part of a plentiful, growing postwar economy, which encouraged a more egocentric generation. Nuclear families were the norm and the world was seen as revolving around their generation. Work was and is a defining part of both their self-worth and their evaluation of others. In essence, they live to work. Some believe that true life/work/family balance is not a reality. They believe in the 8–5 work day. This is one of the biggest differences between this generation and later generations. Some of this generation followed rules set by the Traditionalists, but in what was seen as the "bent" form.

Gen Xers tend to:
- Embrace positive attitude
- Be impatient
- Be goal-oriented
- Multitask
- Think globally
- Be self-reliant
- Prefer informal work environments
- Environment aware
- Believe a job is just that—a job
- Be technology literate
- Believe in balanced lifestyle
- Want a lot to do but the freedom to be autonomous
- Question authority

Generation X was raised in the shadow of the dominant Boomer generation. They lived in environments as children where their parents sacrificed greatly for their companies. Thus, this generation has a tendency to be independent, resilient, and more adaptable than previous generations. In opposition to their parents, they work to live.

Gen Yers (as well as Zers) tend to:
- Exude confidence
- Are social
- Be of moral character
- Be street smart
- Believe in diversity
- Promote collective action
- Have a heroic spirit
- Be tenacious
- Be technology savvy
- Lack in dealing with others and conflict
- Multitask
- Need flexibility

The Y generation is said to be the next powerful and influential generation, as being raised in an "empowerment" parenting style they are not afraid to express themselves. During these empowerment years they were taught that everyone wins and everyone gets a medal. They were nurtured by their parents and maintained structured lives, but they were encouraged to make their own choices and question authority. Like the Baby Boomers, this group was raised in a healthy economy and tend to argue their autonomy in defining the terms and conditions of their employment where they expect to be accommodated.

This generation (as well as X to a lesser degree) is coming into the workforce, with "networking, multiprocessing, and global-minded skills" that the Traditionalists and Baby Boomers could not have imagined. Technology has encouraged an "always connected" mindset that can cause friction between earlier generations. It is this ability to always be available that encourages the Y (and X) generations to rebel against the rigid 8–5 work day.

There is a plethora of information about generational differences and this, too, attributes itself to the diversity dynamic. Avoiding the trap of under-standing generational differences cannot be overstated. It is critical to know the new generation and connect with their preferred style and expectations. It is just as important to understand that your colleagues and students' guardians may be of a different generation. Understanding that they see things differently can help you to accept that what they experienced growing up is real, and as difficult as it is for you to change your mindset, it is just as difficult for them.

When entering into relationships and conversations with others, as a leader who desires positive change, it is important to consider the drive behind their behaviors. Negating these differences leaves you open to increased conflict and, sometimes, increased stress. It is far more productive to be tolerant than to oppose others based on a stereotype that may or may not be valid. It is important to take the time when building trusting relationships in education, where each generation can accentuate the positives of their experiences and work toward the common goal of creating successful learning environments.

*Chapter 12*

# Managing Cultural Differences

Leaders take time to see and learn about the differences between themselves and others, and use this dynamic to encourage positive outcomes. Becoming culturally competent and applying culturally responsive pedagogy are vital to managing the diverse relationships within your classroom. The culture in which a person lives affects attitudes, thoughts, feelings, and actions, whether the person has a developmental disability or not. Being able to bridge the gap between our cultural background and the cultural background of the people we serve will strengthen, support, and facilitate our role in assisting people as they plan their preferred future. There are many benefits in being culturally responsive. Among the benefits is the ability to:

- foster more understanding of the person and how the person operates, feels, and the ways in which the person lives his or her life;
- let people know they are thought of as individuals, as human beings;
- effectively communicate culturally sensitive choices and their consequences; and
- be aware of many possibilities and respond appropriately.

Applying culturally responsive and respectful skills in your classroom increases your likelihood to be responsive to the needs of all of your learners and their families as they make choices and display behaviors, which often are based on a framework influenced by their cultural background.

## Managing Stereotypical Beliefs

Teachers' stereotyping beliefs about schools, families, and education all affect their psychological health as they walk into a classroom of students who often differ much from their own backgrounds, and rarely do we want to acknowledge that this can be problematic in fear of being chastised or judged. Although educational preparation classes about diversity and multicultural issues are standard in teacher preparation, until you are absolutely ready to deal with your beliefs regarding these issues you cannot be as successful as you must become to teach in the present state of education. This takes honesty and courage. If it is easy for you, then you are probably only scratching the surface of knowing who you are psychologically. We encourage you to dig deeper.

Predispositions about what your life will look like, personally and in the classroom, make addressing biases and stereotypical thinking important. Human nature makes openly admitting areas in which you may have biases uncomfortable. However, acknowledging that everyone has predispositions, and that it is normal, is important to your growth as an integrated leader. Not understanding them and being neglectful to truisms that exist within your conscious and subconscious is irresponsible. To become culturally competent starts with crucial self-analysis and is followed with mature application.

Beliefs are based on past experiences and the understanding that our past is constantly changing. So it should be fair to say that preexisting beliefs, too, must be continually restructured and matured. However, change of any sort can increase fear and often stress. The same can be said for changing demographics, economic disparity, and societal tensions within the classroom. The continuum of change has historically fostered climates of distrust and fear between races, genders, communities, and religions. The potential for conflict and discrimination runs high when prejudice and stereotypical beliefs go unchallenged or are ignored. Left unexamined, biased attitudes can lead to biased behaviors, which have the potential to escalate into negative actions toward others, including your students, parents, colleagues, and other important relationships in your life.

Biased behaviors are learned behaviors, even when they may be unconscious and they exasperate the cycle of distrust between beings, and to be a successful teacher you must not only have trust but also know how to gain trust. Bias is also conscious and unconscious. Research suggests that this type of stereotyping is common among U.S. teachers who are white and from the middle- through upper-class socioeconomic groups, which comprises 75.2% of the teacher population (U.S. Department of Education, 2004). By understanding yourself, you will be better able to empathize with your students, who will also come to the classroom with predispositions about education and teachers.

Beliefs that need to be reconstructed or matured do not show that you dislike any particular type of student, but they are real and affect your learning community. However, changing one's belief structures or even admitting that one's belief structures may not be accurate is the **most difficult** to change in all of us. Many times it is not until we are faced with no choice but to adjust our thinking, sometimes feeling forced, that we actually take the steps necessary to do so. Any time one feels cornered about something personal, it can increase stress and emotionally responsive reactions (which we will also address), so prepare for the changes you will experience in the future (which will occur no matter how much training you receive) and find a position of readiness to teach and address issues as they arise. You will be far more prepared than future educators that neglect or are unaware of the need to address displaced expectations and beliefs prior to entering their first classroom.

Like it or not, historically teachers have adamantly denied the need to address "how to teach." Since the 1970s (Lortie, 1975), research has found that future teachers carry beliefs into their programs that are so laced in idealism that they already "feel" like they can teach without anyone's help. Starting the first day of their preparation courses, many future educators reflect similar statements about their predispositions toward preparation, especially in the area of multicultural learner preparation: "This isn't supposed to be in this class"; "I'm not prejudiced—what does this have to do with me?" and "I treat everybody the same... race, class, gender, or even disability doesn't matter... everybody's equal" (p. 37). It is not uncommon for preservice teachers to believe that their teacher preparation program is unneeded and unimportant, as a whole (Mertz & McNeely, 1991) and in specific areas (e.g., theory; Joram & Gabriele, 1998).

Joram and Gabriele (1998) found that preservice teachers had little belief that the foundational courses in their professional development were important and also reported that most of their knowledge about teaching would come from practice in the field or through trial and error when they entered the classroom (Feiman-Nemser, 1990; Joram & Gabriele, 1998). Is this you?

Additional research has also reported that preservice teachers consider their field work to be the primary component of their learning (Joram & Gabriele, 1998; Ross, 1998; Whitbeck, 2000; Zeichner, 1983). Mertz and McNeely (1991) found that 7 out of 10 prospective teachers felt they did not require preparation programs, just practice. Overall preservice teachers were not interested and saw little meaning, in at least a portion of their educational program. Again, is this you?

If it is, hopefully you will soon learn that as diverse and complicated educating learners is today you need **every** tool you can get and that includes the "boring theory stuff." Did you know that many researchers dedicate their lives to helping you to be more successful? Often we forget that theories have been tested, and retested, and retested to give the educator established practices, to give educators a starting point. Researchers do not do what they do to complicate the issues, as much as the overwhelmingly differing perspectives may appear as such. What may seem boring should be invigorating. It should remind you that you have a team that is dedicated to your success. Yes! You have a team—a huge one—working for you. Be mindful of their suggestions and tuck them away for that day you may need that bit of theoretical guidance.

Further, we encourage you, as a future successful leader in education, to learn everything you can. As you approach methods and theories, apply them to the development of your belief structure so that you are not one of the unprepared future teachers. It may be a simple concept, but remember that there will be students uninterested in what you have to teach them, but you know it is important, and often you will feel like you are the only one who appreciates the knowledge you are sharing. So, too, do your teacher preparation instructors, and your team of educational researchers, want you to feel confident and prepared and to be successful! Do not allow yourself to become the apathetic learner whom we are all scared to teach. We all have preexisting beliefs, prejudice, stereotyping behaviors, and even a sense of pride when it comes to something that we feel passionately about. How we deal with them is what affects your teaching and circle of relationships down your future path.

Consider how we deliver information to students. When we disseminate information it is difficult to not include our slant to the information, including our opinions and personal stories. Creatively and motivationally speaking, we are encouraged to use stories to help students identify with what is being learned, but most would agree that we only know our own stories. What about your students' experiences or personal stories? How do yours differ from the students you will teach? Does it matter? Years of successful teachers and researchers say it does.

So how do we understand what biases we as educators reflect in our classrooms? We suggest by addressing the realities of research that identifies what has been happening for years.

Truth: Having lower expectations of and predispositions about achievement toward low socioeconomic status (SES), poverty, and minority students is well documented (Alexander, Entwisle, & Horsey, 1997; Alexander, Entwisle, & Thompson, 1987; Katz, 1999; Olmedo, 1997; Rist, 1970).

Whether we think we will do it or not it is something that must be addressed. Some of these biases include the idea that (whether believed outright or promoted unconsciously) minority students simply do not have the capability to perform at the same levels that middle-class Caucasians perform (Rosser-Cox, 2011). Sometimes it comes in the form of "caring": How can the students do as much as others, when they have so much to deal with? We as teachers find ourselves using empathy of students as an easy way to expect less.

These predispositions appear to be regulated by personal experiences that affect the way we look at student conformity to the educational setting and their family backgrounds. Even the dress and the speech of students have been suggested by research to provoke racist biases from U.S. educators (Alexander et al., 1987, Dietrich, 1998):

> They [teachers] see you and they stereotype you. The teachers think you're in a gang just 'cause the way you dress. It's harder for the black guys and the Mexican guys— especially the Mexican guys. We have this teacher and he has lots of Mexican guys who don't speak English. He doesn't mean to but I think he gets frustrated and takes it out on them... If they can't speak English then they aren't American citizens. That's how I feel about it.—Comment of a student (Dietrich, 1998)

Bias and stereotyping have also undermined additional educational areas. Stereotypical grouping of students by ability (Rist, 1970) is but one of these topics. This so-called grouping is also reflected in the words of Rashlesh (Dietrich, 1998):

> I think they put all those Mexican guys in electives 'cause they can't do anything else.- Comment of a student (Dietrich, 1998).

Biased behavior can be subtle or overt and a teacher's natural altruistic nature lends toward empathy that is often misplaced and used to make excuses for lower student expectations.

Additionally in schools, name-calling and acts of social exclusion are common examples of discriminatory behavior and prejudicial thinking. Although children are not born prejudiced, by preschool they have already acquired stereotypes or negative attitudes toward those they perceive as "others," which is often ignored by educators as "normal" development, but it is not—it is stereotyping. When actually addressed by educators, in an attempt to minimize the development of prejudice, we often teach children to ignore differences and focus only on similarities. However, this "ignoring" of differences is in itself a racist act. Why do we ignore what is different rather than appreciate it?

Being "color-blind" has proven ineffective in all workplaces (years ago) as well as in education and is in actuality a blatant disrespect of differences. However, this belief that being color-blind is responsible still exists in preservice teaching programs today with numerous students and instructors, who are unaware of culturally responsible practices, believing that they should not address differences such as color, race, religion, etc. Have you heard this comment before? "God doesn't see color so why should I?" (Rosser-Cox, 2011). It sounds empathetic and conscientious. Or does it?

Just as common experiences are part of the "glue" that holds communities together, understanding and respecting differences are essential for successful multicultural schools and classrooms. Our history began as a need to make the United States a "melting pot," but today it is evident throughout the literature that the United States is maturing its beliefs and strives for what is now known as the "salad bowl." It is the distinct tastes and colors that make the salad delicious. Consider also a crayon box. Would your students be able to create beautiful and descriptive pictures if we melted all of the colors together? It would be murky and bland, but when we use *all* of the colors—now that's beauty!

Teachers who seek to challenge their stereotypes and biases can also develop better future leaders by influencing students to create positive interpersonal experiences and equitable relationships across cultural barriers. This challenge also offers new teachers a way to learn about other cultures and experiences so that appropriate scaffolding of learning material can be achieved. Understanding that fear is what drives us to negate what we need to understand about others and our environment must stay in front of your sensors at all times. Know what you don't know, and don't be scared to ask questions. One competency in applying culturally responsive pedagogy is the forming of caring relationships, and a relationship cannot reach this level without learning about one another. Do you want to feel comfortable teaching students who differ from you? Then ask them about their lives, interests, motivations, goals, families, needs. Take and make the time! Your attention to this will be a huge step in making you the educational leader that will be successful, and a model for which other teachers may attain.

## Managing the Classroom

*There is no "best method" of dealing with discipline in the classroom; rather there are many different methods for different children in different circumstances.*
—Fred Jones

Managing your classroom is one of the most important skills you will ever obtain. Often, due to negotiated time restraints, preparation programs are unable to focus on this subject until graduate school, and by then you have been chewed up and spit out by a classroom of learners. What makes classroom management important is that you must maintain control of your students without negotiating relationships, which can be tricky. There are many books about learning this skill, but some do not address what we have stressed here—the importance of addressing students' cultural differences. Two of the most prominent management techniques that I (Michelle) have studied, practiced, and later aligned with cultural competence are the management techniques by Dr. Fred Jones and Dr. Harry Wong.

Jones's book, *Tools for Teaching: The Fundamental Skills of Classroom Management,* (2007), has a compelling argument for behaviors a teacher can use without breaking relationships. His techniques have been proven to work and his methods seen as non-threatening to diverse groups of learners. Jones contends that time lost in a classroom due to mismanagement is significant: 50% student misbehavior and being off-task; 30% talking without permission; 19% daydreaming, out of seat, making noises; and 1% serious behavior problems. Although we cannot fully explain his techniques in this text, we would like to highlight some of his techniques and further encourage you to read his book, attend a workshop, or visit a school where this method is employed.

Positive classroom management is built on theoretical underpinnings of Dr. Fred Jones and poses that a relationship exists between the physical arrangement of the classroom and student management; that limit-setting and defusing crisis are accomplished through the effective use of body language; that responsibility training is a process of developing cooperation and motivation; and that classroom management is designed to make misbehavior futile. He reminds us that *calm is strength*. The following are just a few of Dr. Jones's techniques:

- PAT time—a way to reward students for positive behaviors and provide a consequence for poor behaviors that does not invoke intimidation or unhealthy reactions by the teacher or the students.

- "The underlying premise to PAT is this: If the children give me time to teach, then I have time to give them to play an educational game—and I am still teaching, I use PAT as a reward for the time the class earns for positive behavior, minus the negative behavior. They earn minutes/seconds for positive, appropriate behavior, and they lose minutes/seconds for negative, inappropriate behavior. These are minutes earned for the entire class."—Teacher comment
- Using effective body language
  - Eye contact, facial expression (calm/no nonsense), posture and gestures (pointing at a rule on the board), and physical proximity are ways to stop misbehaviors without wasting time.
  - These nonverbal acts usually stop misbehavior and avoid verbal confrontation.
- Dr. Jones suggests several ways to be in charge of your room without being aggressive. One important tool is the use of space. Walking in and out of a student's personal space at just the right time can be helpful to the success of your management technique.
- A guide to arranging your room: Arranging your room in a way that helps you to walk around (also called working a room) comfortably and creates an environment where your students are accommodated decreases the likelihood of abrupt behaviors.
- A guide to creating rules and standards for your classroom
  - Simple, clear, few
  - Posted and taught (students know why)
  - Reinforced consistently, calmly, and promptly
- Positive instructional support
  - Techniques are taught to assist you in moving quickly from student to student (praise/prompt/leave)
  - Have visual instruction plans (VIPs)

Dr. Harry Wong's book, *The First Days of School* (1998), is an insightful book that not only assists in your management development but also addresses what effective teachers do that differs from the rest. Highlights of Wong's guide for teachers include the following:

- The three characteristics of an effective teacher are:
  - has good classroom management skills
  - teaches for mastery
  - has positive expectations for student success

- Treat students as though they already are what they can be, and you help them to be capable of becoming what they will be.
- Call (or write) each home before school begins and again within two weeks. Teachers + Parents = Good Students
- Stand at the door and greet the students.
- Give each student a seating assignment and a seating chart.
- There must be an assignment posted, and in a consistent location, when the students enter the room.
- Position yourself in the room near the students: problems are proportional to distance.
- Credibility: Display your diploma and credentials with pride.
- Dress in a professional manner to model success and expect achievement.
- The three most important things that must be taught the first week of school are discipline, procedures, and routines.
- State your procedures and rehearse them until they become routines.

There are many good books out there that will help you achieve more cultural competence. One common characteristic of excellent teachers is that they believe they are lifelong learners. Take ownership of your own learning and growth.

### Managing Conflict

Conflict is a major deterrent to a balanced lifestyle and being "whole" and is a viable possibility even when the best classroom management techniques are used. Unfortunately, research has also suggested that there is always the potential for conflict between professionals, such as the teacher, and the organizations for which they work (Freidson, 1986; Wallace, 1995) in addition to the students. However, skill can also help you balance this factor with all of your relationships: work colleagues, personal relationships, and student relationships. Research suggests that when a person is unsuspecting of this potential for conflict, there is a higher likelihood that the conflict will take place (Eaton, 1980; Leiter, 1991; Stevens & O'Neill, 1983).

Human service workers (such as educators) have historically not been taught how to work within an organization (Pines, Aronson, & Kafry, 1981; Raelin, 1986), yet that is where they will work, in a school or other educational bureaucracy. This disconnect can be directly related to the overwhelming unpreparedness that educators feel when they enter the profession. They, and now you, were unprepared for the "organization" more so than the learners, which is the norm for what future preparing teachers are asked to learn in the institutions of preparation. Consider your own preparation program. Generally there are two areas of focus in your courses: (1) content (history, math, etc.) and (2) information about how to relate, discipline, assess, and teacher your learners. Thus as a result two areas of importance are often negated in preparation: (1) how to help yourself be what you need to be, and (2) what will "school" look like?

Interpersonal skills, whether from experience or learning, are essential in dealing with conflict between all stakeholders within an organization (Cherniss, 1980; Leiter, 1991). However, you cannot fully manage others if you cannot manage yourself. Managing self develops by being self-aware and knowing what you need to be "best."

Change in itself brings up many questions for a child as well as psychological and motivational implications such as feelings of fear, sorrow, uncertainty, and anxiety. All of these reactions can increase or decrease a child's motivation. For example, a child may become more motivated to gain attention from others or to not be "noticed." These, as we have learned, may be attributed to fulfilling basic needs such as safety and belonging. However, the child may also, unconsciously, decrease motivation to learn or to perform tasks that you may feel are important. Psychologically, the child actually may be incapable of meeting your needs in the classroom based on his or her situation. This is **not** personal. This is a normal human response to trauma, but it must be balanced because you have 25+ other students that must also be managed and educated in a positive learning environment.

Additionally parents of your learners who are experiencing crisis are often blinded due to their own needs and fears. The child who has been historically nurtured by the parents may be seeing and experiencing pressure to understand something that he or she may be unable to do and often feel frustrated and alone. It is important that, although you may not be a counselor, you can be a place of safety and balance for a child who is not coping with change. The following checklist can assist you in supporting a learner who may be experiencing challenging changes:

1. **Be supportive.** Reassure your learner that you care about him or her and that the learner is valued. He or she needs to know that you are looking out for his or her best interests.
2. **Be creative.** The learner may feel at fault so guilt and anger are normal; find encouraging ways (e.g., drawing, educational games, and fun technology assignments) to give him or her a place to set these emotions, even temporarily, aside.

3. **Be reassuring.** If your learner shares his or her situation, reassure your learner that change is emotional and that everyone in the situation has a right to his or her own feelings. Change is not always easy, and your learner must be allowed to feel. Do not inject your personal opinions and always encourage the child that your school counselor is available.
4. **Be clear.** Provide clear and concrete learning instruction that is simple and brief, accepting that the learner may feel overwhelmed. This does not mean you as a teacher must lower your standards; simply acknowledge that what the child is going through may affect your environment.
5. **Never judge.** Never make public personal judgments about lifestyles or cultures. Your opinion may further complicate the confusion a child is experiencing.
6. **Be sensitive.** Each day brings about new challenges for a child in change. Be aware of changes in mood, behaviors, etc. Also avoid terms that may be offensive to the child or family members (e.g., *broken home* or *real parent*). Don't assume that individuals in the same family have the same last name and consider family differences when communicating.
7. **Be welcoming.** Create an environment that welcomes all types of families and encourages involvement of all adults that play an important role in the child's life. In the case of divorce, this includes communicating with both parents. If the divorce is unhealthy or toxic, you may confuse the child more so by only communicating with one parent.
8. **Create a healing environment.** Find ways to encourage your student to laugh and to be successful.
9. **Create a partnership.** Find ways to support the involvement of the parents/family members through parent networking, parent-child home learning activities, and parent participation at school.
10. **Incorporate activities.** Include activities in your daily lessons that encourage understanding of different types of families, increase self-esteem, teach appropriate skills for expressing feelings, and support the positive parent-child relationship.

In some cases, student behaviors can make you feel threatened, and this is also important to consider in the dynamic of being a healthy helper. Understanding how to better respond to radical student behaviors can be helpful. Also remember that just because the behavior may appear radical to you, it may not be considered as such in the home or personal culture of your learner. Suggestions about what to do if a student or other is displaying unexplained aggressive negativity or bias behaviors toward you or your environment that increase your heart rate, make you feel uncomfortable, or increase your negativity about the person personally, rather than the behavior itself:

1. Realize that your amygdala may be being hijacked into a fight-or-flight response and consciously make a decision to not react.
2. Take 4 or 5 deep, cleansing breaths, but we suggest not doing this in a way where the other party notices—this can be an instant trigger for the child to believe you think he or she is wrong or that you do not care about the student.
3. Empathetically consider what has happened and why. What could have possibly occurred in this child's life to increase protective behavior?
4. Interact with the person in a way that makes him or her feel valued: attentively listen, be calm, do not overreact, and do not take it personally.
5. Consider empathetic or humorous comments (based on the appropriateness of the situation or your ability to do so) (Goleman, 1996).
6. After the situation, consider and become aware of what actually triggered your reaction. By better understanding what past experiences have developed your emotional responses, the better you will deal with it if it happens again.
7. Write down methods that could help the situation if it were to arise again.
8. Based on the situation, determine a plan of action to encourage or even improve the relationship.

**Managing Students' Diverse Relationships**

Helping your students to manage relationships is also important to the positive development of your classroom community. As you begin to better manage and form positive relationships with others, your ability to assist students in this process will also positively develop. Apply the strategies you have been taught. Giving your students the ability to be tolerant, understanding, empathetic, and the ability to take risks to find solutions will go a long way in encouraging their confidence to academically achieve as well as create positive models for a successful future. You can be their role model in this process.

Often with school-age children, activities can assist you in helping them to learn important social skills and awareness. Listed below are some learner activities you can use to help students learn more about one another and the world of diversity:

- Ball of Yarn Game—Have your students form a large circle. Have each of them hold their hands in front of them. Begin by tossing a large ball of yarn around the circle, allowing the yarn to continuously unstring. Call out the name of the person you are throwing it to and say something positive about that person. Ask the student to throw to another person and do the same. After a person catches the yarn, he or she should put his or her hands down so people in the circle can make the distinction of who has not caught the ball yet. Continue until everyone in the circle gets a turn. Discuss how the students are all connected and what can be created while working together.
- The Hall of Fame Billboard—Give each of your students a 22"x 28" poster board for them to advertise their pride in their ethnic background. Supply different colored markers, magazines to allow them to cut out pictures, paint, glue, and other materials they can use to design and decorate a billboard that tells who they are. Encourage them to post positive things about their heritage on the billboard. Use this as a time to celebrate different families, cultures, and ethnic backgrounds as students learn about one another.
- Music and Dance Celebrations—Start a monthly club to celebrate a variety of dances from diverse cultures. Invite different students to lead in teaching dances each month. This is a fun and easy way to combine learning about diversity with getting physical exercise. Also encourage trading and sharing ethnic music with fellow students for variety. Be sure to become involved, too, so you can learn more about your students' music and dance preferences, as well as share your own. Who knows, they may actually enjoy some of your country and western or 1970s rock music.
- Tossed Salad Activity—Set aside a day each month where all your students are asked to bring an item to mix into a gigantic tossed salad. Encourage them to join in mixing up the variety of vegetables and fruits as you point out all the different colors of the ingredients being tossed into the salad. Talk about how our society resembles a large tossed salad of colors and flavors of people. Discuss how each one adds to make the salad more interesting and flavorful. You could also

combine this with an ethnic food day where people bring food from a selected culture that is the theme for the day. Put up posters and listen to music of that selected culture.

- Set Up a Pen Pal Program—Setting up a pen pal program is one of the most effective and fun ways to give students a real-life lesson in social studies and geography, as well as language and arts. Many students have reported building lifelong friendships as a result.

Managing your social and student relationships will be a key component to being a successfully integrated leader who is victorious in the classroom. Take the time to learn about those around you and evaluate your actions and behaviors. This will guide you in your journey to the fulfillment you desire in your future career.

## Section III Review

**Section Activities**

**Activity 1**: The list of areas you should continually develop is lengthy and ever-changing. Additionally, it may not be until you actually experience a situation that you understand the importance of being aware. Childhelp Speak Up Be Safe, a child advocate group that includes child welfare professionals, researchers, and volunteers dedicated to child abuse prevention, suggests the following questions that we believe will assist you as you move forward in your development of crucial social awareness and in realizing the implications of social norms rather than ignoring their importance when situations arise:

- Does my community influence the ability for some types of families to manage or cope with stress? How will this affect my classroom?
- What level of poverty exists in the community within which I teach?
- Poverty comes with a great deal of stereotyping. Parents and children living in poverty are rarely ignorant to the inequality between their families and others. Free lunch programs, for example, although created to assist these families, when addressed insensitively can increase the difficulty for these families to trust their school and you.
- What cultural norms exist around the role of the youth in your school's community? Does it support children from all backgrounds?
- What cultural norms exist around how affection is shown or displayed in your school?
- Some cultural norms include physical displays of affection, such as kissing or hugging at every greeting. Although boundaries can be defined in school, reacting instead of responding to a child may encourage confusion and irritation by a child. Sometimes it is how we respond that matters most.
- What parenting norms or values exist? Or is your community so diverse that there are no norms? How does my school address this?
- It is important to be culturally competent and an expert in managing diverse environments. Just because one culture's norms are different from your own does not, or should not, invoke you to "change" them.

- What cultural norms exist around discussing personal or family matters outside of the family?
- What is the community's history with racism or other forms of discrimination?
- What cultural norms exist around the role of the family?
- The role of family differs greatly between cultures. In some cultures parents expect to be notified often about their child; in others, the teacher is considered the expert and contact is not expected. Additionally, in some cultures the definition of family is diverse and those who are included vary greatly.
- What is the perception of educators and the education system in your community? Is there a norm of partnership or alienation? Respect or mistrust?
- What are the existing prevention efforts in the community and the school around child abuse and bullying? Are these efforts visible or does the school appear tight-lipped about these types of issues?
- How is "community" defined where my school is located?
- How is bullying behavior identified in my school? What is the community's history, if any, of bullying on its children?
- How large is the community and what is the perceived level of connectedness between its members?

In many small communities, large extended networks of families may make up a significant proportion of the population, or families that have lived many generations in the same area may be recognized as belonging to that family.

**Activity 2:** Make three columns. In the first column, make a list of the stakeholders in education. In the second column, write why you think it would be important to have a relationship with them. Remember that the word *relationship* does not imply friendship, but the acknowledgment of them in the dynamic of your career is important. In the final column write what barriers you think you might experience in creating a positive relationship with each stakeholder. Form groups and discuss the different lists and why you think they differ.

# SECTION IV

## Developing the Leader in You

*If your actions inspire others to dream more, learn more, do more and become more, you are a leader.*
—John Quincy Adams

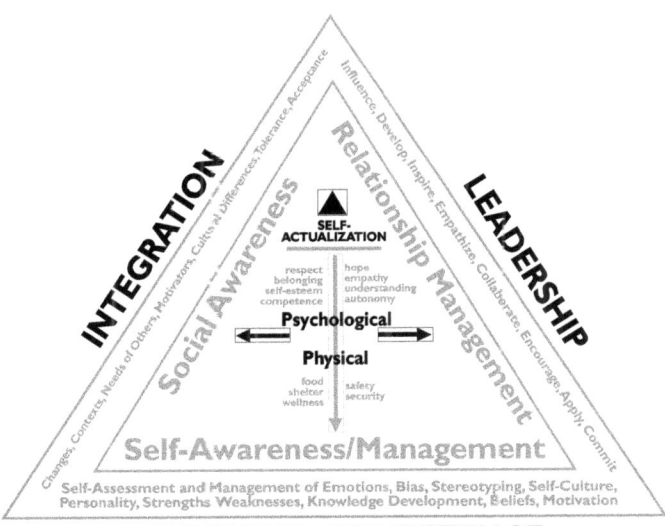

*The purpose of life is a life of purpose.*
—Robert Byrne

Facing changes in life today without a purpose or sense of direction can be a slippery slope. Without it you'll waste a lot of time trying to figure out who you are and what you should be doing. Developing a personal vision can drastically reduce stress and help you create a clearer path for your life. The majority of people today live stale lives clouded by fear simply because they don't have a vision for their future. They can't see past today, so they simply live for the moment, never giving a second thought as to how their actions today will affect their lives tomorrow. Developing a clear personal vision will help open your mind's eye to the possibilities of the future and enable you to view the world of the unseen. Far too many people become jaded by broken dreams and give up on pursuing their goals. Instead, they choose to live in a quiet state of desperation or resignation. Don't allow that to happen to you. Grab hold of a personal vision that opens your mind to possibilities and hopes for a bright future. When you envision a more productive, happier life, you are much more likely to make necessary changes to transform it into a physical reality.

*The first responsibility of a leader is to define reality.*
*The last is to say thank you. In between, the leader is a servant.*
—Max De Pree

An important part of your success as an educator will be determined by your ability to lead. Even if you don't see yourself as a natural-born leader, you can still develop characteristics that great leaders possess. Remember that becoming a great leader is more than simply being at the forefront of the crowd. You must be willing to lead yourself first, and that takes time and effort. By identifying areas in which you lack skills and working to improve and maximize those traits, you will grow into a person to whom others turn when strong leadership is required. You don't need to be liked on a personal level, although most great leaders are. You simply need to have the characteristics that others trust and respect in the leadership role you fulfill. A great leader never rules by fear, but he or she must be willing to be firm in preventing anyone from derailing a team in reaching its ultimate goal and take swift decisive action when it happens. If you aren't confident you won't get anywhere as a leader, but confidence should never be confused with arrogance. Be confident but do so in a calm, collected manner with the aim of doing things right and getting the job done. Rock solid confidence in your ability will inspire dedication, trust, and hard work from your students.

You have only to look around you to witness the constancy and the accelerating rate of change. It is constantly occurring both inside and outside our individual lives and the workplace. Our challenge as integrated educators and leaders is to understand the change process and help students manage it as proactively as possible. You must both accept the inevitability and the fact that resistance to change is normal, not negative. The discussion of resistance needs to take place in an open, nonjudgmental atmosphere and include those who will be affected by the approaching change. If it does not, then discussions will take place in the parking lot, the dorms, the cafeteria, or other venues that will create even more challenges. People fear most what they don't understand. In the heat of resistance, remember: Knowledge is power.

## Something to Think About

Your ability to lead and guide your students is vital. Not only are you affected by your past and current experiences but so are your students. Consider the following letter that was submitted to these authors about their educational experiences and their profound effect on every area of this wonderful person's life:

*Letter from Rachel:*

When I reflect upon my educational experience, three teachers stand out in particular as having made an impact in my life. There were a few who showed great kindness for which I will never forget, and a few who were not so kind and I will equally never forget. I am grateful to them all for planting seeds in my life. Who I am today is a result of how I cultivated those seeds.

The first was my 5th grade English teacher. He introduced me to the world of Edgar Allan Poe, the man who became my most beloved poet. I do not know how the other kids felt of his theatrical readings of "The Raven," but I was in awe. I learned that someone could walk in shadows and write about it beautifully. I loved to write and upon discovering Poe, I found a kindred spirit who also seemed to suffer but was able to express it through words, something I found so cathartic. My English teacher believed in me and encouraged me to write. I also learned that one must not remain in the dark because it is contagious. Light must be brought into the dark or shadow will spread throughout all places of the soul. I needed to learn hope.

My second experience occurred during my freshman year of high school. I examined the schedule for my second semester and noticed I was enrolled in a special education course; something I thought was a mistake. When I approached my homeroom teacher about it he told me he doubted it was a mistake. I protested and he responded that I would never be anything in life without an M.R.S. degree. With a perplexed look on my face I asked what that meant, he said "A Mrs." I assumed he was telling me I would not be anything in life unless I procured a husband of stature to lend value and success to my life. At that moment I could have gone two ways. Either I would fall for his disparaging prophesy, or I would use it as a fuel for the fire I had been fighting most my life, to prove I was somebody. The only way I can describe it is that I had an incessant inner voice for as long as I can remember, a voice that always told me I was meant for something, to have faith in myself. I call it my "knowing." I recently became aware that I made an unnecessary vow that I would have to "prove" myself without ever being a wife. I also realized that if I maintain such a vow, that man wins. Today I try to be mindful of vows I may have subconsciously formed in defense or pain, and instead act on what is truly the desire of my most inner and authentic self. There is no proving or fighting to be done, that is the job of the ego, and the ego has no place in a conscious mind. However, we internalize much of our experience and both the seeds of goodness and seeds of poverty take root, often without our conscious awareness. Unknowingly, I would battle his statement for years to come, even into college. I needed to learn faith.

The third experience occurred while I was working on my bachelor's degree and keenly aware that I approached each semester's enrollment with trepidation. I tried to avoid classes I was "afraid" to take, classes that required presentations, oral quizzes, and group work. As part of my degree, I was required to take Greek or Latin. I tried Latin and dropped out after the second day. The next semester I enrolled in Greek. As the weeks progressed I began showing up later and later to class in an attempt to avoid the oral quizzes. I thought I presented myself as a capable, mature, and articulate young woman, but on the inside I was still the insecure, avoidant, and fearful young girl. One day after class my professor approached me and requested that I come to his office to talk. He told me that I would be a stellar student if I would show up. I broke down in tears and gave him a quick synopsis of my background. He listened, but did not coddle me. He acknowledged my fear, but responded with hope and faith. He said he would help me, tutor me if needed, and that no matter what he was not going to sign my drop slip. That was a defining moment for me, a moment I drew upon often. I needed to learn courage.

Looking back, the profundity of that moment was that I internalized it. Eventually I no longer needed the external pushing and guidance of the teacher, I was able to access my internal guidance system. I began to face challenges as opportunities rather than formidable obstacles. Fear became something to be challenged rather than avoided. This did not happen overnight; until I graduated I approached challenging classes with self-doubt. Even in the beginning stages of my master's degree, I worried about the intensity of classes and what I could handle. And then one day, it was gone. I know this did not happen overnight, but change often seems that way. I recall at some point realizing that there was no class I feared. I knew that with effort, humility, and hard work I could handle any class thrown at me.

*Chapter 13*

# Inevitability of Social Change

*There are two primary choices in life: to accept conditions as they exist
or accept the responsibility for changing them.*
—Denis Waitley

Accepting the inevitability of change influences your ability to become the leader you must become. "No man ever steps in the same river twice, for it's not the same river and he's not the same man" (Heraclitus). Can this be said about changes and life? Nothing is ever the same from day to day. Our choices, our surroundings, our beliefs are constantly changing. The difficulty with this concept is that change has happened so quickly. Adapting to this change, when yet it still changes again, is not an easy task to accomplish, and we must always be aware that change is happening all of the time and that looking forward and being ready is the best way to adapt and assist positive changes, in any context.

Throughout history, the United States has seen drastic changes in population numbers, gender roles, value commitment, religious engagement, civil rights, immigration needs, and economic stability. Family migration patterns and norms have changed quickly and drastically over the past decades. This contextual moderator has affected much of the relative diversity that exists, including beliefs and subsequent behaviors, and you must consider these changes as you strive to become an educator, or at least an educator who desires to have positive outcomes with learners. Understanding how mobility affects your classrooms is only one area that has made teaching complex, but increasingly worthwhile. Societal change does modify how you must look at your environment and is of utmost importance to your success. There are obvious changes that have also occurred in the racial and ethnic composition of public school students over the last three decades due to much to this, which again is a good thing—complex, but good. However, as we have read, other variables have also affected the context of classrooms and the complexities of teaching: an increase in gang activity, increases in youth depression and eating disorders, changes in the meaning of "family," changes in the definition and expectations of male and female roles, and changes in socioeconomics, as well as increasing bombardment of negative accusations toward teachers, parents, and students based on a nonexistent, or at the least inconsistent, vision about what success in education should look like for all.

In 2010, 37.5 million people 1 year and older in the United States changed locations. Among those who moved, 69% stayed within the same county, 17% moved to a different county in the same state, 12% moved to a different state, and 3% moved to the United States from abroad (U.S. Census Bureau, 2011). Additionally, the minority rate for migrating often was twice as high for minorities as it was for white students, and even more prominent among poor and minority students.

Mobility itself has been encouraged by several factors. Increase in split families, welfare reform (Kerbow, 1996; Rumberger, Larson, Ream, & Palardy, 1999), and a "grass is greener" mentality have all played a part in this largely ignored but responsible variable. Additionally, research has suggested that between 30% and 40% of school changes are not associated with residential changes. Factors such as overcrowding, class size reduction, suspension and expulsion policies, and the general academic and social climate, encouraging discontentment, have also contributed to student mobility. Thus, students raised in one cultural environment may be attending school with students and teachers who have an entirely different cultural value system.

This disparity about how schools/teachers should be performing has created cyclical changes in school environments. In response, the overall learning of the student is affected and increased adversity between stakeholders is encouraged.

Student mobility not only varies widely among students but also between schools and other factors. In the Chicago public schools, for example, an average of 80% of students in the district remained in the same school from September 1993 to September 1994 and only 47% remained in the same school over a four-year period. Fifteen percent of the schools lost at least 30% of their students in only one year. According to the Military Child Education Coalition, approximately 800,000 military-connected students make an average of six to nine school changes between kindergarten and high school graduation (Keller, 2003).

Although 13% of these students attend schools run by the Department of Defense, where the curriculum is aimed at reducing negative effects of location changing, 75% of these students have similar challenges faced by other frequently migrating populations. In a 2000 New York study, almost 65% of foster care children were transferred in the middle of the school year. Nationwide, an estimated six million elementary school children change schools each year (Cornille, Boyer, & Smith, 1983). Nineteen percent of the school-aged children move in a single year, and 23% of primary-grade children relocate every year (U.S. Department of Commerce, 1987).

Additionally, research has suggested that the mobility of students can complicate the ability for some students to succeed in school. A 1999 study found that less than half of California high school students who changed schools even once were less likely to graduate as those who did not change schools. Research also indicates that frequent school changes affect students' achievement, even placing a learner a year behind peers (Kerbow, 1996). However, other research that accounted for the background of participants suggested that mobility may be more of a moderator than the root of the problem, noting that mobile students are more likely to be underprivileged families, which research suggests have a lower academic performance overall. Even if research could clearly identify that these types of social issues aligned with mobility are contributing to the causes for lower achievement in students, it does not solve any of the problems. We must examine the negative effects to gain the understanding so that practical solutions can be applied.

Changes in our classrooms are inevitable but making this a more difficult consideration is that much has changed in a very short amount of time. For example, in 2009, some 19% of 5- to 17-year-olds were in families living in poverty, compared with 15% in 2000 and 17% in 1990. In the 2000 census it was found that there were 601,209 committed gay couples in America (Lifetips, 2012) and more same-sex marriages have publically developed in recent years, again affecting the dynamic within public environments. Although this dynamic change is not necessarily negative or positive—it is a change—it affects the attitudes of communities and educators, sometimes negatively. It is simply not a subject that should go unnoticed. Everyone may have differing opinions on changes such as these, but there should be an agreement by all about the effects to education: diversity changes dynamics and this issue is complex and is not simply one of color and ethnicity.

Our societal dysfunction affects the continuum of learning as cultures change living locations, schools, and home environments (due to economic good and bad times). Packing up a moving truck and simply leaving a community has become more acceptable and doable. No longer are the days where families all knew one another, as well as the families who resided before them. No longer does a community hold a unified value system that fully drives the expectations of teachers, parents, and students. When education began, cultural norms were determined by the community that experienced little population change. This can no longer occur with the diverse current cultural make-ups of all communities.

Unlike 50 years ago, when cultural diversity might have included two differing religions in a small town schoolhouse, cultural diversity of school environments and of communities is now a multifaceted culture of norms that are each based on different people and ideas from all walks of life. About one fifth of all Americans move annually (U.S. General Accounting Office, 1994) and according to the 1998 National Assessment of Educational Progress (NAEP), one-third of fourth graders, 19% of eighth graders, and 10% of 12th graders changed schools at least once in the previous two years; reports indicate that frequent migrating students were below grade level, up to 41% of these students (U.S. General Accounting Office, 1994).

Understanding misunderstood conceptions about financial hardships is imperative. As the adage goes, "Bad things happen to *good* people." Many factors contribute to the frequent migration of families, the economy being one, as parents seeking work must, at times, relocate. Parents who are without work and do not want to move their child then face the opposite cynicism in a community, such as stereotyping from others. Often, the majority conclude that these parents do not want to work. However, in actuality, these parents are trying to do what is best for their child, and once a person becomes a parent, there is a great realization that no matter how hard you try you will never get it all correct. Social adjustment to new peers and social expectations are difficult on anyone.

### The Family Dynamic

Additionally the culture of the classroom is being altered by changes in family norms that were originally established largely by the white, middle-class majority (Gorman & Balter, 1997). These "healthy" messages of previous norms do not reflect the cultural diversity found in society today. Cultural norms about parenting practices play an important role in how children are raised. They influence what values parents teach their children, what behaviors are considered appropriate, and which methods are used to teach these values and behaviors (Kim & Hong, 2007; Melendez, 2005; Singh & Clarke, 2006). Cultural norms can influence how we treat a learner as well as other stakeholders. Cultural norms can also affect how these stakeholders respond to you and your way of teaching.

Other changes in the family have also affected education and the learners you will teach. Although statistical data suggest that divorce rates are lowering, some research also suggests it is because fewer are marrying, preferring to live with another. In 2002, the percentage of married people who reach their 5th, 10th, and 15th anniversaries are 82%, 65%, and 52%, respectively. The percentage of married people who reach their 25th, 35th, and 50th anniversaries were 33%, 20%, and 5%, respectively.

The response of women (mothers) to abuse in the home is also a changing factor. According to the National Institute of Child Health and Human Development (NICHD) (2005), the rate at which women are abused has not changed in recent years, but women are far less likely to stay in the abusive relationship. Cherlin (2005) states:

> Women are less dependent on marriage than in previous years, as single women have more employment opportunities than in previous decades and society is more accepting of partners living together outside marriage.

And although this is obviously a healthier thing for the mother and often the child, it is still a traumatic change that increases some of the negative behaviors that are seen during school hours (which we will continue to discuss later in this chapter). Additionally, although women cohabit more often than in the past, based on abusive histories, stereotypes again play a role in the adjustment of this population, based on "norms."

With family cultures changing, how we address learner needs must also change. Children of immigrant parents are one of the fastest growing groups in the United States (Melendez, 2005), so historical norms are not applicable to new cultures of learners. The Census Bureau estimates that the percentage of same-sex couples raising children has more than doubled in just 10 years, from 8% in 2000 to 19% in 2010. Change is all around us if we just take the time to look. It is this dynamic that must be considered, and it is important to become aware of cultural norms that are consciously (and unconsciously) in place within your school. This is a key to becoming culturally competent.

By developing a cultural competency, that is, understanding and respect for culturally based values, beliefs, and behaviors of the community of learners that you have dedicated yourself to, you as a successful educational leader will be more equipped to design, disseminate through life-based scaffolding, and apply effective educational content for your various and diverse cultural groups. You cannot simply accept the culture of the school and its teachers. This may not parallel your learners. Thus, understanding the goals and needs of the learners' parents is valuable.

There are a multitude of strategies that research has cited to assist educators, remembering again that **knowledge is power**. In a study by the Centers for Disease Control and Prevention and the National Center for Injury Prevention Control, entitled *Promoting Healthy Parenting Practices Across Cultural Groups: A CDC Research Brief* (2008), parents of differing cultures were asked about what discipline they preferred to implement with their child. The following strategies were identified as preferred:

(1) Parents from all cultural groups believed signaling (e.g., giving a child "the look" or using a certain tone) was a good response.
(2) Many white parents and some Asian American, Latino, and American Indian parents (primarily mothers) also preferred redirecting a child's attention by changing the condition, or even ignoring negative behaviors. In contrast, some African American parents (both mothers and fathers) preferred a more direct and immediate response to misbehavior.
(3) Verbal reprimands were also supported by differing cultural groups but with distinct boundaries that were concerned about the reprimand not being abusive, which in some cases is defined differently between cultural groups. Specifically, screaming, bullying, and humiliation were not acceptable for all cultural groups in the study. One American Indian father said that this reaction (verbally abusive) "breaks the spirit."
(4) American Indian, white, and African American parents and some Asian American mothers reported that using guilt as a tool was a good response for their children. This is one example that demonstrates that not all practices are accepted by all cultures.

The consideration of adapting parenting interventions to the context of your classroom for specific cultural groups can be intimidating (also noting that these parental preferences are linked to their relationship of caring for their child). Your classrooms are more diverse than many stakeholders and communities realize. In the United States there are more than 50 Latino groups, 60 Asian or Pacific Islander groups, more than 500 American Indian tribes and sub-clans, and numerous mixed-race, religious, and socioeconomic groups. We can no longer force populations to assimilate to the white culture (Kumpfer, 2002) that has historically defined the norms in public education. And if all of these dynamics are not overwhelming by themselves, we have not even begun to address the social awareness of the dynamics that will take place with other variables, such as children of divorce, unhealthy home environments, abuse, hunger, or on the opposite cultural coin, children of privilege and children of parents who intentionally expect white norms to be taking place in your classrooms.

Once we begin to effectively accept that change is constant and nonnegotiable, we can prepare ourselves to be leaders who help to ensure that the changes, throughout society, are based in social justice and equality and compassion for others. You as a future helper—a teacher—have chosen to be one of the most prominent players in the chess game of change. You hold in your hand all of tomorrow's pieces.

### Committing to Positive Change

The permanence of change in your life as a teacher is as true today as it was for the ancient Greek philosopher Heraclitus. You will continually face shifts in technology, governmental regulations, and demographics of students, which will challenge you to understand the dynamics of change. Whatever changes people encounter, there are certain patterns of response that occur and re-occur. It is important for you as a leader in the classroom to understand these basic patterns, since they are normal responses to the change process. Understanding them will allow you to avoid overreacting to behaviors that at times may seem to be resistant or non-adaptive responses.

According to well-known author on leadership and management development Kenneth Blanchard, there are seven elements present in any change in the workplace:[1]

1. **People will feel awkward, ill at ease, and self-conscious.** When people are asked to do things differently, it disrupts their habitual ways of behavior. This tends to make them feel awkward or uncomfortable as they strive to phase out old responses and learn new ones. All people need to feel competent to maintain motivation, and this includes your learners as well as yourself and your colleagues. In most cases, the loss of competence breeds perceptions of inadequacy. People must feel safe to take risks. No one likes to feel judged or laughed at; we all desire the belongingness that affirmation can give to us.
2. **People initially focus on what they have to give up.** Even for changes viewed as positive, such as promotions or job transfers, people will often focus on what they are giving up or losing. As a change catalyst you should be sensitive to the feelings of loss for

old ways of doing things, and not get frustrated at what may seem to be an irrational or tentative response to change. Remember that people must also understand why the change is important as well as see and feel the benefits of the change to lessen the sense of loss in giving up the old.

3. **People will feel alone even if everyone else is going through the same change.** No one can feel what you experience inside and you cannot experience what he or she feels. This can contribute to an increasing sense of isolation for those undergoing change. A part of moving from a sense of belongingness to a healthy self-esteem is one's ability to feel comfortable inside one's own skin. In the case of your students undergoing change, create opportunities for them to feel safe in processing their feelings and affirm that it is perfectly normal to have self-doubt and a sense of aloneness during challenging times. Reassure them that you are on their team. One of your most important roles as a teacher is being a cheerleader for your students!

4. **People can handle only so much change.** History has proven that people who undergo too much change in a short amount of time will often become dysfunctional and/or physically ill. While some changes are beyond our control, it is important not to stack up change after change after change. A little empathy goes a long way here. You may be perfectly comfortable asking someone else to do something you find easy, but do not forget to put yourself in that person's shoes. As a leader you must remember, *"It's not all about you."*

5. **People are at different levels of readiness for change.** Some people thrive on change and others do not. For some change is exciting, while others feel threatened by it. This is also diversity. Change also often elicits different reactions in people:
   - Ridicule or laughter about the notion of the change
   - Denial
   - Opposition (resistance) to the change, sometimes aggressively
   - Acceptance of the change as being inevitable. Often, in time those who resist will accept it as inevitable.

6. **People will be concerned that they don't have enough resources.** Change always takes too much time and costs too much, according to a cynic: a person who knows the cost of everything and the value of nothing. If you are a cynic, stop and think about your goals in education! Although change can be challenging, it is important for you to acknowledge and plan for the additional effort that will be required,

keeping in mind that the purpose of change is to make things better in the long-term. Solicit additional support, reassure your students that scarcity is only a state of mind, teach your students how to be creative problem solvers, and remind yourself to focus on the bright spots, rather than the negative.
7. **Commit yourself to the change.** Your students will have a tendency to go back to the old way, especially if you are not consistent and completely committed to the change.

Consider those people who are more ready for the change to be innovators who will influence others who are less ready. Allowing open discussion will help. Those who have a low threshold for transition can be encouraged by others who thrive on it. As a teacher you can often facilitate the change process easier in your classroom by making alliances with the students who are the "informal" leaders in the class (every group has informal leaders). Get them to champion the change with their peers and watch their influence grow as you delegate leadership responsibilities to those capable of handling them.

### Attrition Rates

One indicator that many teachers are having difficulty accepting, and adapting to, the drastic cycles of change in education is the current attrition rates. The challenges these changes have for them and their profession can be daunting, although educators are more prepared for the classroom and conscious of individual student needs than in our past. Teachers, through multiple strategies including theory based courses and fieldwork experiences, are trained to meet the needs of diverse classroom environments. So why are attrition rates rising?

In our opinion, the constant barrage of negativity about performance outcomes, historically "white" school structure, and the neglect of teachers taking care of themselves first have encouraged many teachers to question their chosen career in fear of being unsuccessful: they are not fully prepared to be a key player for positive change in education. Thus, teachers often quickly resolve their love for teaching for other careers, for the sake of their physical and psychological health, their finances, their personal empowerment, and their need for achieving self-actualization. According to the National Education Association, half of new U.S. teachers are likely to quit within the first five years because of high stress and low salaries (2005). A total of 394,140 teachers changed or left public schools in 1999–2000 (Alliance for Excellent Education, 2005). This is why you must build your foundation upon leadership. You must be equipped for the classroom and your learners in every way.

The inventory of stressors a teacher will experience and must be ready to address is lengthy. You must be ready to change this facet of education, as there are students who still require dedicated teachers to help them to learn, grow, excite them with a passion for learning, and encourage their success. It is important that you know what you are up against before you can meet the many challenges and be successful in your chosen career.

The economy in itself creates instability for career teachers and increases the stress of how teachers are to provide for their families. Budget cuts reduce our teacher numbers and subsequently make teaching more challenging. Between May 2007 and May 2011, the number of teachers in the United States decreased by 223,770 (Mandle, 2012). Thus as safety and security needs become more of a concern for teachers, research suggests that their motivation to do the job they set out to do will also decrease. However, one way to combat this is to become a good saver and spender. Integrated leaders know how to budget, to save, and to make good financial decisions.

### Becoming a Catalyst for Change

As an integrated educational leader you must be willing to be a catalyst for change. According to *Change Anything: The New Science of Personal Success* (Patterson, Grenny, Maxfield, McMillan, & Switzler, 2011), there are six sources that influence change in our lives. These same six sources of influence can be used to either promote a healthy or unhealthy behavior and they are a vital source of empowerment for your development.

- **Personal motivation**—You must tap into existing desires and burning passions if you want to muster up the motivation to change.
- **Personal ability**—Be willing to learn new skills to successfully change. Einstein once said, "We cannot solve our problems with the same thinking we used when we created them."
- **Social motivation**—Habits, especially unhealthy ones, are a social disease. To develop good habits you must turn accomplices into friends who help you make positive changes.
- **Social ability**—Use the support and coaching of those who have made the changes you aspire to make. You already know what you know. Open yourself up to new information and find a mentor to help you learn new approaches.
- **Structural motivation**—Directly link rewards and pleasant thoughts to your new habits through pictures, motivational quotes posted where

you can see them, or predetermined rewards you give to yourself as you attain your goals.
- **Structural ability**—You must change your environment to one that promotes the change you want.

Remember that the success of any change ultimately rests with your willingness to adopt a "burn the ships" mentality. This phrase comes from a historic conquest in 1519 when Spanish Conquistador Hernando Cortez landed in Mexico on the shores of the Yucatan, with only one objective: to find the great treasures kept there by the Aztecs. Cortez's commitment to his mission was legendary and he was an excellent motivator. He convinced more than 500 soldiers and 100 sailors to set sail from Spain to Mexico in search of the world's richest treasure. The historic question is: "How could such a small band of soldiers arriving in a strange country swiftly conquer a large and powerful empire that was in power for more than six centuries?"

For Cortez, the answer was easy. As far as he was concerned it was an all or nothing proposition. He got the "buy in" from his men by simply removing the option of failure. When Cortez and his men arrived on the shores of the Yucatan he rallied them together for one final pep talk before he ordered them to "burn the ships." They were surprised at first, but he repeated himself and said, "If we are going home, we are going home in their ships." With that, they burned their own ships and their commitment was raised to a higher level than any of the men, including Cortez, could have ever imagined.

Amazingly, Cortez's army won one incredible victory after another where others had been unsuccessful for six centuries. Why did they succeed? They had no escape, no plan for retreat. Failure simply wasn't a choice. Their ships were burned. They had no way to get back. Their backs were against the wall. To succeed you must have an attitude much like that. Get rid of your "crutches" or "retreat plans." Do not give yourself an out. It takes inner strength, which you have the ability to develop. The world is becoming smaller. Every day we are competing with people from other cultures who have a "burn the ships" mentality. They want what we have. The golden age of American dominance in the world is drawing to a close. We have no choice but to move forward. As a teacher you are guiding the leaders of our future. Failure is simply not an option.

Notes
1  The seven dynamics of change in bold above are adapted from an article by Ken Blanchard, published in *The Inside Guide*, Oct., 1992.

# Chapter 14

# A Leader with Vision

> *Workers are concerned with time and money. They sit at the back of meetings and put in time. Leaders are concerned with enhancement and cooperation. They have a career, are talented and are professionals.*
> *Some teachers are workers, others are leaders.*
> —Harry Wong, educator, educational speaker, and author

An important part of becoming a fully integrated educational leader is by understanding, developing, and clarifying the vision of our life journey. It is a priority to successfully integrate all of the elements we have addressed in this text. This chapter differs from the previous in that you must become more participatory in your development. No more just reading—you must do. It will be imperative that you address your current definition of success and what that will look like as you move forward.

But just as important is understanding the lack of consistency in education's vision, so you can base your development on this complex reality. As you have read, little is clear in the educational equation, but two things are blatantly obvious: (1) clarity of vision is needed and (2) empowerment of educators is long overdue. Few groups in this nation agree on the vision of education. Visions are molded with the postulation of questions: Why does this nation need children to learn? What are the realities of the global expectations of our youth and strength as a country? On the macro level, we want and need to preserve the health, well-being, and sustainability of our societal quality of life. We must continue to maintain a position of global leadership in the 21st century. On the micro level, we must consider each individual as valuable and an asset.

Researchers and legislators must quit battling over what area of understanding is most important (e.g., cognition, motivation, discipline, stereotyping, historical creation of "school," minority assimilation, majority dominance within a critical race continuum, etc.) and work together to create practical solutions for preparing youth that meet a widely diverse community of weaknesses and strengths. Ways to evaluate and encourage productivity that encourages pride in our system and our perseverance must be considered for successful change to happen.

So, if the educational organization cannot agree on a vision for what education is, what is the vision for your life? Do you have one? What does it look like? You are more than just a teacher. You are a human being with feelings and needs. You must start to clearly define this to help you become more purposeful and ready to serve diverse groups of learners. Are you currently on track to fulfill your life vision, or are you focused on and concerned about the challenges that currently haunt your chosen career? Are you negating your vision of who you are and who you desire to become? Are you currently in negative circumstances so you are just surviving your program of preparation until it is complete? Have you ignored the amount of energy that you must attribute to acutely develop your wholeness as a teacher? Or have you never considered the idea that you even need a vision about what your journey should look like?

The development of a vision is crucial as you consider your future goals and needs. This is a vital part of your growth—a part of finding your intrinsic power to be a successful helper, teacher, and leader by (1) identifying your strengths and weaknesses and (2) establishing visions and goals for both your personal life and your professional life.

### Identifying Our Strengths, Admitting Our Weaknesses

In a world where efficiency and competency rule the workplace (e.g., education) using one's personal strengths is essential. What would happen if you spent more than 75% of each day using your strongest skills and engaged in your favorite tasks, basically doing exactly what you like to do? Would you arrive each day at work with an attitude of positive expectancy and passion? What effect do you think that would have on others in your environment? What about your students?

Gallup researcher Marcus Buckingham (2001) has interviewed thousands of people at every career stage and is widely considered one of the world's leading authorities on human productivity. He reports that organizations focused on cultivating people's strengths rather than simply improving weaknesses stand to dramatically increase efficiency while allowing for maximum personal growth and success. Have you chosen a profession in education because you have passion for teaching and a genuine desire to help students succeed? If that is not the driving force behind your career choice, perhaps you should do something else. You'll be happier and so will your students.

*But* if this is why you did choose your career, we know that you want to be the best that you can be. This is why becoming self-aware is so important. Your physical needs will be addressed first as we better understand what you need so that you may then successfully give your students what they need.

In the past, teachers have been the victims of a decreasingly effective educational system right along with students. It is time for teachers to take back their careers and own their passions for helping others. It is time to be real. It is time to be healthy. It is *time to be successful!* Remember, you cannot give away that which you do not have. To be an effective teacher, leader, and agent of change you must lead by example. If you are not playing to your strengths, if you become emotionally exhausted, if you become overly frustrated, if you are not able to give everything to the process of teaching, how can you inspire your students to give all that they have to learning? You have a choice. Find the power within yourself to become the leader education needs or live life in a vacuum that will deplete why you ever even considered education as a career.

Unfulfilled needs make themselves known through feelings of restlessness: "the person feels on edge, tense, lacking something" (Maslow's hierarchy of needs). If you feel this way, use that feeling as motivation to take actions toward fulfilling those needs. That will propel you to make positive changes and seek greater happiness in the things you do. Self-actualization is only experienced when you successfully fulfill your other needs. Be aware, however, that this is not a destination or stopping point, but a continual journey filled with challenges and opportunities. Enjoy the process and be encouraged by these words from Helen Keller: "Life is either a daring adventure or nothing. To keep our faces toward change and behave like free spirits in the presence of fate is strength undefeatable."

The key to finding your vision and becoming a *leader* goes back, first, to knowing yourself. You must honestly evaluate yourself, which is not always as easy as it sounds. Answering the following questions can you help you gain greater self-awareness:

1. What are my personal strengths? What are my weaknesses?
2. What is my personality type?
3. Am I an extrovert or introvert? How does being with people make

me feel? (Energized? Drained of energy?) Do I handle being with young people better than adults my own age? Why?

4. Am I a "detail"-oriented person who assesses my immediate surroundings strictly through the five senses, or would I prefer to focus on the big picture and rely on personal intuition? What are the benefits and weaknesses of how I assess?
5. Am I primarily a thinker or feeler? (For example, do you make decisions based on rational, analytical thoughts or are you influenced more by what you feel at the "gut" level?)
6. Do I require order and predictability in my life or do I prefer spontaneity and the excitement of uncertainty? What does this say about me?
7. What biases and stereotypical beliefs do you hold? In other words, what qualities do you most like to see in others? What qualities make you feel uncomfortable or agitated?
8. What motivates me? Does it differ depending on the situation? Why?
9. How do I most like to be recognized or rewarded for my efforts? (By affirming words or public acknowledgment; by receiving gifts of appreciation from others; or by acts of service others perform for you?) Why?
10. What do I fear most in life? Why?
11. What are my dreams for the future? Do they complement my goals to become a leader in education? How?
12. When I disagree with someone or things don't go my way, how do I respond? (Be honest with yourself.)
13. How would others describe my emotional maturity and behavior? How can I develop my maturity and behavior?

### Creating a Personal/Professional Vision

Numerous experts in the leadership and personal development fields emphasize how important it is to create a vision for your life. Like a road map that guides you to the destination you have set for yourself, a compelling vision will help you go far beyond where you'd be without one. It will enable you to get the most out of life without simply leaving the future to chance. In fact, successful people don't believe in chance—they choose to shape their future by creating a vision and setting out to achieve it. If you don't create your own vision, others will direct your life for you. Do not be like the masses of individuals who late in their lives say, "If only..."

Your vision is simply a picture of what success looks like to you, an idea of what you want to achieve both personally and professionally. Do you want to make a lasting impact in the lives of your students? Raise successful, well-adjusted children? Write a book? Be fit and healthy? Travel to foreign countries? Learn a second language? Help others fulfill their dreams? What are you good at? What do you love to do? These are the types of questions that are essential for identifying your vision.

Invest in your personal vision by writing some personal intention statements and goals designed to move you toward it. You may have heard it said that your goals should be specific, measurable, attainable, relevant, and time-driven (commonly referred to as SMART goals by "realists"). We agree in part, but we also believe your goals should stretch and inspire you to live with passion and courage. Reflect for a moment on these words by performance coach Brendon Burchard (2012):

> No one joins the major leagues to bunt. Those living a Charged Life see the crowds on their feet, chanting, calling for greatness, and they want to swing big, go for the fences, and sprint around the bases with a reckless abandon that the "realists" would call madness. Real desire is like that: wanting nothing less than the home run and the global contribution. It's that level of drive that incites us to take chances, to give our best efforts and go for broke, not out of foolhardiness but out of blatant disregard for the naysayers and a grand desire to do something that counts. (pp. 156–157)

The first step in creating a vision is to perform an environment scan that includes evaluating the past, the external factors that have existed, and the trends that have occurred that affect the context of the vision. In this case, you are creating your vision as an educational leader. This step has been detailed throughout this text. You now know where education started—where it has been—and where it is possibly going. We have noted trends throughout history that have exasperated the academic issues we currently are facing. Although there is no end to what can be considered in the complex history of education, and we feel quite certain we have not addressed everything, we do hope that the information we have introduced has enlightened you to the mistakes of our past so that we can have a better future.

Based on the SOAR model of visioning (Strengths, Opportunities, Aspirations, and Results) you can now begin to develop your personal vision. The SOAR framework helps identify and tap into your internal assets, core strengths, aspirations, and opportunities for achieving measurable results and impact. SOAR fosters a constructive, growth-oriented, and possibility-focused understanding of your potential to become an educational leader. The next step would be to create an accurate and thorough personal assessment to help guide you in the process.

|  | Strengths | Opportunities |
|---|---|---|
| **Strategic Inquiry** | What are my greatest assets? | What are the best possible opportunities? |
| **Appreciative Intent** | Aspirations<br>What is my preferred future? | Results<br>What are the measurable results, impact? |

Listed below are some questions in various areas that are designed to help you gain clarity to develop your vision:

**Personal Values**
1. What is most important in your life?
2. What are the things you most enjoy doing?
3. What makes you happy?
4. What gives you a sense of achievement or personal mastery?
5. What accomplishment are you most proud of?
6. What causes are you most passionate about?
7. What do you enjoy so much that you could see yourself doing it the rest of your life?

**Personal Dreams/Goals**
1. What would you like to be doing 5 to 10 years from now?
2. Who are the people you most admire and what qualities do they possess that you want to emulate?
3. When you dream about being successful what does that look like and what would need to happen to make it possible?
4. What are you doing now to achieve your dream?
5. What do you want to be remembered for?
6. Whose lives do you most want to inspire or influence?

**Personal Strengths**
1. What things do you perform well?
2. What topics do you love to learn about?
3. What would you consider to be your natural talents or "gifts"?
4. What stimulates your strongest interests or passions?
5. What personal qualities make you unique?
6. How can you use your unique qualities to enhance your career as a teacher?
7. Who can you form partnerships with to be more accountable to your goals?

**Personal Weaknesses**
1. What would you like to stop doing?
2. What are your blind spots?
3. What mistakes do you repeat over and over?
4. How do you sabotage your success?
5. How do you contribute to situations that undermine healthy relationships?
6. What excuses do you make for not accomplishing your goals or keeping your commitments?

**Personal Challenges**
1. What are you saying "yes" to that you should be saying "no"?
2. What are you saying "no" to that you should be saying "yes"?
3. What triggers your hot buttons?
4. What gets your life out of balance?
5. Who influences you in negative ways?
6. What are your greatest fears about failure and/or success?
7. What recurring patterns do you need to avoid or change?
8. What bothers you most about other people?

**Opportunities**
1. What opportunities have I experienced to help me attain my goals?
2. What opportunities should I seek out that will help me to attain my goals?
3. Who are the people who will serve as sources of support and encouragement in the pursuit of my goals?

We suggest you go through the questions above slowly in multiple sessions with times of reflection between to help you become better aware of where you are now and where you want to be in life. Self-awareness, as addressed earlier in Section II, is an important key to personal success and fulfillment. Be aware of any self-criticism or self-limiting beliefs that come up during this process. Begin with the assumption that you are worthy of every aspiration you have. It does not serve the world for you to think less of yourself. How will you inspire your students to reach for their dreams if you are not reaching for yours?

### Implementing and Maintaining Your Vision

There are a number of different ways to proceed. Listed below are some steps you can take to formulate, implement, and maintain your personal and professional vision:

1. Go through the questions above and produce a written list that reveals your values, dreams, desires, personal strengths, weakness, challenges, and opportunities. From that list you should be able to identify
   - the things you have passion for;
   - what you have natural talents or skills to perform well; and
   - actions that provide rewards both personally and professionally. Your individual "sweet spot" will lie somewhere within the intersection of those three areas.
2. Engage a friend to go through the list with you to give accurate feedback and a realistic assessment of how you answered the questions.
3. Create a vision board filled with affirming statements and pictures of what you want in life and place it where you'll see it often. Be sure to use words and pictures that elicit enthusiasm and passion.
4. Write a paragraph vividly describing your life vision of what you want to accomplish. Place it in your day planner or personal journal and read it daily.
5. Set some goals that will inspire you to action toward the fulfillment of your vision in the areas of family, career, faith, health, or whatever else is important to you.
6. Ask a friend or colleague to be an accountability partner. Give them permission to inquire regularly about your progress and to be bluntly honest if they see you lapse into periods of distraction, apathy, or plain laziness.
7. Regularly evaluate and manage priorities. Continually ask yourself, "Is this really what I want to be doing?" Everything you do should move you toward your intended destiny.
8. Celebrate your successes and do not just wait for the homeruns. Celebrate your base hits, too. Reward can be a tremendous motivator.
9. Maintain a grateful attitude. Based on the law of attraction, whatever we appreciate in our lives will grow. Continually speak positive words affirming your personal worthiness to fulfill an outstanding vision.
10. Act "as if" you have already accomplished your vision and do not allow fear to derail your success. Take action and the courage will follow.

To summarize, a vision will help you understand where you are today, where you are going tomorrow, and what you need to be doing along the way. To accomplish it you must be willing to prepare and work hard. You must be willing to be extremely honest to yourself, about yourself. There may be trials, tests, or risks encountered along the way and you may have to face down some huge fears as well. No one said achieving a great vision is easy, but be assured that each one of the challenges will help you grow stronger. You must be willing to fail, sometimes repeatedly, but keep pursuing your vision. As long as you are trying, you are not a failure. And maybe one day, just maybe, you will discover that instead of you building your vision, it has begun to build you.

### The Leader in You

Historically teachers taught. If you knew your content, that was enough. Unfortunately it is no longer "enough." You must be a manager, a content expert, a creative thinker, and a firm negotiator. All of these requirements confirm that no longer can we be just the educator. We must find the strength in ourselves to be the integrated educational leader, as it will take strong leaders to help our youth become well-balanced and confident adults. However, as you have read, this is not easy. It will take dedication. You must be tenacious. You must be willing. You must be confident. Workers are concerned with time and money. They sit at the back of meetings and put in time. Leaders are concerned with enhancement and cooperation. They have a career, are talented, and are professionals. Some teachers are workers, others are leaders (Wong & Wong, 2001). To make positive changes in education, you must become a leader.

To be an effective educator you must clearly possess the ability to lead. Being a great leader is more than simply standing in front of a group. Real leaders are known by the actions they take. Too often we assume that someone looks or sounds like a leader, but do we actually look at what they do behind the scenes? Do we know how they prepared? How they planned? How they goal set?

According to Matthew Swyers of *Inc.* (2012) leaders have four common traits: they aspire, they plan, they inspire, and they execute. Sounds just like a teacher! It does not matter if you are quiet or if you are charismatic, if you are cautious or a risk-taker. Leaders come in different packages and how they do the following may look different, but they do them. How will you do it?

**Aspire.** Great leaders have high expectations—for themselves and for others. They reach higher than others. They do not believe in accepting mediocrity.

> But if you aspire for greatness, even if you come up short, more likely than not you will still achieve a level greater than that which you knew you could reach. Great leaders always aim for goals higher than others think can be achieved. (Swyers, 2012)

**Plan.** To achieve greatness a leader must have a plan. Planning keeps us moving forward to the finish line.

> A goal without a plan is just a wish. —Antoine de Saint-Exupéry

**Inspire.** Before a leader can execute any plan, he or she must inspire those around him or her—help them to believe in the plan, take ownership of the plan, realize the hope that is within the plan. If you truly want your students and your classroom to be successful—healthy, safe, academically prosperous, and developmentally encouraging—you will need to inspire your students to want that, too.

> What you do makes a difference, and you have to decide what kind of difference you want to make. —Jane Goodall

**Execute.** You can do all of the above but if you fail to execute, the energy spent on the previous actions will be moot. Ultimately you must take action to reach your goal. Make and keep clear commitments, be accountable, communicate honestly and professionally, and **always** follow through.

> Whatever you do will be insignificant, but it is very important that you do it. —Mahatma Gandhi

Chapter 15

# Integrate and Lead

Becoming a successfully integrated educational leader has many facets, as we have discussed. Deciding purposefully to increase your success is the key. Intentional thoughts and the power you have to make things happen in your life and in the life of others are becoming a popular subject in many contexts (Dyer, 2005). Whether you believe in this idea on a spiritual level or as just a higher level of goal-setting, it can be said that without intention we have no vision. The following sections will recap what intentions you are encouraged to purposefully address in your life as an educator so that you find the power within yourself to become successful in your chosen career and self-development, as well as in the life of your learners.

The past is what it is. We cannot change it. All we can do is learn from it to make positive changes, but there will always be some who would have us never change. From the beginning of the European settlement in this country, the forcing of majority norms has been an issue. We have based our educational goals on the economic needs of the nation and we have neglected the educators who have been charged with developing our learners.

We encourage you to continue your journey and learn what events have affected today's educational system. Too often, as we have seen, we have neglectfully ignored our past actions, only to commit them again. To be a leader you must be willing to integrate your understanding of the past with the numerous skills that it will take to be successful.

Applying critical pedagogy and diversity management maturity to your skill set is also vital to your educational leadership development success. Understand that the need to belong is something we all desire and that to do this in diverse environments it takes thoughtfulness and knowledge. It is easy to disconnect from what we do not understand, whether in fear of offending another or that the task is too complicated. However, without strategically and intentionally applying cultural competency you will be unable to be successful with your learners, as we have seen from our past struggles.

Take the time. Read. Learn. Empathize. Consider. Know yourself. Know your biases. Know your weaknesses. When you have begun to critically look at yourself, it is then that you will have the ability to be the critical educator that is needed in today's schools. Developing cultural competence results in an ability to understand, communicate with, and effectively interact with people across cultures and is essential to becoming a successful leader in education. Remember that being culturally competent includes the following:

- The valuing of diversity
- Self-assessment of your own culture
- Understanding and awareness of the dynamics of cultural interactions
- Development of your cultural knowledge that is continual
- Positive adaption to diversity
- Acceptance of your role as a change agent and your power of influence as an educator

Becoming culturally competent in your classroom is not an option and it is not easy. Cultural competence is never fully realized, achieved, or completed, but rather cultural competence is a lifelong process that encourages positive leadership focused on positive changes. Educators will always encounter diverse learners, classrooms, families, and communities. It is vital to your successful classroom to apply cultural competence as an ongoing learning process for everyone in your contexts.

Remember that understanding yourself, your beliefs, biases, needs, and desires is as important as understanding those around you to becoming a leader. However, understanding that your first basic requirement is to satisfy your physiological needs is essential and often negated. You need healthy food, clean drinking water, and adequate shelter, as well as protection from diseases and autoimmune disorders, for wellness and motivation. Deficiencies in any of those areas can result in a diminished quality of living and even a shortened lifespan. You cannot perform at your best as a teacher if you are malnourished or physically ill. So you simply cannot afford to neglect your health. Eat a balanced and nutritious diet, exercise regularly, manage your weight, monitor your stress levels, and get regular medical checkups. Those actions are the greatest insurance you can give yourself against physical health problems.

Physical safety is also important as you address your needs; be free from the threats of physical harm can occur in your personal and professional life, and from many sources. Safety threats could come from other people, such as a stranger who threatens you or an intimate partner that emotionally breaks down your confidence, or it could come from the environment, such as being trapped in a burning building or working in a school where aggressive behavior is ignored. Risks to your physical or psychological health can be blatant or subversive. Whether in your personal life or in your work life, you must be aware and take care to eliminate certain risks within your environment to stay out of harm's way.

Being safe psychologically is also just as important but more often ignored. You can feel just as unsafe when faced with the taunts of a bully as you would be facing the knife of a mugger. Bullies in your environment may include abusive school administrators, peers, and even some students. If you see bullying going on anywhere, never ignore it. Seek help and alert the proper authorities. Toxic relationships can also decrease your psychological health as well as your self-esteem. Your career as a teacher is too important. Young lives are in your hands. Evaluate your relationships and make pertinent choices.

Have you heard the saying, "When you let go of negative people in your life, positive ones show up"? This is true and although difficult, it is important as you will encounter many negative situations in your chosen career: abused or malnourished children, family disputes, and in some cases, the loss of a great learner through accidental death or disease. You cannot afford to have negatives in your life. Finding a positive balance is crucial to assist you in stress and health wellness.

Understanding your need to belong to a specific social group or community is also important to your success. Here is where we formally cross from physical to psychological needs. Belonging to a group can add more meaning and direction to your life as well as a sense of identity. It can also boost your feelings of moral support from which you can draw strength in times of crisis. And finally, belonging to a group produces feelings of being wanted and loved, which makes you feel more valuable. Do not neglect your need to be a part of your school community, which includes your colleagues and students. When you feel like you "belong" you also boost your self-esteem and efficacy, which is another important facet of becoming the integrated leader in education.

Self-esteem is made up of two primary components: self-acceptance and self-love. Self-acceptance is the ability to acknowledge both your strengths and weaknesses and accept them as equally valid parts of who you are; self-love is the ability to be kind to yourself regardless of how many mistakes you make or how well you perform. It is such an easy concept to understand, but yet many never attend to its attainment. When you feel great about yourself, you are free to make mistakes, take risks, think outside of the box, be creative, and be giving of your time, energy, and self.

It is also important to note that you not only must be able to lead others but also be willing to lead yourself. No one succeeds in life by simply following. Sometimes you must have the courage to strike out on a bold new path into uncharted territories. Listed below are some steps that will help:

- Truth is not absolute but rather subjective based on changes in thinking. Consider Copernicus, Galileo, Da Vinci, Edison, and other great inventors, or Columbus, Lewis and Clark, Livingston, and other explorers, or Gandhi, King, or Mandela and all the champions of social change who have affected our world. Some may argue that these people happened to be in the right place at the right time. Maybe so, but if they hadn't had their eyes open to new possibilities it wouldn't have mattered if they were in the right place. As a great leader you must keep your eyes open and live in the question, "Who are the Galileos and Columbuses of today?" They are here. It is up to you to recognize and inspire them.
- Develop an insatiable appetite for learning through every source you can find. Someone once said, "When you're done learning, you're done." That is true! The greatest leaders are the most enthusiastic students. Continually seek to expand your horizons, both internally and externally. Feed your mind with new knowledge and expand your social connections as well. Seek out and meet new people as you immerse yourself in diverse social situations that broaden your view of the world. You never know when these new experiences will catapult you to new levels of leadership.
- Look beyond traditional paths of learning. Don't simply read books in the literary canon or the bestsellers list. Seek out seminars hosted by unconventional thinkers, teachers, and writers who allow room for questioning and debate. If you want to be a leader for positive change and innovation expand your thinking and look for answers from the most unsuspecting places.
- There are no leadership manuals that will provide instructions for every situation you encounter. You must have the courage to improvise based on your best judgment. Will you make mistakes? Absolutely! And do not make excuses when you do. Simply learn and make adjustments to

do better next time. Remember: Success comes from good judgment; good judgment comes from experience; and experience comes from bad judgment. Look at problems from all angles and solicit feedback from every direction.
- Find at least one person to help every day, even if there is no apparent advantage to you. That means giving of your time, energy, or money to further another person's success. Sometimes it will be a personal action for someone you care about and other times it could mean helping someone you don't know or particularly like. If you make it a point to help one person every day, then soon those thoughtful actions will transform into a habit, which will inspire others around you to do the same. Just imagine how much better the world would be if we all did a little more each day to help one another.

Awareness of your surroundings as well as how to manage them has also been introduced to you as a future leader in education and will play a key role in a successful career. To increase your ability to make good decisions, manage your emotions, and apply practical strategies, you must know what you are up against. Managing relationships in education can be challenging, but the reward will be your happiness and fulfillment in a career that you love. Take the time to understand, to care, to empathize, to communicate, and to be thankful. Without these you can truly never be a leader.

Social awareness is being able to observe other people and recognize and even appreciate their individuality. In a word it is *empathy*. The empathetic leader can read a person's facial expressions and other nonverbal signals, in addition to listening to the inflection of their voice, to understand what the individual is feeling. The ability to empathize is especially important for teachers. The better you understand your students, the better you will be at helping them achieve learning objectives.

Your effectiveness as a leader will be much stronger through incorporating the power of influence rather than simply the power of authority. What makes a leader influential? Trust. Here are some practical tips to build trust:

- Listen with both your ears and eyes. Do not mentally rehearse what you are going to say in response. Do not interrupt or rush to give advice or try to fix problems. Do not change the subject. Simply allow the person to have his or her moment while you fully engage in what is being said. Then ask questions to clarify you understand what the message really is.

- Pay attention to the person's tone of voice to hear the hidden emotions behind what they are saying. Watch their body language, especially the face and posture. This is the way people often communicate what they think or feel, even when their verbal communication says something different. Are they frowning or showing frustration? Do they come across as fearful or apprehensive? Are they slouched or holding their head down? Any of those gestures indicate a message they may not be speaking. When you hear a tone of voice or observe a body gesture you are not sure about, do not make any assumptions. Ask the person what it means.
- Words only account for 7% of the total message that people receive. The other 93% of the message is contained in the tone of voice (38%) and body language (55%) (Mehrabian, 2009). For effective and accurate communication about emotions, those three parts of the message need to be congruent with each other. For example, a person might display the following:
    - Verbal: "I don't have a problem with you!"
    - Nonverbal signs: He avoids eye contact; his forehead is furled and he looks angry; his arms are crossed, revealing a closed body language.

If this type of scenario happens, there is sufficient indication that his words do not accurately reveal his feelings. It is important to note that in respect to Mehrabian's studies, the experiments dealt with communications of feelings and attitudes (i.e., like versus dislike), and a disproportionate influence of voice tone and body language becomes effective only when the situation is ambiguous. Such ambiguity is likely to appear when the words spoken are inconsistent with the tone of voice or body language of the speaker. When that happens, ask the person what those indicators mean.

- Don't take phone calls, check your email, look at your watch, or engage in other distracting behavior while trying to hold a meaningful conversation. Put yourself in the other person's shoes (another definition for empathy). How would you feel if someone did that to you? Look directly at the person and call the person by name. A person's name is one of the sweetest names they will hear, especially if it is spoken nicely. When you address a person by name it sends a message that you care about the person as an individual. Ask questions about things that are important to him or her such as family, hobbies, aspirations, or challenges. And never forget to smile.

You can consciously choose how you engage with other people, and how to use the power of social awareness and empathy to relate to others. Train you mind by setting an intention and practicing the tips above to connect with others in meaningful and powerful ways. You must first understand others before expecting them to understand you. As a teacher and leader, this skill is fundamental to leading and influencing others.

There are many definitions of the meaning of success; however, the following incorporates much of the sited meanings in the literature and from spiritual resources. Ron Haynes (2005) contends that Remember that you and only you can define what success is. It will differ, at least a little, for everyone. Additionally success may be defined differently for you in different contexts. As an educator you may define success in one way. As a community leader, another. As a parent, yet another. However, all of these reside under one big umbrella. This umbrella is your life and you will, at some point, need to define what success is in general—for your life, your journey. However, to have a completely successful life we contend that you will need to consider these six components:

Can anyone truly consider themselves successful if they lack this ingredient? Can a leader lead without this? People around the world are constantly searching for peace of mind: a freedom from fear, worry, anger, and guilt. People seek peace of mind through many channels, some destructive and some worthwhile. Some seek peace of mind through faith, some through money, others in relationships, others in work, and still others seek to fill this void through participation in vices such as gambling or drugs. Success, no matter how you define it, must have peace of mind in the mix; otherwise, your success will be bland and watered down.

"Success" without good health and the energy to enjoy life is not success at all; it is just a shell of what it can be. Any success without health and energy is like a high performance car with no gasoline in the tank.

We all need to be loved and no matter how much financial success someone enjoys, it is a hollow feeling if you have no one to share it with.

That is, freedom from thinking about money all the time. Not necessarily being "rich," but having enough money to pay your bills, feed your family, and take care of basic necessities.

Humans need to feel as if they are making a difference. We desperately want to improve ourselves, or someone, or something. It is just human nature. Set clear goals so that you too will make a difference.

Also called self-actualization, this is the concept of "being all you can be," of feeling like you matter and that you are making a difference. This is the feeling that you are not just going through the motions for no reason, that what you do and who you are are of vital importance. If you have the first five components, but feel unfulfilled and useless, you cannot enjoy the full measure of success.

You do have the power within yourself to be an integrated leader in education, no matter your background, past mistakes, past triumphs, your level of bias, your "natural" talent. If you intentionally focus on what success looks like and how to achieve it with your students you will be successful. The only thing that is holding back the educators of today is permission to be leaders. We encourage you as you continue on your journey to approach everything you do, everything you learn, as something that you will apply to your skill set. You will apply it to your self-awareness. You will apply it to your management of others. You will apply it to your relationships.

If you want to be the kind of teacher that does make a difference, then you must decide to be sacrificial in your pride. You must be willing to learn what you think you already know. You must be willing to lift and encourage others. And you must be willing to be honest with yourself. The components that make up the Integrated Educational Leadership Model are not new. This model includes all of the tools that teachers have been receiving for years. But, when they are woven together and approached as a way to find self-actualization and hope in a career that has been under scrutiny and has faced numerous challenges for many years, it is exciting.

A fully integrated leader is one who has learned how to integrate the following qualities into a part of who they are:

- The identification of personal strengths, weaknesses, values, and passions, along with an authenticity that evokes the trust of others.
- The ability to communicate effectively with empathy and build relationships through the power of influence.
- The demonstration of competency with the ability to apply what you have learned without allowing preexisting beliefs to manage your knowledge for you.

This person balances directive/authoritative/self-confident style with collaboration, encouragement, empathy, and concern. A tilt too far in either direction can lead to an imbalance. If a leader is relationship oriented, he or she cannot make hard decisions or command the authority he or she needs to lead effectively. This leader may find difficulty in inspiring and motivating people. Sometimes leaders have to possess the courage to make tough decisions.

Trying to please everyone ends up pleasing no one. On the other hand, if a leader is so authoritative or controlling that people become afraid to raise questions or disagree, then inspiration and motivation become diminished as well. There is a difference between compliance and commitment. If a leader is always forcing compliance to a given set rules, what will happen if he or she leaves the room? Leaders who are obsessed with command and control send a message that they do not trust people to make good decisions. When people are treated like they are untrustworthy, they often became exactly that.

An integrated leadership style is one that combines the best of both styles, bathed in cultural competency. Depending on the situation, one style might be more appropriate than another, but the integrated leader doesn't always default to one particular personal preference. With an integrated style, the focus is on collaboration (win/win), rather than compromise (win/lose). It can be competitive yet collaborative, focused and diffused. The integrated leader is rational and objective yet subjective and operates intuitively, balancing action with deliberation.

If you lead with an integrated style, you will build and maintain an environment of trust. To influence people to accept your directives and commit to work toward common goals practice the following actions:

- Establish clear expectations of codes of conduct (group values) and they are important.
- Commit to these expectations.
- Set specific, achievable goals and provide the resources along with the skills your learners need to attain them.
- Clarify the rewards versus consequences for standards of work performance and emphasize that each is the result of their personal choices of actions.
- Tell people, including your learners, the truth and never compromise your own integrity. People are always watching you and actions will speak much louder than words. Also never ask others to compromise their individual integrity.
- Continually share information openly. Communication should always be a two-way process. Listen to what others have to say and respect their perspective.
- Be a servant leader. Put aside your own ego and act in the best interest of others and never expect more from them than you are willing to give yourself.

Commit to becoming a fully integrated leader. Provide a vision for the future and motivate others by making them feel important and appreciated, especially your learners. Always act ethically, be true to your own values, and lead by example. Display a personal commitment to continuous learning and self-improvement, and nurture an environment where others are inspired to continuously learn and improve as well. Be a leader that others choose to follow.

Choosing to be a leader, as we have explained, takes the ability for you to integrate numerous skills and take ownership of your success. The power within you exists to make a difference in improving education for everyone. You must be willing to accept your challenge and be willing to never stop learning to accomplish your goals, your vision. Tomorrow's learners need teachers willing to make the difference, which means that all aspects of your life must be considered to encourage health, balance, and positive self-encouragement. You are exactly what our future needs, and you must protect yourself from the negative implications of our past, the media, the lack of vision, and the inconsistencies of what success is. Choose now to become this leader. Make your vision count. Use the Integrated Educational Leadership Model to intentionally choose your journey—one that is positive, fulfilling, and successful. Integration of all you learn must be intentional and purposeful:

- Develop cultural competency, empathy, and maturity
- Become self-aware and take ownership of managing yourself: "If you want to manage somebody, manage yourself. Do that well and you'll be ready to stop managing. And start leading."
    - Address your needs
    - Know who you are
    - Be self-determined by effectively cultivating your needs for autonomy, competency, and belonging
    - Become a positive influence on cultural competency and diversity management
- Become socially aware
    - Acknowledge others' needs
- Manage your relationships
    - In your classrooms
    - In your personal life
    - A culturally competent environment must have clearly defined goals that include accountability and evaluation based on the identified community, considering others, and accepting feedback from everyone.

- Focus on your future
  - Be intentional
  - Be focused
  - Be purposeful

Teachers do make a difference and you, too, will make a difference, but the challenges are increasing. It is important that you realize your value *and* its importance to address appropriately these challenges. As you continue to prepare, be open to changes in what you think, what you want to believe. Those involved in your training want you to be successful. Find the gem in every situation, because even in the most unobvious places, there are things we can learn about ourselves, about others, about making a difference.

Throughout the writing of this manuscript, hundreds of stories from students and teachers have been sent to us. These stories include teachers who have literally saved students from harm, inspired students to be more, encouraged students to believe in themselves. Stories from teachers have also been numerous: teachers who have been touched by their students and their families; teachers who have dedicated themselves to the long days, emotional see-saws, and little appreciation—all to make a difference. One story we received included a teacher who had taught for 50 years; now that is dedication!

We encourage you to make it look and feel fabulous and fulfilled! To pave your path, it will take more from you every day. More. But you will make a difference as you develop yourself as a leader through the power you have within, and the inner power you will develop by becoming an integrated educational leader can move mountains; you just have to be aware of what your mountain looks like.

We end this with our gratefulness to you—a future teacher who wants to be the best—and encourage you to do just that. Become the Integrated Educational Leader that your learners need. In the words of Woodrow Wilson:

> *"You are not here merely to make a living. You are here in order to enable the world to live more amply, with greater vision, with a finer spirit of hope and achievement. You are here to enrich the world, and you impoverish yourself if you forget the errand."*

## Section IV Review

**Section Activities**

**Activity 1**: Form a discussion group or consider these questions individually:
- What are the changes that have taken place in the past 10 years that have profoundly affected the way you live today?
- How have those changes affected you in a positive way?
- What are the changes that you anticipate happening in the next 10 years?
- What are your greatest fears concerning those changes?
- How can you begin now to prepare for those and transform them into a positive?

**Activity 2**: Vision points to lead in a small group or reflect on individually:
- Spend time thinking about what you want your life to look like 10–20 years from now. If you don't know what you want, how can you get there?
- Give yourself permission to dream big. Don't shoot down a dream for tomorrow just because you think it's too far outside your reach today. Anything is possible. Conceive, believe, and achieve, in that order.
- Close your eyes and mentally picture yourself at some point in the future. Imagine being completely fulfilled and content with your life. Where are you? What are you doing? Who are you with?

**Activity 3**: Do you have the desire to become a great leader? Listed below are some key leadership traits to discuss and work on with your students:

1. Have you clearly articulated your vision? As a leader, you must communicate your vision to those you want to follow you. First paint a picture with words. Speak it, write it, draw it, or whatever methods you can use to clearly convey what you want. As they say, "A picture is worth a thousand words." Second, ask your students to describe, in their own words, what they understand about your vision. How close is it to what you thought they understood? Are they on the same page

as you? Also keep in mind that you should reevaluate periodically to stay current with the changing times. Remember to involve others in keeping you up to date if you truly want them to buy in. It must be their vision, too.

2. Do you exude enthusiasm? Your passion is infectious. If your students catch it, they'll go to the ends of earth because of it. You've got to light the "fire in their bellies," to get them to feel passion about your vision. This is such a key part of being a great leader that if you don't have it, you simply won't be effective. Think of all the great leaders throughout history and try to name one that didn't possess great passion. When you talk about your vision for their future, let your passion shine through. Others will feel it and want to get on board with you. If you don't have passion, how can expect them to catch it? On a scale from 1 to 10, how would others rate your passion level? What do you need to do to get it to at least an 8?

3. Do you have character that others trust and respect? Who you are speaks much louder than the words you say. Without character, all the other traits will be negated. That is because your character strengths and limitations will play a critical role in your leadership influence. People, especially children, mimic what we do rather than what we say. Keep in mind that others are always watching you, even when you aren't aware. Be authentic, accountable, and willing to own and grow from your mistakes. How do you respond to feedback? Do you have a peer that you trust and respect who will serve as an accountability partner?

4. Do you focus on building people? As an educator your first responsibility is to educate and grow your students. How do you do that? You start by setting clear expectations and then delegating responsibility to your students and letting them run with it. Don't breathe down their necks or stand over their shoulders, but do make yourself available if questions or problems arise. Teach your team to analyze solutions and give them the freedom to work through their own decisions. When they fall behind, don't start pointing fingers. That is when you need to inspire confidence the most by letting them know you support them and are ready to help. Don't forget to use humor to keep their spirits up during tough times. When a crisis hits, they will look to you to be a tower of strength and endurance. What are you doing to grow your students? How are you preparing them with life skills to make wise decisions and responsible choices as adults?

5. Are you a transactional or transformational decision maker? How are major decisions made in your classes? What process do you use for making them? For example, do you discuss strategies with your students and create a list of pros and cons about choices, along with the rewards and consequences for choices? Transactional decision makers are "my way or the highway" types of leaders who garner compliance more than commitment. There are times when that style may be appropriate, say, if you're a drill sergeant preparing your recruits to go into battle. But rarely will this be the case. On the other hand, transformational decision makers are more democratic and lead by influence derived from offering choices. If you adopt this style, your students will much more likely be committed to the desired outcome. Would you consider yourself to be primarily a transactional or a transformational leader? How's that working for you? More importantly, how's that working for your students?

# APPENDIX

## Mental Health Sources

The following organizations have developed materials about mental illnesses and their treatment that may be useful to you or your students. Much of the information is available on the World Wide Web. Phone numbers are also provided here for your reference.

American Academy of Child and Adolescent Psychiatry (AACAP)
http://www.aacap.org
1-202-966-7300
The AACAP is the leading national professional medical association dedicated to treating and improving the quality of life of children, adolescents, and families affected by mental, behavioral, or developmental disorders. The organization includes over 6,500 child and adolescent psychiatrists and other interested physicians. This site provides information about child and adolescent psychiatry, fact sheets for parents and caregivers, updates on current research on children's mental health, and information on managed care. It also includes guidelines for seeking a child or adolescent psychiatrist and a referral directory.

American Psychiatric Association (APA)
http://www.psych.org
1-703-907-7300
Over 38,000 U.S. and international physicians are members of the APA making it the world's largest psychiatric organization. The vision of the organization is to ensure that high-quality psychiatric diagnosis and treatment is available and accessible for all people who have a mental disorder. The Web site includes information about mental illnesses for the public, advice for choosing a psychiatrist, breaking news about mental illnesses, advocacy information to reduce stigma associated with mental illness, and books and other publications related to mental illness.

Attention Deficit Information Network Inc. (AD-IN)
http://www.addinfonetwork.com
1-781-455-9895
AD-IN is a nonprofit, volunteer organization that offers support and information to families of children with ADD, adults with ADD, and mental health professionals. The AD-IN network of parent and adult support chapters throughout the United States provides information on training programs and speakers. AD-IN also presents conferences and workshops for parents and professionals on current issues, research, and treatments for ADD.

Center for Mental Health Services (CMHS)
http://www.mentalhealth.org/cmhs/
1-800-789-2647
The CMHS, a component of the U.S. Department of Health and Human Services, is charged with leading the national system that delivers mental health services. The mission of the center is to provide treatment and support services needed by adults and children with mental disorders and serious emotional problems.

Children and Adults with Attention-Deficit/Hyperactivity Disorder (CHADD)
http://www.chadd.org
1-800-233-4050
CHADD is a major advocate and key information source for people dealing with attention disorders. The organization sponsors support groups and publishes two newsletters concerning attention disorders for parents and professionals. In addition to providing general information on ADHD, the organization offers referrals to CHADD chapters, branches, and other organizations that serve people with ADHD.

Depression and Bipolar Support Alliance (DBSA)
http://www.DBSAlliance.org
1-800-826-3632
The mission of DBSA is to improve the lives of people living with mood disorders. The organization seeks to educate patients, families, and the public concerning the nature of depressive illnesses. DBSA maintains an extensive catalog of helpful books, as well as a list of support groups throughout the United States.

National Alliance for the Mentally Ill (NAMI)
http://www.nami.org
HelpLine: 1-800-950-NAMI (6264)
NAMI is a nonprofit, grassroots, self-help support and advocacy organization of families and friends of people with severe mental illnesses such as schizophrenia, major depression, bipolar disorder, obsessive-compulsive disorder, and anxiety disorders. This site includes links to local affiliates and support groups, an 800-number help line, information about mental illnesses and their treatment, and brief articles describing the results of research studies on mental illnesses and their treatment.

National Alliance for Research on Schizophrenia and Depression (NARSAD)
http://www.narsad.org
1-800-829-8289
NARSAD is an organization of concerned families linked with professionals to raise and distribute funds for scientific research into the causes, cures, treatments, and prevention of brain disorders, especially schizophrenia, depression, and bipolar disorder.

National Institute of Mental Health (NIMH)
http://www.nimh.nih.gov
1-301-443-4513
1-866-615-NIMH (6464)
The mission of the NIMH is to diminish the burden of mental illness through research. This site provides current and authoritative information about the latest research on mental illness.

National Mental Health Association (NMHA)
http://www.nmha.org
1-800-969-NMHA (6642)
The NMHA is the oldest and largest nonprofit organization in the United States that addresses all aspects of mental health and mental illness. This site provides information about a variety of mental illnesses and their treatments, as well as a directory of local NMHA affiliates. The directory will help you locate mental health resources that are relatively near your school. This site also includes news regarding the advocacy efforts of the NMHA and a list of additional mental health resources.

National Mental Health Consumers' Self-Help Clearinghouse
http://www.mhselfhelp.org
1-800-553-4key (4539)
The National Mental Health Consumers' Self-Help Clearinghouse is a consumer-run, national technical-assistance center that helps connect individuals with self-help and advocacy resources. The organization also provides expertise to self-help groups and other peer-run services for mental health consumers.

Suicide Prevention: United States National Suicide and Crisis Hotlines
National Suicide Prevention Hotline
http://suicidehotlines.com/national.html
1-800-SUICIDE/1-800-784-2433
For more information about child traumatic stress and the National Child Traumatic Stress Network, visit www.NCTSNet.org or e-mail info@NCTSNet.org

# REFERENCES

Abraham, R. (1999). Emotional intelligence in organizations: A conceptualization. *Genetic, Social & General Psychology Monographs, 125*(2), 209–225.

Adams, J. S. 1965. Inequity in social exchange. *Advances in Experimental Social Psychology. 62.* 335-343.

Alexander, K., Entwisle, D., & Horsey, C.. (1997). From first grade forward: Early foundations of high school dropout. *Sociology of Education, 70*(2), 87–107.

Alexander, K., Entwisle, D., & Thompson, M. (1987). School performance, status relations, and the structure of sentiment: Bringing the teacher back in. *American Sociological Review, 52*(5), 665–682.

Alliance for Excellent Education. (2005). *Teacher attrition: A costly loss to the nation and to the states.* Retrieved from http://www.all4ed.org/files/archive/publications/

Allinder, R. M. (1994). The relationship between efficacy and the instructional practices of special education teachers and consultants. *Teacher Education and Special Education, 17*(2), 86–95.

Altemeyer, R. A. (1988). *Enemies of freedom: Understanding right-wing authoritarianism.* San Francisco: Jossey-Bass.

American Psychological Association. (2007). *Stress survey: Stress a major health problem in the U.S.* APA Help Center. Retrieved from http://www.apahelpcenter.org

American Psychological Association. (2008). *Stress in America.* Retrieved from http://apahelpcenter.mediaroom.com

American Psychological Association (2013). *Stress: The different kinds of stress.* Retrieved from http://www.apa.org/helpcenter/stress-kinds.aspx

Amunts, K., Kedo, O., Kindler, M., Pieperhoff, P., Mohlberg, H., Shah, N., Zilles, K. (2005). Cytoarchitectonic mapping of the human amygdala, hippocampal region and entorhinal cortex: Intersubject variability and probability maps. *Anatomy and Embryology, 210* (5), 343–352.

Anderson, D. W. (2003). Special education as reconciliation. *Journal of Education & Christian Belief, 7*(1), 23-35.

Ashton, P. T., & Webb, R. B. (1986). *Making a difference: Teachers' sense of efficacy and student achievement.* New York: Longman.

Associated Press. (2012). *US poverty rate to hit highest level since 1965, economists say.* Retrieved from http://www.cnbc.com/

Ball, D. (1988). Unlearning to teach mathematics. *Learning of Mathematics, 8*(1), 40–48.

Bandura, A. (1997). *Self efficacy: The exercise of control.* New York: W. H. Freeman and Company.

Banks, J. (2002). *Diversity within unity: Essential principles for teaching and learning in a multicultural society.* New Horizons for Learning. Retrieved from http://www.nsrfharmony.org/fac_equity/diversity_unity.pdf

Banks, J. (2004). Multicultural education: Historical development, dimensions, and practice. In J. A. Banks, & C. A. M. Banks (Eds.), *Handbook of research on multicultural education* (2nd ed., pp. 3-29). San Francisco: Jossey-Bass.

Barnes, D. (1992). *From communication to curriculum.* Portsmouth, NH: Heinemann.

Beck, M., & Malley, J. (1998). A pedagogy of belonging. *Reclaiming Children and Youth, 7*(3), 133–137.

Blanchard, K. (1992). The seven dynamics of change. *The Inside Guide.* Retrieved from http://www.theresourcechannel.com.au/the-inside-guide.

Bohannan, P. (1995). *How culture works.* New York: Free Press.

Borg, G. (1998). *Borg's Perceived Exertion and Pain Scales.* Champaign, IL: Human Kinetics

Bowler, R. M., Smith, M. W., Schwarzer, R., Perez-Arce, P., & Kreutzer, R. A. (2002). Neuropsychological and academic characteristics of Mexican-American children: A longitudinal study. *Applied Psychology: An International Review, 51*(3), 458–478.

Brewster, C., & Railsback, J. (2003). *Building trusting relationships for school improvement: Implications for principals and teachers.* Portland, OR: Northwest Regional Educational Laboratory.

Bryant-Davis, T., & Ocampo, C. (2005). Racist incident–based trauma. *The Counseling Psychologist, 33*(4), 479–500.

Buckingham, M. (2001). *Now, discover your strengths.* New York: Simon & Schuster.

Burchard, B. (2012). *The charge.* New York: Free Press.

Bureau of Justice Statistics. (2012). *Measuring the prevalence of crime with the national crime victimization survey.* Retrieved from http://bjs.ojp.usdoj.gov/

Caprara, G. V., Barbaranelli, C., Borgogni, L., & Steca, P. (2003). Efficacy beliefs as determinants of teachers' job satisfaction. *Journal of Educational Psychology, 95*(4), 821–832.

Carmeli, A., & Josman, Z. E. (2006). The relationship among emotional intelligence, task performance, and organizational citizenship behaviors. *Human Performance, 19*(4), 403–419.

Carpenter, D., & Ramirez, A. (2007). More than one gap: Dropout rate gaps between and among Black, Hispanic, and White students. *Journal of Advanced Academics, 19*(1), 32–64.

Carpenter, D., II, Ramirez, A., & Severn, L. (2006). Gap or gaps: Challenging the singular definition of the achievement gap. *Education and Urban Society, 39* (1), 113–127.

Carpenter, J. W. (2010). Interview. *Teach for America.* Retrieved from http://www.teachforamerica.org/

Carroll, T. (2004). *The high cost of teacher turnover.* Policy brief prepared for the National Commission on Teaching and America's Future.

Center for Immigration Study. (2007). *Immigrants in the United States.* Retrieved on July 1, 2012, from http://www.cis.org/

Centers for Disease Control and Prevention (1999). *Strategies for preventing job stress suggested by CDC in new publication.* Retrieved from http://www.cdc.gov/niosh/updates/stresrel.html

Centers for Disease Control and Prevention and the National Center for Injury Prevention Control. (2008). *Promoting healthy parenting practices across cultural groups: A CDC research brief.* Retrieved from http://www.cdc.gov/ncipc/pub-res/

Chapman, C., Laird, J., Ifill, N., & Kewal-Ramani, A. (2011). *Trends in High School Dropout and Completion Rates in the United States: 1972–2009* (NCES 2012-006). U.S. Department of Education. Washington, DC: National Center for Education Statistics. Retrieved from http://nces.ed.gov/pubsearch

Chapman, D., Perry G., & Strine T. (2005). The vital link between chronic disease and depressive disorders. *Preventing Chronic Disorders, 2(1).* Retrieved from http://www.cdc.gov/

Charach, A., Pepler, D., & Ziegler, S. (1995). Bullying at school—a Canadian perspective: A survey of problems and suggestions for intervention. *Education Canada, 35*(1), 12–18.

Cherlin, A. (2005). American marriage in the early twenty-first century. *The Future of Children, 15*(2), 33–55.

Cherniss, C. (1980). *Professional burnout in human service organizations.* New York: Praeger.

Cherniss, C. (2000). Social and emotional competence in the workplace. In R. Bar-on & J. D. A. Parker (Eds.), *The handbook of emotional intelligence* (pp. 433–458). San Francisco: Jossey-Bass.

Cochran-Smith, M. (1997). Knowledge, skills, and experiences for culturally diverse learners: A perspective for practicing teachers. In J. J. Irvine (Ed.), *Critical knowledge for diverse teachers & learners* (pp. 27–87). Washington, DC: American Association of Colleges for Teacher Education.

Connolly, J., & Viswesvaran, C. (2000). The role of affectivity in job satisfaction: A metaanalysis. *Personality and Individual Differences, 29,* 265–281.

Cornille, T., Boyer, A. E., & Smith, C. K. (1983). Schools and newcomers: A national survey of innovative programs. *Personnel Digest, 62,* 229–236.

Costa, P. T., Jr., & Mc Crae, R. R. (1992). Four ways five factors are basic. *Personality and Individual Differences, 13,* 653–665.

Craig, W., & Pepler, D. (1997). Observations of bullying and victimization in the schoolyard. *Canadian Journal of School Psychology, 2,* 41–60.

Craig, W. M., Pepler, D. J., & Atlas, R. (2000). Observations of bullying on the playground and in the classroom. *International Journal of School Psychology, 21,* 22–36.

Crandall, J. (1981). *Theory and measurement of social interest.* New York: Columbia University Press.

Crimes Against Children Research Center at the University of New Hampshire (2000). *Internet.* Retrieved from http://www.unh.edu/ccrc/internet-crimes/

Cummins, J. (1986). Empowering minority students: A framework for intervention. *Harvard Educational Review, 56*(1), 18–36.

Cummins, J. (1992). Bilingual education and English immersion: The Ramírez report in theoretical perspective. *Bilingual Research Journal, 16*(1), 95–104.

Darling-Hammond, L. (1997). *The right to learn: A blueprint for creating schools that work.* San Francisco: Jossey-Bass.

Darling-Hammond, L. (2006a). No Child Left Behind and high school reform. *Harvard Educational Review, 76*(4), 642–667.

Darling-Hammond, L. (2006b). *Powerful teacher education: Lessons from exemplary programs.* San Francisco: John Wiley.

Darling-Hammond, L. (2007). Evaluating No Child Left Behind. *The Nation.* Retrieved from http://www.thenation.com/doc/20070521.

Deci, E. L., & Ryan, R. M. (1985). *Intrinsic motivation and self-determination in human behavior.* New York: Plenum.

Deci, E., & Ryan, R. (2000). The "what" and "why" of goal pursuits: Human needs and the self-determination of behavior. *Psychological Inquiry, 11*(4), 227–268.

Deci, E. L., Ryan, R. M., Gagné, M., Leone, D. R., Usunov, J., & Kornazheva, B. P. (2001). Need satisfaction, motivation, and well-being in the work organizations of a former Eastern Bloc country. *Personality and Social Psychology Bulletin, 27*(8), 930–942.

DeVoe, J. F., & Kaffenberger, S. K. (2005). *Student reports of bullying: Results from the 2001 School Crime Supplement to the National Crime Victimization Survey* (NCES 2005-310). Washington, DC: U.S. Department of Education.

Dietrich, L. (1998). *Chicana adolescents: Bitches, 'ho's, and schoolgirls.* (PUB CITY): Greenwood.

Dimaggio, G., Lysaker, P., Carcione, A., Nicolò, G., & Semerari, A. (2008). Know yourself and you shall know the other... to a certain extent: Multiple paths of influence of self-reflection on mindreading. *Consciousness and Cognition, 17(3),* 778-789.

Dominice, P. (2000). *Learning from our lives: Using educational biographies with adults.* SanFrancisco, CA.: Jossey-Bass.

Dyer, W. (2005). *Power of intention.* Hay House.

Eaton, J. (1980). Stress in social work practice. In C. L. Cooper & J. Marshall (Eds.), *White collar and professional stress* (pp. 167–185). Chichester: John Wiley.

Eigenberger, M. E. (1998). Fear as a correlate of authoritarianism. *Psychological Reports, 83,* 1395–1409.

Faber, C. (1991). Is local control of the schools still a viable option? *Harvard Journal of Law,* 447.

Farkas, S., Johnson, J., Foleno, T. (2000). *A sense of calling: Who teaches and why. A report from public agenda.* Retrieved from http://www.publicagenda.org/

Feiman-Nemser, S. (1990). Teacher preparation: Structural and conceptual alternatives. In W. Houston (Ed.), *Handbook of research on teacher education.* New York: Macmillan.

Feiman-Nemser, S., McDiarmid, G. W., Melnick, S. L. & Parker, M. (1989). *Changing beginning teachers' conceptions: a description of an introductory teacher education course.* East Lansing, MI: National Center for Research in Teacher Education, Michigan State University.

Fetler, M. (1999). High school staff characteristics and mathematics test results. *Education Policy Analysis Archives, 7*(9), 1-23.

Foster, M. (1995). African American teachers and culturally relevant pedagogy. In J. A. Banks & C. A. M. Banks (Eds.), *Handbook of Research on Multicultural Education* (pp. 570–581). New York: Macmillan.

Freidson, E. (1986). *Professional powers: A study of the institutionalization of formal knowledge.* Chicago: University of Chicago Press.

Frey, K. S., Hirschstein, M. K., Snell, J. L., Edstrom, L. V., MacKenzie, E. P., & Broderick, C. J. (2005). Reducing playground bullying and supporting beliefs: An experimental trial of the steps to respect program. *Developmental Psychology, 41(3),*479-490.

Friedman, M., & Rosenman, R. (1974). *Type A behavior and your heart.* Greenwich, CT: Fawcett Crest.

Furnham, A. (1999). Personality and creativity. *Perceptual and Motor Skills, 88,* 407–408.

Garcia, E. (1991). *Education of linguistically and culturally diverse students: Effective instructional practices.* National Center for Research on Cultural Diversity and Second Language Learning: University of California. Retrieved from http://repositories.cdlib.org/

Garcia, E. (1994). *Understanding and meeting the challenge of student diversity.* Boston: Houghton Mifflin.

Garcia, S., & Malkin, D. (1993). Toward defining programs and services for culturally and linguistically diverse learners in special education. *Teaching Exceptional Children, 26*(1), 52–58.

Garfinkel, B., Hoberman, H., Parsons, J., & Walker, J. (1986). *Adolescent stress, depression and suicide: Minnesota study.* United States. Congress. House Select Committee on Children, Youth, and Families.

Garner, R. (2005). Nearly half of teachers have suffered from mental illness. *The Independent.* Retrieved from http://www.independent.co.uk/news.

Gay, G. (2000). *Culturally responsive teaching: Theory, research, and practice.* New York: Teachers College Press.

Gay G. (2002). Culturally responsive teaching in special education for ethnically diverse students: Setting the stage. *International Journal of Qualitative Studies in Education, 15*(6), 613–629.

Georgia Bureau of Investigation (GBI). (2011). *Special investigation into CRCT cheating at APS.* Retrieved from http://www.ajc.com/news/volume-1-of-special-1000798.html

Gibbs, C. (2005). Teachers' cultural self-efficacy: Teaching and learning in multicultural settings. *New Zealand Journal of Educational Studies, 40*(1/2), 101- 112.

Gibson, S., & Dembo, M. (1984). Teacher efficacy: A construct validation. *Journal of Educational Psychology, 76*(4), 569–582.

Glass, L. (1995). Toxic People. New York: Simon & Schuster

Gleitman H., Fridlund, A., & Reisberg, D. (2004). *Psychology* (6th ed.). New York: Norton.

Goddard, R. D. (2001). Collective efficacy: A neglected construct in the study of schools and student achievement. *Journal of Educational Psychology, 93*(3), 467–476.

Goddard, R., Hoy, W., & Woolfolk Hoy, A. (2000). Collective teacher efficacy: Its meaning, measure, and impact on student achievement. *American Educational Research Journal, 37*(2), 479–507.

Gold, Y., & Roth, R. A. (1993). *Teachers managing stress and preventing burnout: The professional health solution.* Washington, DC: The Falmer Press.

Goldstein, L. (1999). The relational zone: The role of caring relationships in the co-construction of mind. *American Educational Research Journal, 36*(3), 647-673.

Goleman, D. (1995). *Emotional intelligence: Why it can matter more than IQ for character, health and lifelong achievement.* Bantam Books, New York.

Goleman, D. (1996). *Emotional intelligence: Why it can matter more than IQ.* New York: Bantam.

Goleman, D. (2011). *The brain and emotional intelligence: New insights.* Northampton, MA: More Than Sound.

Good, T. L. (2012). Two decades of research on teacher expectations: Findings and future directions. *Journal of Teacher Education, 63*(4), 947-961.

Goodenow, C. (1993). The psychological sense of school membership among adolescents. *Psychology in the Schools, 10*(1), 79–90.
Gopaul-McNicol, S., & Thomas-Presswood, T. N. (1998). *Working with linguistically and culturally different children: Innovative clinical and educational approaches.* Boston: Allyn & Bacon.
Gorman, J., & Balter, L. (1997). Culturally sensitive parent education: A critical review of quantitative research. *Review of Educational Research, 67*(3), 339–369.
Gornick, J. (2001). Restructuring gender relations and employment: The decline of the male breadwinner. (edited by Rosemary Crompton) *American Journal of Sociology, 106(5),* 1472-1474.
Grant, C. & Secada, W. (1990). Preparing teachers for diversity. In W. Robert Houston (Ed.). *Handbook of research in teacher education.* New York: MacMillan.
Grau, R., Salanova, M., & Peiró, J. M. (2000). Modulatory effects of self-efficacy in occupational stress. *Psychology Notes,* 18(1), 57-75.
Gray, S. (2005). *An enquiry into continuing professional development for teachers.* University of Cambridge. Retrieved from http://gtcni.openrepository.com
Griffin, G. (1999). *The education of teachers.* Chicago: University of Chicago Press.
Guild, P. (2001). Diversity, learning style and culture. *New Horizons for Learning.* Retrieved from http://www.newhorizons.org/strategies/styles/guild.htm
Gusdorf, G. (1980). Conditions and limits of autobiography. 1956. In J. Olney (Ed.), *Autobiography: Essays theoretical and critical* (pp. 28-48). Princeton, NJ: Princeton University Press.
Guskey, T. R. (1988). Teacher efficacy, self-concept, and attitudes toward the implementation of instructional innovation. *Teachers & Teacher Education, 4*(1), 63–69.
Hackman, J. R., & Oldham, G. R. (1980). *Work redesign.* Reading, MA: Addison-Wesley.
Hagell, A. (2012). *Changing adolescence: Social trends and mental health.* Bristol: Policy Press.
Hart, P. M. (1999). Predicting employee life satisfaction: A coherent model of personality, work, and nonwork experiences, and domain satisfactions. *Journal of Applied Psychology, 84,* 564–584.
Harvard Business Review. (2003). The 2003 HBR breakthrough ideas for tomorrow's list. *Harvard Business Review, 81*(4), 92–98.
Haynes, R. (2005). How do you define success. *The Wisdom Journal.* Retrieved from http://www.thewisdomjournal.com
Hinduja, S. & Patchin, J. W. (2012). *School climate 2.0: Preventing cyberbullying and sexting one classroom at a time.* Thousand Oaks, CA: Sage Publications.
Hinton, S., & Stockburger, M. (1991). *Personality trait and professional choice among preservice teachers in eastern Kentucky.* Research paper presented at Eastern

Kentucky University (ERIC Document Reproduction Service No. ED 341672).

Hofstede, G. (2003). *Culture's consequences: Comparing values, behaviors, institutions, and organizations across nations.* Thousand Oaks, CA: Sage Publications.

Hoy, W. K,. & Sweetland, S. R. (2001). Designing better schools: The meaning and measure of enabling school structures. Educational Administration Quarterly, 37, 296-321.

Hoy, W. K., & Tschannen-Moran, M. (1999). Five faces of trust: An empirical confirmation in urban elementary schools. Journal of School Leadership, 9, 184-208.

Hoy, W. K., & Tschannen-Moran, M. (2001). *The conceptualization and measurement of faculty trust in schools: The omnibus T-scale.* Retrieved from www.coe.ohio-state.edu

Hoy, W. K., & Tschannen-Moran, M. (2003). The conceptualization and measurement of faculty trust in schools: The omnibus T-Scale. In W. K. Hoy & C. Miskel (Eds.), Studies in leading and organizing schools (pp. 181-208). Greenwich CT: Information Age.

Inc. Magazine. (2012). Retrieved from www.inc.com.

Ingersoll, R. (2003). *In no dream denied.* National Commission on Teaching and America's Future. Retrieved from www.nctaf.org

International Labour Organization (ILO). (1986). *Workplace health promotion and well-being.* Retrieved from http://www.ilo.org/

International Labour Organization (ILO). (1992). *Workplace health promotion and well-being.* Retrieved from http://www.ilo.org/

Irvine, J. J. (1992). *Making teacher education culturally responsive.* In M.E. Dilworth (Ed.), Diversity in teacher education: New expectations (pp. 79-82). San Francisco, CA: Jossey-Bass.

i.Safe America. (2004). Retrieved from http://www.isafe.org/

Jansen, A., Nguyen, X., Karpitsky, V., & Mettenleiter, M. (1995). Central command neurons of the sympathetic nervous system: Basis of the fight-or-flight response. *Science Magazine, 5236*(27), 1-18.

Jones, F. (1987). *Positive classroom management.* New York: McGraw Hill.

Jones, F. (2007). *Fred Jones tools for teaching: Discipline, instruction, motivation.* Fred Jones Publishing.

Joram, E., & Gabriele, A. (1998). Preservice teacher's prior beliefs: Transforming obstacles into opportunities. *Teaching and Teacher Education, 14*(2), 175–191.

Kagan, D. M. (1992). Implications of research on teacher belief. Educational Psychologist, 27, 65-90.

Kamaron Institute, School Surveys (2007–2009). Retrieved from http://kamaron.org/Cyber-Bullying-Articles-Facts.

Katz, S. (1999). Teaching in tensions: Latino immigrant youth, their teachers and

the structures of schooling. *Teachers College Record, 100*(4), 809–841.
Keller, M. (2003). *Military education coalition.* Retrieved from http://www.militarychild.org/
Kerbow, D. (1996). Patterns of urban student mobility and local school reform. *Journal for Students Placed at Risk, 1,* 147–169.
Kessler, R. C., Chiu, W. T., Demler, O., & Walters, E. E. (2005). Prevalence, severity, and comorbidity of 12-month DSM-IV disorders in the national comorbidity survey replication. *Archives of General Psychiatry, 62,* 617–627.
Kieschke, U., & Schaarschmidt, U. (2008). Professional commitment and health among teachers in Germany. A typological approach. *Learning & Instruction,*18, 429-437.
Kim, E., & Hong, S. (2007). First generation Korean American parents' perceptions of discipline. *Journal of Professional Nursing. 27*(1), 60–68.
Kline, M. (2012). *Searching for budget cuts.* Retrieved from http://www.academia.org/
Kounin, J. (1971/1977). *Discipline and group management in classrooms.* New York: Holt.
Kowalski, R., Limber, S. P., Scheck, A., Redfearn, M., Allen, J., Calloway, A., … Vernon, L. (2005, August). *Electronic bullying among school-aged children and youth.* Paper presented at the annual meeting of the American Psychological Association. Washington, DC.
Kumashiro, K. (2012). *Bad teacher! How blaming teachers distorts the bigger picture.* New York: Teachers College Press.
Kumpfer, K. L. (2002). Additional tools for measuring vulnerability to substance abuse. *Contemporary Psychology, 47* (1), 82–85.
Ladson-Billings, G. 1994. The Dreamkeepers: Successful Teachers of African American Children. San Francisco: Jossey-Bass
Ladson-Billings, G. (1995). But that's just good teaching! The case for culturally relevant pedagogy. *Theory into Practice, 34*(3), 159–165.
Ladson-Billings, G. (1997). *The dreamkeepers.* San Francisco: Jossey-Bass.
Ladson-Billings, G. J. (2001). *Crossing over to Canaan: The journey of new teachers in diverse classrooms.* San Francisco, CA: Jossey-Bass.
Ladson-Billings, G., & Tate, W. F. (1995). Toward a critical race theory of education. *Teachers College Record, 9*(1)7, 47–68.
Latham G. P. (2007). *Work motivation: History, theory, research, and practice.* Thousand Oaks: SAGE.
Leiter, M. (1991). The dream denied: Professional burnout and the constraints of human service organizations. *Canadian Psychology, 32,* 547.
Leiter, M. P., & Schaufeli, W. B. (1996). Consistency of the burnout construct across occupations. *Anxiety, Stress, & Coping, 9,* 229-243.
Lifetips. (2012). *Life tips.* Retrieved from www.gaymarriage.lifetips.com
Long, M. (1996). The role of the linguistic environment in second language

acquisition. In W. Ritchie & T. Bhatia (Eds.), *Handbook of Second Language Acquisition*, pp. 413-468. San Diego: Academic Press.

Lopes, P. N., Grewal, D., Kadis, J., Gall, M., & Salovey, P. (2006). Evidence that emotional intelligence is related to job performance and affect and attitudes at work. *Psicothema*, 18, 132-138.

Lopez, M.H. & Velasco, G. (2011). *The toll of the great recession childhood poverty among Hispanics sets record, leads nation. The toll of the great recession.* Pew Hispanic Center. Retrieved from http://pewhispanic.org/reports/report.php?ReportID=147

Lortie, D. (1975). *Schoolteacher: A sociological study.* Chicago: University of Chicago Press.

Maddocks, J. (2007). *A three-month pre- and post-study applying the human element to developing emotional intelligence.* Retrieved from www.emotionalintelligence.com.uk

Mandle, J. (2012). The missing teachers. *The Huffington Post.* Retrieved from http://www.huffingtonpost.com/jay-mandle/

Marbley, A. F., Bonner, F. A., II, McKisick, S., Henfield, M. S., Watts, L. M., & Shen, Y.-J. (2007). Interfacing cultural specific and black pedagogy with counseling: A proposed diversity-sensitive training model for preparing pre-service teachers for diverse learners. *Multicultural Education*, 14(3), 8–16.

Marlene, A. (2012). *Ready to exceed your own expectations and those of others?* Retrieved from http://www.audreymarlene-lifecoach.com/news-articles.html

Maslow, A. H. (1943). A theory of human motivation. *Psychological Review*, 50(4), 370–396.

Maslow, A. (1971). *The farther reaches of human nature.* New York: Viking Press.

McInerney, M., & Hamilton, J. L. (2007). Elementary and middle schools technical assistance center: An approach to support the effective implementation of scientifically based practices in special education. *Exceptional Children*, 73(1), 242–255.

McNeely, S., & Mertz, N. (1990). *Cognitive constructs of pre-service teachers: Research on how student teachers think about teaching.* (ED322116) Presented at the American Educational Research Association (AERA), Boston, MA.

Mehrabian, A. (2009). *"Silent messages"—A wealth of information about nonverbal communication (body language).* Los Angeles, CA: Author.

Mehta, S. (2012). Personality of teachers. *International Journal of Business and Management Tomorrow (2)*2, 1–8.

Melendez, L. (2005). Parental beliefs and practices around early self-regulation: The impact of culture and immigration. *Journal of Infants and Young Children*, 18(2), 136–146.

Mertz, N., & McNeely, S. (1991). *Cognitive constructs of pre-service teachers: How students think about teaching before formal preparation.* (ED331810). Paper presented at American Educational Research Association (AERA), Chicago, IL.

Mertz, N., & McNeely, S. (1992). *Pre-existing teaching constructs: How students "see" teaching prior to training.* (ERIC Document Reproduction Service ED346075). Paper presented at American Educational Research Association (AERA), San Francisco, CA.

MetLife. (2005). Retrieved form https://www.metlife.com/metlife-foundation/what-we-do/student-achievement/survey-american-teacher.html?WT.mc_id=vu1101

Miller, L., Smith, A. D., & Rothstein, L. (1994). *An action plan to manage the stress in your life.* New York: Pocket Books.

Mockabee, S. (2007). A question of authority: Religion and cultural conflict in the 2004 election. *Political Behavior, 29,* 221–248.

Moll, L., Amanti, C., Neff, D., & Gonzalez, N. (1992). Funds of knowledge: Using qualitative approach to connect to homes and families. *Theory Into Practice, 33(2),* 132-141.

Moroz, K. (2005). *The effects of psychological trauma on children and adolescents.* A report prepared for the Vermont Agency of Human Services Department of Health Division of Mental Health Child, Adolescent and Family Unit. Retrieved from http://mentalhealth.vermont.gov/

Mossholder, K. V., Bedein, A. G., & Armenakis, A. A. (1982). *Employee organization linkages: The psychology of commitment and turnover.* New York: Academic Press.

Murphy, K., Delli, L. A., & Edwards, M. (2004). The good teacher and good teaching: Comparing beliefs of second-grade students, preservice teachers, and inservice teachers. *Journal of Experimental Education, 72(2),* 69–92.

Murray, B. & Fortinberry, A. (2005). *Depression and fact stats.* Retrieved from http://www.upliftprogram.com/

Murray, C. J., & Lopez, A. D. (1996). *The global burden of disease: A comprehensive assessment of mortality and disability from diseases, injuries and risk factors in 1990 and projected to 2020.* Geneva, Switzerland: World Health Organization.

Musher-Eizenman, D. R., Holub, S. C., Miller, A. B., Goldstein, S. E., & Edwards-Leeper, L. (2004). Body size stigmatization in preschool children: The role of control attributions. *Journal of Pediatric Psychology, 29,* 613–620.

Myatt, M. (2012). *Forbes 10 communication secrets of great leaders.* Retrieved from http://www.forbes.com/

Nadler, L. (2009). *What was I thinking? Handling the hijack.* Retrieved from www.truenorthleadership.com.

National Alliance on Mental Illness. (2013). *Depression in children and adolescents fact sheet.* Retrieved from www.nami.org.

National Association of Colleges and Employers. (2012). *NACE salary survey*. Retrieved from http://www.naceweb.org/salary-survey-data/

National Center for Educational Statistics (NCES). (2001). *The condition of education*. Retrieved from http://nces.ed.gov/

National Center for Educational Statistics (NCES). (2011). *Digest of educational statistics*. Retrieved from http://nces.ed.gov/

National Commission on Teaching & America's Future (NCTAF). (2004). *Who will teach? Experience matters*. A report from The National Commission on Teaching and America's Future. Retrieved from http://nctaf.org/wp-content/uploads/2012/01/NCTAF-Who-Will-Teach-Experience-Matters-2010-Report.pdf

National Education Association (NEA) Policy Brief. (2008). *Promoting educators cultural competence to better serve culturally diverse students*. Retrieved from http://www.nea.org

National Education Association (NEA). (2012). *Rankings of the states 2012 and estimates of school statistics 2013*. Retreived from http://www.nea.org/home/

National Institute of Child Health and Human Development (NICHD). (2005). *Abused women less likely to be married or in long-term relationships*. Retrieved from http://www.nichd.nih.gov/news/releases/abused_women.cfm

NBC News (2012). Retrieved from http://usnews.nbcnews.com/_news/2012/06/08/12124259-teacher-put-on-leave-after-allegation-of-racist-remark?lite

Nelson, D. L., & Simmons, B. L. (2004). *Eustress: An elusive construct an engaging pursuit*. P. L. Perrewé & D. C. Ganster, eds. Oxford, UK: Elsevier Jai.

Neuman, S.B. (1999). Books make a difference: A study of access to literacy. *Reading Research Quarterly, 34*, 286-301.

Niemeyer, A., Wong, M., & Westerhaus K. (2009). Parental involvement, familismo, and academic performance in Hispanic and Caucasian adolescents. *North American Journal of Psychology, 11*(3), 613–631.

Olmedo, I. (1997). Voices of our past: Using oral history to explore funds of knowledge within a Puerto Rican family. *Anthropology and Education Quarterly, 28*(4), 550–573.

Pajares, M. F. (1992). Teacher's beliefs and educational research: Cleaning up a messy construct. *Review of Educational Research, 62*(3), 307–322.

Palmer, P. J. (1998) *The courage to teach. Exploring the inner landscape of a teacher's life*. San Francisco: Jossey-Bass.

Pang, V. O., & Sablan, V. A. (1998). Teacher efficacy: How do teachers feel about their abilities to teach African American students? In M. E. Dilworth (Eds.), *Being responsive to cultural differences–how teachers learn* (pp. 39–58). Thousand Oaks, CA: Corwin Press.

Parker, S., Axtel, C., & Turner, N. (2001). Designing a safer workplace: Importance of job autonomy, communication quality, and supportive supervisors. *Journal of Occupational Health Psychology, 6*(3), 211–228.

Parker, S. K., & Wall, T. D. (1998). *Job and work design*. London: Sage.

Patchin, J. W., & Hinduja, S. (2012). Traditional and nontraditional bullying among youth: A test of general strain theory. *Youth and Society, 43*(2), 727–775.

Patterson K., Grenny J., Maxfield D., McMillan R., & Switzler A. (2011). *Change anything: The new science of personal success*. New York: Business Plus.

Pelletier, K. R. (1977). *Mind as healer, mind as slayer*. New York: Dell.

Pines, A. (1993). Burnout: An existential perspective. In W. B. Schaufeli, D. Maslach, & T. Marek (Eds.), *Professional burnout: Research developments in theory and research*. Washington, D.C.: Taylor & Francis

Pines, A. M., Aronson, E., & Kafry, D. (1981). *Burnout: From tedium to personal growth*. New York: Free Press.

Podell, D., & Soodak, L. (1993). Teacher efficacy and bias in special education referrals. *Journal of Educational Research, 86*(4), 247–253.

Puhl, R.M., Andreyeva1, T. & Brownell, K D (2008). Perceptions of weight discrimination: prevalence and comparison to race and gender discrimination in America. *International Journal of Obesity*, 32, 992–1000.

Raelin, J. A. (1986). *The clash of cultures: Managers managing professionals*. Boston, MA: Harvard Business School Press.

Reeve, J., Jang, H., Carrell, D., Jeon, S., & Barch, J. (2004). Enhancing students' engagement by increasing teachers' autonomy support. *Motivation and Emotion, 28*(2), 147–169.

Reid, T. R. (2005). Spanish at school translates to suspension. *Washington Post*. Retrieved from http://www.washingtonpost.com

Reyhner, J. (2001). Cultural survival vs. forced assimilation: The renewed war on diversity. *Cultural Survival Quarterly, 25*(2), 22–25.

Reynolds, A. J. (1992). Comparing measures of parental involvement and their effects on academic achievement. *Early Childhood Research Quarterly, 7*(3), 441–462.

Richards, C., & Killen, R. (1994). *Collaborative solutions to key problems in the practicum*. ERIC Document Reproduction No. ED 376141.

Richardson, V. (1996). The role of attitudes and beliefs in learning to teach. In J. Sikula (Ed.), *The handbook of research in teacher education* (2nd ed., pp. 102–119). New York: Macmillan.

Rilling J, Gutman D, Zeh T, Pagnoni G, Berns G, Kilts C. (2002). A neural basis for social cooperation. *Neuron*. 35(2), 395-405.

Rist, R. C. (1970). Student social class and teacher expectations. *Harvard Educational Review, 40*(3), 411–451.

Rosenstock, L. (2012). Stress in the workplace. *Health Advocate*. Retrieved from http://www.readbag.com/healthadvocate-downloads-webinars-stress-workplace.

Ross, J. A. (1998). The antecedents and consequences of teacher efficacy. In J. Brophy (Ed.), *Advances in Research on Teaching* (pp. 49–74). Greenwich, CT: JAI Press.

Ross, M. (n.d.). Cyber Bullying Articles & Facts. Retrieved from http://kamaron.org/Cyber-Bullying-Articles-Facts.

Rosser, M. L., & Nelson, R. (2012). Gaining applicable knowledge in the university online environment: An exploratory case study. *International Journal of the Academy of Organizational Behavior Management*, (3). 79-115.

Rosser-Cox, M. L. (2011). *Cultural responsiveness and motivation in preparing teachers*. Saarbrücken, Germany: Lambert Academic Publishing.

Rothschild, M. (2008). School superintendent threatened over Pledge of Allegiance in Spanish. *The Progressive*. Retrieved from http://www.progressive.org/

Rumberger, R. W., Larson, K. A., Ream, R. K., & Palardy, G. J. (1999). *The educational consequences of mobility for California students and schools*. Berkeley, CA: Policy Analysis for California Education.

Rusting, C. L., & DeHart, T. (2000). Retrieving positive memories to regulate negative mood: Consequences for mood congruent memory. *Journal of Personality and Social Psychology, 78*, 737–752.

Ryan, R., & Deci, E. (2000). Self-determination theory and the facilitation of intrinsic motivation, social development, and well-being. *American Psychologist, 55*(1), 68–78.

Ryan, R. M., & La Guardia, J. G. (2000). What is being optimized over development?: A self-determination theory perspective on basic psychological needs across the life span. In S. Qualls & N. Abeles (Eds.), *Psychology and the aging revolution* (pp. 145–172). Washington, DC: APA Books.

Saarni, C. (2000). Emotional competence: A developmental perspective. In R. Baron & J. D. A. Parker (Eds.), *The handbook of emotional intelligence* (pp. 68–91). San Francisco: Jossey-Bass.

Scantlebury, (INITIALS). (2009). *Gender bias in teaching*. Retrieved from http://www.education.com/

Selye, H. (1974). *Stress without distress*. Philadelphia: J. B. Lippincott Co.

Singh, R., & Clarke, G. (2006). Power and parenting assessments: The intersecting levels of culture, race, class, and gender. *Clinical Child Psychology and Psychiatry, 11*(1), 9–25.

Smith, T. (2000). *Taking America's Pulse II*. Report for the National Conference for Community and Justice. Retrieved from http://www.racematters.org/takingamericaspulse.htm

*Stanford Psychological Encyclopedia*. Retrieved from https://lib.stanford.edu/psychology/. 66.

Steele, C. M. (1997). A threat in the air: How stereotypes shape intellectual identity and performance. *American Psychologist, 52*, 613–629.

Steele, C. M., & Aronson, J. (1995). Stereotype threat and the intellectual test-performance of African-Americans. *Journal of Personality and Social Psychology, 69*(5), 797–811.

Stein, M., & Wang, M. (1988). Teacher development and school improvement: The process of teacher change. *Teaching and Teacher Education, 4*(2), 171–187.

Stenner, K. (2005). *The authoritarian dynamic.* Cambridge: Cambridge University Press.

Stevens, G. B., & O'Neill, P. (1983). Expectation and burnout in the developmental disabilities field. *American Journal of Community Psychology, 11*, 615–627.

Stevens, T., Olivárez, A., & Hamman, D. (2006). The role of cognition, motivation, and emotion in explaining the mathematics achievement gap between Hispanic and white students. *Hispanic Journal of Behavioral Sciences, 28*(2), 161–186.

Stockdale, B. (2012). *Survivor traits: What they are, what they do, and how to get them.* Retrieved from http://www.brendastockdale.com/

Swyers, M. (2012). *Leaders and common traits.* Inc. Magazine. Retrieved from http://www.inc.com/matthew-swyers/4-traits-of-great-leaders.html

Taylor, E. W. (1998). *The theory and practice of transformative learning: A critical review.* (Information Series No. 374). Columbus, OH: ERIC Clearinghouse on Adult, Career, and Vocational Education.

Terr, L. (1992). Too scared to cry: Psychic trauma in childhood. New York: Basic Books

Thomas, R. (2006). *Building on the promise of diversity: How we can move to the next level in our workplaces, our communities, and our society.* Toronto, ON: AMACOM: a division of American Management Association.

Thompson, S., Gee, J., & Gee, B. (2004). *Highly qualified for successful teaching: Characteristics every teacher should possess.* Retrieved at http://www.usca.edu/essays/vol102004/

Thoreson, C., & Mahoney, M. J. (1974). *Behavioral self-control.* New York: Holt, Rinehart and Winston.

Tiezzi, L., & Cross, B. (1997). Utilizing research on prospective teachers' beliefs to inform urban field experiences. *The Urban Review, 29(2)*, 113-125.

Troman, G., & Woods, P. (2000). Careers under stress: Teacher adaptations at a time of intensive reform. *Journal of Educational Change, 1*, 253-275.

Troman, G., & Woods, P. (2001). *Primary teachers' stress.* New York: Routledge/Falmer.

Tschannen-Moran, M., & Hoy, W. K. (1997). Trust in schools: A conceptual and empirical analysis. *Journal of Educational Administration, 36*(4), 334–353.

Tschannen-Moran, M., Woolfolk Hoy, A., & Hoy, W. K. (1998). Teacher efficacy: Its meaning and measure. *Review of Educational Research, 68*(2), 202–248.

United Nations Joint Staff Pension Fund (n.d.). *Overcoming generational gap in the workplace.* Retrieved from http://www.un.org/

University of Illinois Counseling Center. (n.d.). *Cultural transistion and adaptation.* Retrieved from http://www.counselingcenter.illinois.edu/?page_id=133

U.S. Budget, Historical Tables. (2006). Retrieved from http://www.ed.gov/

U.S. Department of Commerce. (1987). *Report on migration.* Retrieved from http://www.census.gov/

U.S. Department of Education. (1999). *Teacher quality: A report on the preparation and qualifications of public school teachers.* Office of Educational Research and Improvement. Washington DC. Retrieved from http://nces.ed.gov/

U.S. Department of Education. (2002). The final report and findings of the safe school initiative: Implications for the prevention of school attacks in the United States. Retrieved from http://www.ed.gov

U.S. Department of Education, National Center for Education Statistics. (2004). *Schools and Staffing Survey. Public School Teacher, BIA School Teacher, and Private School Teacher Data Files.* Washington D.C. Retrieved from http://nces.ed.gov/

U.S. Department of Education, National Center for Education Statistics. (2012). *The Condition of Education 2012* (NCES 2012-045), Indicator 33.

U.S. Department of Health and Human Services. (1999). *Mental health: A report of the surgeon general.* Rockville, MD: U.S. Department of Health and Human Services; Substance Abuse and Mental Health Services Administration, Center for Mental Health Services, National Institutes of Health, National Institute of Mental Health.

U.S. General Accounting Office. (1994). *Fact sheet.* Retrieved from http://www.gao.gov/

USA Today. (2008). *Idaho student says teacher tossed his Mexican flag in trash.* Retrieved from http://usatoday30.usatoday.com/news/nation/

Useem, E., Offenberg, R., & Farley, E. (2007). Closing the teacher quality gap in Philadelphia: New hope and old hurdles. Philadelphia: *Research for Action.* Retrieved from http://pdf.researchforaction.org/

Vallerand, R. J., Fortier, M. S., & Guay, F. (1997). Self-determination and persistence in a real-life setting: Toward a motivational model of high school dropout. *Journal of Personality and Social Psychology, 72(5),* 1161-1176.

Vygotsky, L. S. (1978). *Mind in society: The development of higher psychological processes* (M. Cole, V. John-Steiner, S. Scribner, & E. Souberman, Eds. and Trans.). Cambridge, MA: Harvard University.

Wallace, J. (1995). Organizational and professional commitment in professional and nonprofessional organizations. *Administrative Science Quarterly, 40,* 228–255.

Weissmann, J. (2012). *Occupy kindergarten: The rich-poor divide starts with education.* Retrieved from http://www.theatlantic.com

Westen, D., Blagov, P. S., Harenski, K., Kilts, C., & Hamann, S. (2006). Neural bases of motivated reasoning. *Journal of Cognitive Neuroscience, 18(11),* 1947-1958.

Weyrich, P. (1999). *A letter from Paul Weyrich.* Retrieved from www.busmanagement.com

Wharam, J. (2009). *Emotional Intelligence: Journey to the Centre of Yourself.* New Alresford, United Kingdom: John Hunt Publishing.

Whitbeck, D. A. (2000). Born to be a teacher: What am I doing in a college of education? *Journal of Research in Childhood Education, 15*(1), 129–136.

White-Clark, R. (2005). Training teachers to succeed in a multicultural classroom. *Principal.* Published by the National Association of Elementary School Principals. Retrieved from http://www.naesp.org/

Wise, T. (2010). *Color blind: The rise of post-racial politics and the retreat from racial equality.* San Francisco: City Lights Publishers.

Wong, H. (1998). *The first days of school: How to be an effective teacher.* Mountain View, CA: Harry K Wong Publications, Inc.

Wong, H. K., Wong, R. T. (2001). How to be an effective teacher: The first days of school. Mountain View, CA: Harry K. Wong, Publications, Inc.

World Health Organization. (2001). *Strengthening mental health promotion.* Geneva, World Health Organization (Fact sheet no. 220).

Yokota, J. (1995). *Literacy development for students of diverse populations.* In S. B. Wepner, J. T. Feeley, & D. S. Strickland (Eds.), The administration and supervision of reading programs (pp. 239-254). New York, NY: Teachers College Press.

Zeichner, K. (1983). Myths and realities: Field-based experience in teacher education. *Journal of Teacher Education, 31(6),* 45–55.

Zeichner, K., & Gore, M. (1990). *Teacher socialization.* In W. R. Houston (Ed.), *Handbook of Research on Teacher Education* (pp. 329–348). New York: Macmillan.

Zimmerman, B., & Kitsatas, A. (1997). Developmental phases in self-regulation: Shifting from process to outcome goals. *Journal of Educational Psychology, 89(1),* 29-36.

# ABOUT THE AUTHORS

**Michelle L. Rosser, Ph. D.**

Dr. Rosser is a professor at Ashford University serving in the Department of Psychology. She teaches and researches in the areas of Organizational and Educational Psychology. Currently Michelle is on the Editorial Review Boards for the International Journal of the Academy of Organizational Behavior Management and the International Journal of Organizational Behavior and Human Resource Management, as well as a member of the American Educational Research Association and the National Consortium for Instruction and Learning.

**Tom Massey, Ph.D.**

Dr. Massey is an author and transformational speaker who inspires and enlightens with his humorous teaching style and captivating stories that paint word pictures of optimism for the future. He has a high-energy presence that engages people to reach for the best in themselves! In addition to writing seven books on success and leadership, Tom has more than twenty years experience in teaching individuals and organizations to maximize performance. He lives and breathes the strategies he shares.

Critical Pedagogical Perspectives

Greg S. Goodman, *General Editor*

*Educational Psychology: Critical Pedagogical Perspectives* is a series of relevant and dynamic works by scholars and practitioners of critical pedagogy, critical constructivism, and educational psychology. Reflecting a multitude of social, political, and intellectual developments prompted by the mentor Paulo Freire, books in the series enliven the educator's process with theory and practice that promote personal agency, social justice, and academic achievement. Often countering the dominant discourse with provocative and yet practical alternatives, *Educational Psychology: Critical Pedagogical Perspectives* speaks to educators on the forefront of social change and those who champion social justice.

For further information about the series and submitting manuscripts, please contact:

> Dr. Greg S. Goodman
> Department of Education
> Clarion University
> Clarion, Pennsylvania
> *ggoodman@clarion.edu*

To order other books in this series, please contact our Customer Service Department at:

> (800) 770-LANG (within the U.S.)
> (212) 647-7706 (outside the U.S.)
> (212) 647-7707 FAX

Or browse online by series at:

> www.peterlang.com

www.ingramcontent.com/pod-product-compliance
Ingram Content Group UK Ltd.
Pitfield, Milton Keynes, MK11 3LW, UK
UKHW022238230426
12048UKWH00018BA/1340